THE CHAMPIONS OF PHILADELPHIA

The Greatest Eagles, Phillies, Sixers, and Flyers Teams

By Rich Westcott
Foreword by Pat Williams

SPORTS
PUBLISHING

Sports Publishing books may be purchased in bulk at special discounts for sales promotion, corporate gifts, fund-raising, or educational purposes. Special editions can also be created to specifications. For details, contact the Special Sales Department, Sports Publishing, 307 West 36th Street, 11th Floor, New York, NY 10018 or sportspubbooks@skyhorsepublishing.com.

Sports Publishing® is a registered trademark of Skyhorse Publishing, Inc.®, a Delaware corporation.

Visit our website at www.sportspubbooks.com.

10 9 8 7 6 5 4 3 2 1

Library of Congress Cataloging-in-Publication Data is available on file.

Cover design by Tom Lau
Cover photo credit AP Images

ISBN: 978-1-61321-804-4
Ebook ISBN: 978-1-61321-850-1

Printed in the United States of America

DEDICATION

This book represents a special personal milestone inasmuch as it's the 25th one I've authored. For that reason, I'd like my family to help celebrate this happy occasion by dedicating the book to them.

To my wife Lois.

To my children Chris, Susan, Lora, and Amy.

To my grandchildren Samantha, Harrison, Erica, Rachel, Nicole, Margot, Will, Adrienne, and Georgia.

All of you have made special contributions to my life, and I am grateful that you have been such a major part of it.

CONTENTS

Acknowledgments vii

Foreword ix

Introduction xiii

1   The Athletics Win Their First World Series 1

2   Another World Series Victory for the A's 17

3   The Athletics Rule Baseball Once Again 32

4   The Yellow Jackets Are the City's First NFL Champion 48

5   The Athletics Finally Go Back on Top 64

6   The A's Win Their Fifth World Series 81

7   Warriors Become Pro Basketball's First Champs 98

8   The Eagles Win the NFL Title in a Blizzard 114

9   Eagles Repeat as Champions in the Rain 130

10 Local Boys Make Good for the Warriors 147

11 Eagles Win the Crown with a Storied Finish 165

12 76ers Become One of Basketball's Greatest Teams 182

13 Flyers Deliver the City's First Stanley Cup 200

14 Flyers Capture Second Straight Stanley Cup 217

15 World Series Winners At Last 233

16 76ers Dominate the NBA for Their Second Title 250

17 Phillies End a Twenty-Eight-Year Drought
    with Series Win 266

18 Other Pro Teams That Won Championships 283

    Other Books by Rich Westcott 299

    Sources 300

ACKNOWLEDGMENTS

Because I have seen and covered many of the teams and players discussed herein, it has been a special pleasure to write a book that documents their championship seasons. This has been a project, though, that could never have been done without the help of many others.

Foremost, I would like to thank all of the people connected with these teams who have been interviewed. Fortunately, players from teams dating back to the 1940s on up to the most recent teams were available. This group includes more than fifty players, managers, and others, all of whom generously contributed their time, insights, and comments

I would also like to extend a special thanks to my friend Pat Williams, who not only wrote the foreword but provided a considerable amount of help in various other ways. Pat is certainly one of the true legends in the local sports field, with connections not only to basketball but also to baseball.

A number of others provided special assistance in this project, not the least of whom were Jim Gallagher, Sam Carchidi, Bob Warrington, Keith Javic, and Jim Rosin. Thank you, my friends, so very much. I would also like to extend my thanks for the invaluable help provided by Skip Clayton,

Brenda Wright-Galloway, Zack Hill, Mike Mackrides, Brian McBride, John Nash, Rich Pagano, Harvey Pollack, Raymond Ridder, Susan Steigman, Al Tielemans, Bob Vanderhost, Bill Werndel, and Brent Winkler. And finally, a special note of thanks to editor Julie Ganz and all the staff at Skyhorse Publishing, who helped to make this such an exciting project.

Of course, I could never write a book without the help of my dear wife, Lois, who has always has been a huge pillar of support in this sometimes difficult project. Her unyielding encouragement, support, interest, and patience have been invaluable aids to the authoring of this book.

FOREWORD

By Pat Williams

I was hooked on sports at an early age. In 1947, I went to see my first major league baseball game at Shibe Park. I was captivated by baseball, and became a great admirer of Connie Mack.

Even then, I had heard many references to his championship teams. I was fascinated by those 1910, 1911, and 1913 teams, and the teams of 1929, 1930, and 1931. I would have given anything to have been old enough to have seen those teams and players.

But I had to be patient. The first time I came into contact with a championship team was in 1956. I was in 10th grade. The Warriors had a great team that year, winning the championship. I took it all in, watching Paul Arizin, Tom Gola, Neil Johnston, Jack George, and Joe Graboski. My dad had tickets for the final game and we sat in the upper deck watching the Warriors beat the Ft. Wayne Pistons at Convention Hall. What a thrill it was to see a Philadelphia team win a championship.

I came home from college one winter a few years later, and my dad took me to Franklin Field, where we saw the Eagles win the title against the Green Bay Packers. It was a very cold day. I can still see Ted Dean breaking into the open and taking off, and Chuck Bednarik tackling Jim Taylor to save the game. Now, all these years later, I still cherish the glow of that game.

I was not living in the area when the Warriors won the championship in 1966–67. But in 1974, I came back to Philly to interview for a job with the 76ers, and all over the city there was a buzz going on about the Flyers. I thought, *Wow—they could win the championship.* And darned if they didn't. Then with Bobby Clarke and Bernie Parent leading the way, they did it again the following year. They had a parade, both years, and what a parade it was. What a great two years that was for the Flyers.

The next thing you know, the Phillies won the World Series in 1980. I was there at Veterans Stadium the night they won. I'll never forget it—the police dogs, horses, Pete Rose and Bob Boone collaborating on the foul ball, and Tug McGraw coming out of the bullpen. It had never happened before for the Phillies in almost 100 years.

Then in 1982, Moses Malone arrived, and everything turned out right for the 76ers. They were injury-free and not one thing went wrong all season. It was a Cinderella season, capped by a sweep of the Los Angeles Lakers and another incredible parade. I'll never forget it. Going down Broad Street, I never saw so many people in my life.

It took a while, but Philadelphia finally got another championship team in 2008 when the Phillies beat the Tampa Bay Rays to win the World Series. I was ensconced in Florida by then, but I've always been a Philadelphia fan, and I rejoiced like I was right there. Everybody loved those Phillies, and then they had a fantastic parade.

Those parades are absolutely beautiful. Everybody loves our parades and two million or so people always turn out for one. There's a bigger turnout for parades in Philadelphia than anywhere else in the country. Just think, when the San Francisco Giants won the World Series in 2014, about 200,000 turned out to see their parade. What's that tell you?

I'm thinking, we ought to have a parade every year. Let's make it an annual ritual. But you have to realize, it's hard to win a title. In addition to having the talent, everything has to go right. The team has to be extremely motivated. There can't be any letdowns. You can't have any major injuries.

But we've had some great teams. And the pages of this book give fans the chance to read about those teams. *The Champions of Philadelphia* highlights the greatest Philadelphia teams and moments in the history of professional sports.

There have been many of these great teams, starting in 1910 with Connie Mack's Athletics and going on up to Charlie Manuel's 2008 Phillies, with many wonderful highlights in between.

My good friend Rich Westcott is the ultimate author on all things related to Philadelphia sports. Over the years, no one has covered Philadelphia sports history like he has. I have read every book he's written, and the one that you're about to read is his best work yet.

I sat down with this book the minute I got it, and in two sessions I had read it from cover to cover. So get ready for a terrific read. You, too, will find that *The Champions of Philadelphia* is a book that you will have a very difficult time putting down as you celebrate the greatest teams in the history of Philadelphia sports. And when you finally finish reading this book, you are going to say, "Let's win one again as soon as possible."

INTRODUCTION

Among the great sports cities in the United States, Philadelphia ranks as one of the best. It has been like that for more than two centuries.

This is a city where sports were known to have been played as long ago as the 1700s. It is one of just eight cities in the country that currently has a team from each of the four top professional leagues (along with New York, Boston, Washington, Chicago, Detroit, Atlanta, and Dallas). It's one of only five cities that have major league baseball, basketball, football, ice hockey, and soccer teams. And its history is filled with great players, great teams, and memorable events.

Indeed, sports in Philadelphia has been one of the dominant features in a city that has been a leader in many different areas of history.

This, after all, is where the Declaration of Independence was written and signed. It was the nation's first capital. Philadelphia is the birthplace of the American flag, as well as the country's first modern bank, electronic computer, locomotive, zoo, volunteer fire company, trade union, farmers' market, stock exchange, magazine, and professional surgery.

The city is the home of the world-famous Philadelphia Orchestra, the internationally renowned Museum of Art, Fairmount Park, which is the largest inner-city park in the country, and the legendary Mummers Parade. Cheesesteaks, soft pretzels, scrapple, and carbonated water originated in the area.

The Cradle of Liberty, a city that had its start in 1682 when William Penn arrived, featured rowing and horse-racing in the 1700s. Soon afterward, polo and cricket became popular. A form of baseball was first known to be played in 1830, after which the sport exploded onto the scene with hundreds of club teams performing throughout the city and suburbs. Boxing became popular in the 1850s, tennis took hold in the city in the 1880s, and golf became fashionable in the 1890s.

In 1876, the University of Pennsylvania fielded the area's first football team. In 1895, the nation's first college basketball game took place, with Haverford College defeating Temple University, 6–4. The Penn Relays and the Devon Horse Show both began in 1895. The first Army-Navy football game was held in the city in 1899. And in the early 1900s, professional auto races were held on the streets of the city.

In the world of major professional sports teams, a squad from Philadelphia called the Athletics was part of baseball's first pro league and the first pennant-winner of the National Association of Professional Base Ball Players, formed in 1871. Five years later, the National League was created and the circuit's very first game, pitting another team called the Athletics and the Boston Red Caps, was played in Philadelphia in 1876.

A new team called the Phillies joined the National League in 1883. Now, 133 seasons later, only one team (Chicago Cubs) in Major League Baseball has spent more consecutive years playing as a one-city club. In 1901, yet another Athletics team was a charter member of the American League. They left the city after the 1954 season, moving to Kansas City and later to Oakland.

In football, the National Football League was formed in 1920. No teams represented Philadelphia until the previously independent Frankford Yellow Jackets joined the league in 1924. That team folded during the 1931 season. Two years later, another Philadelphia team called the Eagles was formed, and it has been a key member of the local sports scene ever since then.

The Basketball Association of America began in 1946, and one of its original teams was the Warriors. The BAA merged with the National Basketball League in 1949 to form the National Basketball Association. The Warriors remained in the league until moving to San Francisco in 1961. Then in 1964, a new team came to town when the Syracuse Nats became the 76ers.

The National Hockey League started in 1917. But except for the 1930–31 season when a team called the Quakers played in the league, Philadelphia, although it had numerous professional teams over the years, did not have another team in the NHL until the 1966–67 season, when the Flyers became one of six new teams to join the league.

Since the start of the twentieth century, 17 teams have won championships in the city's four major professional sports.

While that falls well below New York's leading total, it is a figure that includes a glittering list of exciting, enormously popular, and memorable teams, each with its own collection of spectacular players.

Of course, Philadelphia teams have often not ranked among the leaders of their respective sports. Indeed, there have been many dismal times in the annals of local sports. But the teams that have won championships and even the many others that advanced to championship games and did not win have all played magnificently while bringing honor and distinction to a city where sports have always ranked higher among the region's population than virtually any other endeavor.

The leader among Philadelphia's champions is the Athletics. The team won American League pennants nine times—in 1902, 1905, 1910, 1911, 1913, 1914, 1929, 1930, and 1931. In five of those years, the A's also won the World Series.

Next come the Eagles. While going to the NFL finals six times—in 1947, 1948, 1949, 1960, 1981, and 2005, including two trips to the Super Bowl—they have won three league championships.

The Phillies captured National League flags seven times—in 1915, 1950, 1980, 1983, 1993, 2008, and 2009, winning the World Series twice.

In journeys to the finals in 1946–47, 1947–48, and 1955–56, the Warriors won two titles. The 76ers also were two-time winners in the NBA after going to the last round in 1966–67, 1977–78, 1982–83, and 2000–01.

The Flyers took home the Stanley Cup twice following trips to the NHL's deciding round in 1973–74 and 1974–75, while also advancing to the finals five times—in 1976, 1979, 1984, 1987, and 1997.

And the Yellow Jackets won the NFL crown in 1926 in an era before there were postseason battles.

Overall, these champions represent the finest in Philadelphia sports history.

Their victories, whether at Shibe Park, Franklin Field, Veterans Stadium, Citizens Bank Park, the Arena, Convention Hall, the Spectrum, or Frankford Stadium, produced some of the most spectacular events in the city's long and rich sports history.

Over the years, good fortune has allowed me to see many of Philadelphia's pro champions. Originally, I saw some of those teams as a youth when my father took me to watch games. Others, I covered and wrote about in later years as an adult. In all cases, the special memories of these teams have produced lingering images. They are images that will never be forgotten.

Think of the players who have defined these teams—Eddie Collins, Jimmie Foxx, Steve Van Buren, Chuck Bednarik, Robin Roberts, Mike Schmidt, Ryan Howard, Joe Fulks, Paul Arizin, Wilt Chamberlain, Julius Erving, Bobby Clark, Bernie Parent, and Houston Stockton—and you have some of the greatest athletes ever to take part in their respective sports.

And the managers and coaches, in particular, Connie Mack, Greasy Neale, Buck Shaw, Dallas Green, Charlie

Manuel, Eddie Gottlieb, Alex Hannum, and Fred Shero, comprise some of their game's finest leaders of all time.

The Champions of Philadelphia does not include the numerous noteworthy minor pro teams in many different sports that have won championships, although they are cited in the final chapter. Nor does it cover the vast number of great college teams in the region that have won major championships. Their achievements, of course, and those of the thousands of semi-pro and amateur teams that have called Philadelphia home, add tremendously to the city's reputation as one of the leading and most enduring sports locations in the nation.

This book, though, is an attempt to document the achievements of Philadelphia's most successful top-level professional teams. Some won championships long ago. Others won titles more recently. The ways in which their games have been played have changed considerably over the years. But regardless of the circumstances surrounding each team's success, the city has been the home of 17 sensational teams, and they all have contributed immeasurably to Philadelphia's long and unforgettable sports history.

—Rich Westcott, Summer 2015

THE ATHLETICS WIN THEIR FIRST WORLD SERIES

1 In the early years of the American League, no baseball team was more successful than the Philadelphia Athletics. This was a team that after the league's 14th season had won six pennants and three World Series. No team in either league came close to that record.

While the Athletics had won American League pennants in 1902 when there was no World Series and in 1905 when they lost in the Series to the New York Giants, it was the 1910 team that pushed the A's to a higher level.

That club paved the way for the A's to win three World Series over a four-year period and four pennants through 1914. And it did it with an outstanding group of players that made it one of the league's first great teams.

The 1910 Athletics set a new American League record by winning 102 games during the regular season. They finished 14½ games ahead of the second-place New York Highlanders, and they crushed the Chicago Cubs, who were playing in their third World Series since 1906, four games to one in the Fall Classic.

In addition to manager Connie Mack, the A's had four future Hall of Fame players—pitchers Charles (Chief) Bender and Eddie Plank, second baseman Eddie Collins, and third baseman Frank (Home Run) Baker—on the team. They had one player—first baseman Harry Davis—who had won four American League home run titles and another—Baker—who later would also win four home run crowns. And they had the makings of what would soon be called "The $100,000 Infield," which one year later would consist of Baker, shortstop Jack Barry, Collins, and first baseman Stuffy McInnis.

The Athletics famed $100,000 infield, so named because it was thought to be worth that sum, stands with center fielder Danny Murphy (middle), formerly the team's second baseman. The infield in 1910 included (from left) Eddie Collins, Jack Barry, Frank Baker, and Stuffy McInnis.
Courtesy of Bob Warrington

The A's home ballpark was just one year old and when it was built was considered the finest baseball stadium in the country. Shibe Park, named after the Athletics' majority owner Ben Shibe and standing at 21st Street and Lehigh Avenue in North Philadelphia, had been constructed at a cost of $315,248.69 and opened in 1909. The first ballpark built with steel and concrete, it would start a trend in which twelve more stadiums around the country would be built the same way, including Fenway Park, Wrigley Field, and Ebbetts Field.

Originally, Shibe Park had a seating capacity of 23,000 with an area behind ropes across the outfield holding another 10,000. That was a considerable difference from Columbia Park, the A's original field at 29th Street and Columbia Avenue, which could accommodate just 9,500 spectators and was deemed too small to hold the burgeoning group of Athletics fans.

When it opened in 1909, Philadelphia mayor John Reyburn called Shibe Park "a pride of the city." American League president Ban Johnson gushed that "Shibe Park is the greatest place of its character in the world." And *Evening Telegraph* reporter William Weart wrote that the ballpark "was built for the masses as well as the classes, and had more room for the poor man than for the rich one" because baseball is a "people's sport."

One year after the opening-day hoopla, the Athletics, who had finished second, just three and one-half games behind the Detroit Tigers in Shibe Park's first season, were ready to go again. At that point, the A's popularity among baseball fans had increased considerably in Philadelphia as the Phillies dawdled in mediocrity.

Mack, who owned 25 percent of the team (while the Shibe family, headed by Ben Shibe, had 50 percent of the stock and sports writers Sam (Butch) Jones of the Associated Press and Frank Hough with the *Philadelphia Inquirer* each owned 12½ percent), had made a few changes in what had been the starting lineup just two years earlier when the A's finished sixth. In particular, Jack Lapp had become the starting catcher, and Barry was now the shortstop.

Barry's keystone partner was Collins, whom Mack had signed out of Columbia University. Nicknamed "Cocky," Collins had originally played at the age of nineteen in 1906 under the assumed name of Sullivan, used because he still had one year of eligibility left at Columbia. During a twenty-five-year career in the majors, Collins would be regarded as one of the best and most intelligent players who ever stepped on the field. An exceptional fielder as well as a hitter, he would finish his career with a .333 batting average. Later he would become the general manager of the Boston Red Sox and the person who signed Ted Williams.

Baker was another key performer. A slugger who starting in 1911 won four straight home run crowns—thus earning him his nickname—he used a 52-ounce bat and hit .307 during a thirteen-year career in the big leagues, during which time he also led the league in RBIs three times. He was also a top defensive player who led the league in fielding percentage twice. He had been the first player to hit a ball over Shibe Park's right field wall in 1909.

Davis was one of the league's premier sluggers, having won home run titles in 1904 through 1907. A Philadelphia native who wound up playing 22 years in the majors, during which time he had a .277 career batting average with 75 home runs, Davis was in his last year as an A's regular in 1910, after which he would be replaced by McInnis.

Outfielders Rube Oldring, Topsy Hartsel, and Danny Murphy were all veteran players who performed admirably during long careers in the majors. Both Amos Strunk, a young reserve, and Murphy were Philadelphia natives. The latter had been a second baseman, but was converted to an outfielder after Collins's arrival. The only problem with the A's roster is that some of its players were getting older. Davis and Hartsel were both thirty-six and Plank was thirty-five.

The Athletics' pitching staff featured Plank, Bender, Jack Coombs, and Cy Morgan, each of whom won in double figures in 1910. Behind the plate, Lapp, the main catcher, shared duties with four other backstops during the season, including the veteran Ira Thomas.

Plank, who would win in double figures sixteen straight times, including eight 20-plus-win seasons, had joined the Athletics in 1901. The following year, he began a streak of four straight seasons as a 20-game winner. Ultimately, he would win 326 games during a seventeen-year career, becoming the first lefthanded hurler to win 300 games.

Bender had joined the A's in 1903. Part Chippewa, he had attended Carlisle Indian School (later to become Dickinson College). He won in double figures in eleven of his first twelve seasons during a sixteen-year career that netted him 212 wins. Coombs was the Athletics' other top hurler, who later earned 159 wins in fourteen seasons.

Chief Bender was one of the stars of the Athletics pitching staff, posting a 23–5 record with a 1.58 ERA.
Courtesy of Rich Westcott

Mack, who had been with the team since its inception in 1901, the year in which the American League began, built this A's team with special care. He would go on to manage the Athletics for fifty years, focusing on quickness and finesse and making sure that his players kept their heads in the game and never stopped thinking. Mack emphasized to his players that they should always hustle, even to the point that the Athletics often scored from second base on fly balls to the outfield or took two bases on sacrifice bunts.

A future member of the first class inducted into the Hall of Fame, Mack had begun his career in 1886 as a catcher. Eventually, he became one of the most influential people in baseball and a towering figure in the evolution of the game. He would go on to win more games (3,731) and lose more (3,948) than any skipper in big league history.

The Athletics held spring training at Atlanta, Georgia. Then, following the traditional City Series against the Phillies, which ended with each team winning three games, they traveled to Washington to open the season against the Senators and ace pitcher Walter Johnson.

Particularly noteworthy was that President Howard Taft became the first chief executive to throw out the first ball, a tradition that lasted until 1971. Taft, Vice President James Sherman, and various other cabinet officers and their wives had come to the game as spectators, but when the President was discovered in the crowd, he was asked to make the first pitch.

Johnson, in his first of what would be fourteen opening day starts, blanked the A's on one hit as the Senators copped a 3–0 decision. The lone hit, a blooper by Baker down the right field line, would've been an easy out, but the Senators' Doc Gessler tripped over a fan standing along the retaining rope before he could get to the ball. Plank took the loss for the A's.

After their opener, the Athletics went on to win 18 of their next 22 games, including seven in a row in early May. The streak was broken by a 1–1 tie with the Cleveland Naps on May 10, after which the A's won six straight games.

One of those wins came on May 12 when Bender fired a no-hitter against the second-place Naps before just 4,000 fans at Shibe Park. The Athletics won, 4–0, as Bender, the second A's pitcher to toss a no-hitter (Weldon Henley was the first one in 1905), struck out four and walked one in a lineup that featured future Hall of Famer Napolean Lajoie. Glittering catches by Oldring in center field and Murphy in right helped to preserve Bender's sparkling feat.

Soon afterward, the team became firmly entrenched in first place, and except for five days in June after they had lost four straight games and the Highlanders moved into the lead for one day, the A's would remain there the rest of the season.

The A's went back into first for good on June 21 with the help of four straight wins over the Highlanders. Six days later, they had a three-game lead before finishing the month with a 38–21 record and a one-game cushion.

Starting on July 1 with a doubleheader sweep of New York, the A's won 17 of their next 20 games and held a 7½-game lead by July 20. Then they lost six of their next 10 games (one tie) before ending July with a 60–30 mark and a six-game lead.

By the end of July, Mack had made what would become a momentous move with future ramifications. He traded a hard-hitting minor league outfielder, who had played in just 10 games for the A's over the two previous seasons but was now performing in New Orleans in the Southern League, to Cleveland for outfielder Bris Lord. Another localite from Upland in Delaware County, Lord had played early in his career with the A's. After the trade, he went on to become a key part of the A's outfield, while the outfielder for whom he was swapped went on to become one of baseball's all-time great hitters. His name was Joe Jackson—later nicknamed Shoeless Joe—a magnificent hitter who earned everlasting notoriety for his role in the Black Sox scandal of 1919, when the Chicago White Sox threw the World Series to the Cincinnati Reds.

From the beginning of August on, the Athletics were virtually unstoppable. One noticeable exception, however, came on August 4, when Coombs and Ed Walsh of the White Sox both pitched 16 scoreless innings in a game that ended in a 0–0 tie. Coombs struck out 18 and yielded just three hits in his part of the marathon.

On August 13 in the second game of a doubleheader, the Athletics walloped Cleveland, 14–1. Three days later, they plastered the Naps again, 18–3, their highest run total of the season. Ultimately, they won 22 of 29 games in August to finish the month with an 82–37 record and an 11-game lead.

By mid-September, the lead was all the way up to 16 games after a 10–0 whitewash of the Detroit Tigers. The Athletics clinched the pennant on September 21, despite managing only a 0–0 tie with Cleveland. Then on October 1, A's pitcher Clarence Russell beat the Boston Red Sox, 3–0, to give his team its 100th win. The win was the only one in Russell's big league career.

One week later, the Athletics finished the season, sweeping the Red Sox in four games before losing their final two outings to New York.

The Athletics' final record of 102–48 gave them a 14½ game edge over the Highlanders, who finished second with an 88–63 mark, three and one-half games ahead of Ty Cobb's third-place Tigers. The record wins would stand only until 1912, when the New York Giants broke it with 103.

It was a marvelous season for the Athletics. The team led the American League in batting average (.266) and fielding percentage (.965), and the pitching staff was first in complete games (123), shutouts (24), and strikeouts (789), and had the league's lowest earned run average (1.79). The team drew 588,095 fans for the season while posting a 57–19 record at home. The A's notched a 52–24 record in the first half and a 50–24 slate in the second half.

While finishing fourth in the league with a .324 batting average, Collins led the AL in stolen bases with 81, and was third in hits (188) and RBIs (81). Murphy hit .300 and tied for second in the league in triples (18), was third in slugging average (.436), and fifth in total bases (244) and doubles (28).

Oldring, enjoying the best season of a fine career, hit .308 before breaking a leg late in the season. Baker hit .283 with two home runs, while Barry hit .259, Davis .248, and Lord, who moved into the starting lineup in place of Hartsel, hit .280.

Out on the mound, the Athletics fielded a staff that would be considered one of the best in baseball history. Coombs, who had been mostly mediocre in previous years, posted a dazzling 31–9 record while leading the league in wins and shutouts (13), tying for first in games pitched (45), and ranking second in complete games (35) and ERA (1.30), and third in innings pitched (353), winning percentage (.775), and strikeouts (224). An extremely knowledgeable ballplayer, he would go on to coach a number of college teams, including the one at Duke University.

Bender posted a 23–5 record with a 1.58 ERA while leading the league in winning percentage (.821), placing fourth in wins, and fifth in strikeouts (155). Morgan compiled an 18–12 record with a 1.55 ERA and Plank, who Mack called "the greatest lefthanded pitcher in the major leagues," went 16–10 with a 2.01 ERA.

It was an amazing season all around for the Athletics. But it got better in the postseason when the A's faced the Cubs in the World Series.

The Cubs, managed by Frank Chance of "Tinker-to-Evers-to-Chance" fame, had run away with the National League pennant, compiling a 104–50 record while finishing 13 games ahead of the second-place Giants and 17½ games in front of the third-place Pittsburgh Pirates (the Phillies finished fourth that year, 25½ games out of first with a 78–75 record). For the Cubs, it was their fourth World Series venture (two Series wins) since 1906.

At the beginning of the season, Chicago still had Chance at first (he was also serving as manager at the time), Johnny Evers was at second, and Joe Tinker at shortstop in what was one of the most widely heralded double play combinations of all time. Chance (.298), Tinker (.288), and Evers (.263) were joined by right fielder Frank (Wildfire) Shulte, who hit .301 and tied for the league lead with 10 home runs, and center fielder Solly Hofman (.325) as the top Cubs hitters. Evers, however, broke a leg late in the season and was replaced by Heinie Zimmerman, and Chance often substituted Harry Steinfeld at third.

Future Hall of Famer Mordecai (Three-Finger) Brown (25–13) and rookie phenom Len (King) Cole (20–4), two of the top hurlers in the league, headed a strong Chicago pitching staff that also included Harry McIntire (13–9), Orval Overall (12–6), and Ed Reulbach (12–8), who once had fired two shutouts in one day.

There was one problem, though, with starting the Series. The American League season had ended one week before the National League campaign did, forcing the Athletics to sit idly until the games began. Not wishing to watch his team go stale, Mack asked AL president Ban Johnson if he could line up a team of all-stars who would face the A's during the week to keep them fresh. Johnson agreed, and a team that featured Ty Cobb, Tris Speaker, Ed Walsh, and Walter Johnson was formed. The teams met five times, and the all-stars won four games.

Finally, on October 17, the Series was ready to begin. Playing at Shibe Park before a crowd of 26,891, the game was the first Series game ever recorded on film. That, however, created a problem as Chance and umpire Hank O'Day vehemently protested the presence of a movie camera on the field. After a lengthy argument with league officials, the game finally began with the camera permitted for use.

Men dressed in suits and ties lined Lehigh Avenue as they prepared to enter Shibe Park during the 1910 World Series.
Courtesy of Rich Westcott

The Athletics opened the scoring in the second inning off Overall with Baker hitting a ground-rule double into the crowd rimming the outfield and scoring on Murphy's subsequent single. Murphy then stole second, moved to third on Barry's grounder, and scored on a single by Bender. Doubles by Lord and Baker added another run in the third, and then in the eighth Baker drove home Collins with his third double of the game. The Cubs scored in the ninth, but that was it as Bender yielded just three hits and struck out eight in the A's 4–1 victory.

Coombs and Brown were on the mound for the second game, but despite the credentials of both hurlers, it was no contest as the Athletics romped to a 9–3 victory while bashing 14 hits. The A's led just 3–2 after six innings, but a six-run explosion in the bottom of the seventh that featured doubles by Davis, Murphy, and Strunk got the job done. Coombs went the distance for the win, although he gave up eight hits and walked nine. The Cubs left 14 runners on base.

Two days later, the Series moved to Chicago's West Side Park. Mack had a surprise. With Plank suffering from a sore arm, The Tall Tactician started Coombs again. Facing Reulbach, the A's righthander allowed six hits and struck out eight and the Athletics' bats exploded for 15 hits as they waltzed to a 12–5 victory. Davis, Barry, and Coombs each had three hits for the A's. Murphy's three-run homer in the third broke a 3–3 tie and sparked a five-run inning. Chance was ejected from the game after arguing that the homer should've been called a ground-rule double.

Bender was back on the mound for Game Four against Cole. After seven innings, the Athletics clung to a 3–2 lead. They loaded the bases in the eighth, but Thomas's double-play grounder ended the inning. Then the Cubs tied the score in the bottom of the ninth on Chance's RBIs triple. They clinched their only victory of the Series in the 10th as Schulte's single drove in the deciding run off Bender to give Chicago a 4–3 win.

Still in Chicago, Game Five on October 23 began with another amazing pitching selection. Coombs got the call for his third start in five days. The Cubs countered with Brown, who had pitched two innings of relief the previous day. Lapp's single gave the A's a 2–1 lead in the fifth, then they nailed down the verdict with a five-run eighth that featured RBIs doubles by Lord and Collins. The inning came to a climax as Zimmerman's wild throw allowed two runs to score and a wild pitch brought in another. Coombs gave up nine hits and struck out four to get his third win of the Series.

The Athletics had their first World Series victory. Jubilation reigned in the clubhouse and Ban Johnson even came in to participate. Then, when the team returned to Philadelphia, the city staged a banquet in the team's honor. The *Philadelphia Times*, one of the city's daily newspapers, published a special World Series edition that sold more than 300,000 copies.

Among the Series statistics, Collins (.429), Baker (.409), Coombs (.385), Davis (.353), and Murphy (.350) led the team in hitting, with Murphy collecting eight RBIs and the only home run of the Series. The Athletics hit .316 as a team, while the Cubs, led by Chance and Schulte (both .353), batted .222.

Coombs pitched three complete games while allowing 23 hits, 10 runs (3.33 ERA), striking out 17, and walking 14. Bender, the only other pitcher used by Mack, allowed 12 hits, struck out 14, and walked four in 18⅔ innings (1.93 ERA). Brown, who appeared in three games for the Cubs, gave up

Jack Coombs led the Athletics pitching staff with a dazzling 31–9 record and a 1.30 ERA, plus three of his team's four wins in the World Series.
Courtesy of Bob Warrington

23 hits and 16 runs in 18 innings while striking out 14 and walking seven.

From a total gate receipts of $173,980 (total attendance 124,222), each A's player received $2,062.79. Each Cub got $1,375.16. But the A's bank accounts would soon increase.

ANOTHER WORLD SERIES VICTORY FOR THE A'S

2 By the time the 1911 season began, there was little doubt about which team was the best in the American League. The Philadelphia Athletics won that distinction by a landslide. They had become the dominant force in the league, and there was virtually no competition.

In the previous nine seasons, the Athletics had won three pennants and one World Series. True, the Detroit Tigers had captured three straight pennants, but they had also lost three straight World Series. And in 1911, they would finish a whopping 13½ games behind the A's, who were on their way to three World Series victories over a four-year period.

The A's had also become the favorite team in Philadelphia, moving ahead of the Phillies, who since their arrival in the city in 1883 had yet to win a pennant, and who were in the midst of a period when they finished above fourth place just once between 1902 and 1911. To illustrate the point, in most seasons the Athletics were drawing about twice the number of fans to their games as the Phils were to theirs. In 1910, the A's had attracted 588,095 fans while the Phillies had a total attendance of 296,597.

That didn't stop the teams from meeting in the annual City Series, though. Having started in 1903, the clash between the city's two major league teams was always a special event in Philadelphia baseball circles. In 1911, the Athletics won three of the five games played.

Playing at the 23,000-seat Shibe Park in the ballpark's third year of operation, the 1911 A's were a distinguished mix of veteran and young players in their early years in the big leagues. Pitcher Eddie Plank at age thirty-six, and first baseman Harry Davis and outfielder Topsy Hartsel, both thirty-seven, were the oldest players on the team. Outfielder Danny Murphy was thirty-five, and second baseman Eddie Collins was thirty-four. Conversely, infielder Stuffy McInnis was twenty and outfielder Amos Strunk was twenty-one.

Athletics players prepare to take batting practice prior to a game at Shibe Park.
Courtesy of Bob Warrington

Interestingly, five members of the 1911 Athletics were natives of the Philadelphia area. Davis, Murphy, and Strunk were all born in Philadelphia, outfielder Bris Lord was from

Upland, and catcher Jack Lapp came from Fraser. In addition, in a day when few players went to college, the team had five players who had attended college, including Collins (Columbia), shortstop Jack Barry (Holy Cross), Plank (Gettysburg), and pitchers Jack Coombs (Colby) and Chief Bender (Carlisle).

"The A's have been the training school for more great players than any other city in the country," Connie Mack wrote in his book, *My 66 Years in the Big Leagues*. "We have taken boys from schools and colleges and have made them world famous."

No one was quicker to agree with that summation than Collins. "We learned baseball at Connie's knee," he proclaimed. To this, Ty Cobb later added toward the end of his 24-year career, "I wish I had started under Connie Mack."

The starting lineup in 1911 was the same as it had been the year before, with two exceptions. Mack replaced the aging Davis with McInnis at first base. Although he was basically a shortstop who had played infrequently in his first two seasons with the A's, McInnis was regarded by Mack as potentially an excellent hitter who despite his 5-foot, 9-inch height and lack of playing experience—he had played only 57 games in his first two years in the majors—could handle the job at first base because he was an outstanding fielder who was quick and agile.

The shift brought what was basically an end to the illustrious career of Davis, who had made his big league debut in 1895 and who had at one point won four straight home run titles. The Girard College graduate would become manager of the Cleveland Naps in 1912 before returning to the A's as a player-coach.

McInnis's conversion to a first baseman launched another prominent phase of Athletics history. Joining Frank Baker at third, Barry at short, and Collins at second, McInnis became part of what would be called "The $100,000 Infield." It was a term that was viewed as a combined salary the four could command and that characterized what has often been described as one of baseball's greatest infields.

"I do not believe the game has ever seen anything better," Mack wrote in 1950. "Today, any one of those men would bring far more than $100,000 on the open market. They might have even been called a 'Million Dollar Infield.' Together, they formed the greatest quartet in baseball."

Mack, who was said to be the first manager to send out scouts to search for young players, also made Lord his regular left fielder in place of Hartsel, who had been in the majors since 1898 and with the A's since 1902. Lord, a big leaguer since 1905 when he started out with the A's, had returned to the team during the 1910 season in the notorious swap for Shoeless Joe Jackson. He would go on to have by far his best season in 1911.

The Athletics roster had one other highly significant characteristic. In Collins, Baker, Plank, and Bender it contained four future Hall of Famers.

The team's success would not be so predictable as the 1911 season began. After spending an uneventful spring training session at Savannah, Georgia, the Athletics returned home and lost their opener on April 12 at Shibe Park to the New York Yankees, 2–1. They wound up getting swept in the three-game series with the Yanks, then after a 1–0 victory over the Boston Red Sox, went on to lose six of their first seven games.

After sinking as low as seventh place, the A's then won 12 of their next 15 games, including a 17–13 slugfest over the St. Louis Browns. But they managed to get no higher than third place, and after a six-game losing streak, they tumbled back to fifth place, losing 13 of 15 games and tumbling 12 games out of first.

Meanwhile, the Tigers won 21 of their first 23 games. Led once again by Ty Cobb, who would go on to hit .420 that year, future Hall of Fame outfielder Sam Crawford, and first baseman Jim Delahanty (the brother of the renowned former Phillies slugger Ed Delahanty), Detroit appeared ready to dominate the league with nobody standing in the way.

That likelihood ultimately disappeared, however, in late May. On May 20, after losing two straight to Detroit, the Athletics outswatted the Tigers, 14–12. The win launched a streak in which the A's won 24 of 27 games, twice winning seven in a row. By the end of the streak on June 22, the A's had moved into second place, just one and one-half games behind Detroit.

After two losses to Boston, the Athletics won 10 of their next 12 games and after a doubleheader win over the Yankees on July 4, they roosted in first place for one day. Unfortunately, seven losses in the next nine games, including a four-game sweep by the Tigers, bounced them back to second place, five and one-half games out of first.

From then on, though, losing became an unfamiliar word in the A's vocabulary. Starting on July 15, they won 14 of 19 games, and at the end of an August 4 doubleheader victory over the Browns, the A's again took over first place. This time, they would stay there for the rest of the season.

The Mackmen wound up winning 17 of 26 games in August, ending the month with a four and one-half-game lead over the rapidly fading Tigers. Then, they started September with doubleheader wins over Boston, 1–0 and 3–1 behind Bender and Plank. The A's went on to win 15 of 17 games, and by September 24, following a 5–3 decision over the Naps, their lead was up to 11 games.

The Athletics won 38 of their final 54 games, including 21 of 27 in September. They clinched the pennant on September 26 with an 11–5 victory over the Tigers in a game in which Baker smacked two home runs and two doubles. The season ended on October 6 with a 5–4 victory over the Yankees, giving the A's a final record of 101–50 and a 13½ game lead over Detroit, which finished with an 89–65 record as Cobb hit an amazing .420 for the season. Cleveland was third with an 80–73 mark, 22 games out of first.

The A's, who posted a 52–22 record in the second half after going 49–28 in the first half, led the league in runs (861), batting average (.296), home runs (35), and fielding percentage (.965) while allowing the fewest runs (602) to the opposition. During the season, they attracted a total attendance of 605,749.

In what would become the first of four straight home run titles, Baker led the league with 11 four-baggers while batting .334, collecting 115 RBIs, which tied with Crawford for second in the league behind Cobb (144), and slamming the league's third-highest number of doubles (42), and fourth-highest number of hits (198). Baker's glittering season caused Mack to say that, "we brought him to Philadelphia when other managers were overlooking him. In my opinion, he had everything." To that, sportswriter Fred Leib added: "Many a time with the Mackmen far behind, a long-distance swat from Baker's war club put the White Jumbos back in the game."

Collins finished with a .365 batting average, fourth best in the league, while scoring 92 runs and driving in 73. Three other starters also hit above .300, including Murphy (.329),

Second baseman Eddie Collins hit .365 in 1911, the fourth best batting average in the league.
Courtesy of Bob Warrington

McInnis (.321), and Lord (.310). Rube Oldring hit .297, Barry .265, and Ira Thomas, who appeared in the most games at catcher, hit .273, while Lapp hit .353 in a reserve role.

Among pitchers, Coombs had his second straight spectacular season with a 28–12 record while leading the league in wins. He placed second in games (47) and innings pitched (337), tied for third in complete games (26), and placed fourth in strikeouts (185).

Plank (23–8) and Bender (17–5) also had masterful seasons, with the former tying for first in shutouts (six) and fourth in wins, and placing fourth in ERA (2.10). Furthermore, Plank relieved in 10 games and was later credited with four saves. Bender led the league in winning percentage (.773) while posting a 2.16 ERA in 31 games.

En route to becoming one of baseball's winningest lefthanders with 327 career wins, Eddie Plank posted a 23–8 record in 1911.
Baseball Hall of Fame and Museum

Among other hurlers, Cy Morgan recorded a 15–7 record while Harry Krause went 11–8.

Once again, the American League season ended one week before the National League campaign was over. The A's were forced to play against another league All-Star team, and this time they won two of four games.

The World Series finally started on October 14. The opponent was the New York Giants, the A's old nemesis who had squashed them in five games in the 1905 World Series with the A's getting shut out four times, including three times by Christy Mathewson in what was one of the greatest pitching feats of all time.

In 1911, Mathewson, unquestionably one of the best pitchers in baseball, had posted a 26–13 record with a league-leading 1.99 ERA while his lefthanded counterpart Rube Marquard had gone 24–7 while topping the circuit in strikeouts (237). The Giants pitching staff led the league in ERA (2.69), complete games (95), and strikeouts (771) while allowing the fewest runs (542) of any team in the league.

At the plate, the Giants led the league in hitting with a .279 team batting average. Catcher Chief Meyers led the way with a .332 mark, followed by second baseman Larry Doyle with a .310 average, third baseman Fred Snodgrass with a .294 average, and right fielder Red Murray with a .291 mark. The Giants stole 347 bases, an amazing total for that era or any other.

Overall, the Giants had posted a 99–54 record under manager John McGraw, winning 20 of their last 24 games and finishing seven and one-half games ahead of the Chicago Cubs and 14½ above the Pittsburgh Pirates. Between their two pennants, the Giants had finished below third place only once, and were regarded as a formidable opponent for the high-ranking Athletics.

McGraw, of course, had already endeared himself to the Athletics by having his team wear specially designed black uniforms in the 1905 Series and by declaring that his opponents were nothing but a band of "white elephants." Although that description was said derogatorily, Mack took advantage of it, and forever after, his team used a white elephant as its symbol.

The Series set a number of precedents that became regular features at future World Series. For one, it was ruled that the playing field must be kept clear of fans without seats, a practice that had existed since the early days of baseball. Also, for the first time, there was extended media coverage of a World Series, with some fifty telegraphers sending play-by-play accounts and articles by reporters in attendance throughout the country. Some of the writers also penned ghost-written syndicated newspaper columns using the bylines of prominent players.

The Series began at the Polo Grounds, which had been rebuilt after experiencing two major fires during the season, with Mathewson facing Bender on the mound. A then-record crowd of 38,281 was on hand as the Giants captured a 2–1 decision, despite an 11-strikeout five-hitter by Bender. Mathewson, called by Mack "the greatest pitcher who ever lived," fanned five and yielded six hits, but the Giants won on Josh Devore's RBIs single in the seventh inning.

Plank was on the mound for the A's and Marquard toed the rubber for the Giants two days later when the Series moved to Shibe Park. This time, the Athletics captured the win, 3–1, when Baker broke a 1–1 tie with a two-run homer over the right field fence. Plank, gaining the first Series win of his career, allowed five hits and fanned eight, and Marquard hurled a four-hitter while striking out four in seven innings.

Back at the Polo Grounds for Game Three, Coombs was on the mound for the Athletics against Mathewson, who was pitching with just two days' rest. Once again, the A's got the upper hand with a 3–2 victory in 11 innings. After scoring an unearned run in the third inning, the Giants held a 1–0 lead until the A's tied the score in the ninth on another clutch home run by Baker. Two innings later, two Giants errors and singles by Collins, Baker, and Davis gave the A's a 3–1 lead. The Giants scored in the bottom of the 11th, but Coombs held on, going the distance with a sizzling performance while allowing just three hits and fanning seven.

Game Four was scheduled for Shibe Park on October 18, but the game was called off because of rain. The rain continued the next day, as well as the day after that. Finally, after constant rain, a field too wet to play on, and Sunday games outlawed in Pennsylvania, the Series resumed after a six-day wait on October 24. Gasoline was burned on the water-soaked field to help dry it out.

Again, Bender faced Mathewson. The Giants took the lead with two runs in the first inning, but the A's came back with three in the fourth, with consecutive doubles by Baker, Murphy, and Davis driving in the runs. A sacrifice fly by Thomas in the fifth finished the scoring, giving the A's a 4–2 win and putting them on the brink of another World Series victory. Bender allowed seven hits over nine innings, while Mathewson was touched for 10 hits, including seven doubles, in seven innings. Three of those hits were by Barry. During the game, A's fans taunted McGraw so loudly that he stayed in the dugout and never appeared on the field for the rest of the game.

The teams returned to the Polo Grounds for Game Five on October 25 with Coombs facing Marquard. Oldring's three-run homer in the third inning gave the A's an early lead and knocked out Marquard. But the Giants scored once in the seventh and two times in the ninth when pitcher Otis (Doc) Crandall slammed a run-scoring double, then scored himself on Devore's single to tie the score. By then, Coombs had pulled a ligament in his groin when he caught his spikes on the mound while making a pitch in the sixth inning. Working in obvious pain, he refused to be replaced by a pinch-runner in the 10th inning.

Ultimately, Plank relieved and in the bottom of the 10th, with Doyle on third and dusk engulfing the field, Fred Merkle sent a fly ball to short right. Murphy made the catch and threw home to Lapp. Doyle slid, appearing to beat the throw. Thinking he was safe and that the Giants had won the game, Lapp left the field. Only trouble was, umpire Bill Klem had made no call. He said later, that he was waiting for Lapp to tag Doyle, who had missed the plate. Mack had also noticed this, but fearing that a protest might start a riot since Giants fans were already swarming the field, he said nothing. Thus, the run stood, and the Giants were still alive with a 4–3 victory.

New York's hopes ended, however, the following day before a surprisingly small crowd of 20,485—the lowest of the Series—at Shibe Park. This time, instead of close games that had dominated the Series, the Athletics surged to a 13–2 triumph to win their second straight Fall Classic. With Bender on the mound once again, the A's gained a 1–1 tie in the third on Lord's RBI double. The A's then kayoed Giants starter Red Ames with a four-run fourth inning made possible by hits by Baker and Murphy and two Giants errors.

The A's added another run in the sixth, then clinched the victory with seven runs in the seventh on six singles, a double, an error, and a wild pitch. Murphy finished with four hits, while Lord had three as the A's slammed 13 hits. Bender went the distance to get the win, allowing just four safeties and fanning five.

That win and his other records over the years prompted Mack to write many years later that Bender was, "the greatest one-game pitcher, the greatest money pitcher baseball ever has known."

The Athletics walked off with four wins in six games, whipping what Mack called "the unbeatable Giants." And for the second year in a row, they ruled the baseball world. They did it by dominating a team managed by one of the game's greatest pilots and that was by far the best in the National League.

Even McGraw himself couldn't keep from complimenting the Athletics on their victory, citing the team's keystone combination of Barry and Collins as a key element in the win. They canceled out the Giants' noted hit-and-run game because of their quickness and deception, he said.

Unquestionably, the hitting star of the Series was Baker. Not only did he lead all batters with a .375 average, but his two home runs were major factors in two A's victories, earning him the nickname of "Home Run" Baker, a label that would stay with him the rest of his career. "Never did a young slugger live up to his reputation more than Baker in the World Series," Mack said many years later.

"It was a big event in those days of the dead ball when a batter made a home run," Mack said. "It was more than an event; it was sensational. It was a calamity for the Giants."

Frank Baker forever after became know as "Home Run" Baker after his home runs won two World Series games for the A's.
Baseball Hall of Fame and Museum.

Barry (.368), Murphy (.304), and Collins (.286), called by Mack "the greatest second baseman who ever lived," also greatly aided the Athletics' cause. As a team, the A's hit .244.

The A's used just three pitchers during the entire Series. Together, Bender, Coombs, and Plank compiled a 1.29 ERA while holding the Giants to a team batting average of .175 with no home runs. While winning two of three decisions, Bender struck out 20 and allowed 16 hits and six runs in 26 innings of work. Coombs, the winner in his only decision, fanned 16 and allowed 11 hits and five runs in 20 innings, while Plank whiffed eight and yielded six hits and two runs with a 1–1 record in nine and two-thirds innings.

On the Giants' side, Doyle (.304) and Meyers (.300) were the batting leaders, but no other regular hit as high as .200. Mathewson was the only Giants pitcher to register strikeout totals in double figures with 13, but he gave up 25 hits and eight runs in 27 innings. Like Mathewson, Marquard pitched in three games, but lasted only 11⅔ innings while allowing nine hits and six runs.

The A's took home a winner's share of $3,655 per player, while the Giants earned $2,436 each.

It was a brilliant victory for the Athletics. As the season ended, they had not only won 203 games over a two-year period, but had captured two American League pennants and two World Series. Clearly, Connie Mack's A's were the titans of baseball. "Our teams were world-beaters," he said.

How right he was.

THE ATHLETICS RULE BASEBALL ONCE AGAIN

3 By 1913, the Philadelphia Athletics had established themselves as the premier franchise in the American League. Since the league began in 1901, the Athletics had won four pennants and two World Series, a record unmatched by any other team in the circuit.

With World Series victories in both 1910 and 1911, the Athletics had seemingly created a dynasty that could last for a long time. But an interruption in that premise had occurred in 1912 when the team unexpectedly crumbled and finished a distant third, 15 games behind the Boston Red Sox, who went on to win the World Series over the New York Giants.

No one was more stunned by the A's weak finish than Connie Mack. "Our 1912 A's were one of the greatest teams of all time," he wrote many years later. "But there is one hazard that is hard to jump. That is overconfidence. Two straight pennants and two World Series victories made the boys feel they couldn't lose. Our boys had a feeling of cockiness that invariably results in a tumble."

The tumble, though, did not last long. One year later, the Athletics regained their position at the top of the league, reclaiming the American League pennant and then winning the World Series. "They quickly picked themselves up again and played with a vengeance," Mack explained.

For Mack, the 1913 season also represented the start of a major change in his bank account. The previous winter, using a $113,300 loan from principal owner Ben Shibe, he had bought out the shares of two of the team's original stockholders, Frank Hough and Sam (Butch) Jones. The two were local sports writers, Hough with the *Philadelphia Inquirer* and Jones with Associated Press. When the A's were formed in 1901, each wound up with a 12½ percent share in the team with Mack owning 25 percent and Shibe owning 50 percent—incredible by today's standards.

By buying out Hough and Jones, who had helped put the team together, Mack became 50 percent owner of the A's. Mack's sons Roy and Earle were added to the team's board

Connie Mack managed from the dugout, always wearing a dress shirt and tie while directing his team by waving his scorecard.
Courtesy of Special Collections Research Center, Temple University Libraries

of directors, and a new company, American Baseball Club of Philadelphia, was formed and incorporated. Shibe was extremely pleased with the deal because it provided assurance that the highly regarded Mack would not be lured away by another team.

A few months later, Mack took the team to San Antonio, Texas, for spring training. There, away from the glare of the spotlight, Mack cracked down on his players' smugness and complacency, and worked them as hard as he had in any previous training camp.

By the time the team left Texas, it had what appeared to be a new attitude, one that had erased the players' inclination for lackadaisical play, as well as the feeling, as Mack said, "that we can win when we have to."

When the Athletics arrived back in Philadelphia, they encountered another change from previous seasons. Shibe Park had undergone its first major alteration. At a cost of $76,000, a roof had been built over the uncovered bleachers down the left and right field lines, and new bleachers holding some 1,000 spectators had been added across the outfield from left to the flagpole in center field.

The Athletics had one more duty before the season began. They had to meet the Phillies in what was now the 11th year of the City Series. The teams played six games, splitting the contests between Shibe Park and the newly named Baker Bowl, with the Athletics winning five and one game ending in a tie.

As it had been through much of their first 12 years in the league, the Athletics' starting lineup was extremely strong.

It had good hitting, fielding, and baserunning. Indeed, there was hardly a weakness among the eight starting positions.

Most noteworthy, of course, was the infield of Stuffy McInnis at first base, Eddie Collins at second, Jack Barry at shortstop, and Frank (Home Run) Baker at third. The group was called "The $100,000 Infield," and it is a widely held view that there has never been a better infield in major league history.

The quartet had first played together as a group in 1911 when McInnis replaced four-time home run king Harry Davis. An excellent fielder, McInnis had originally played mostly at shortstop and third base, but when Davis retired, Mack moved him to first where, despite being just 5-feet, 9-inches tall, his quickness and agility allowed him to catch throws over his head as well as just about anywhere else. He was also a fine hitter who would hit .308 in 19 years in the big leagues.

Barry, another of six college players on the roster, having attended Holy Cross College, was the least known of the infielders. Though he was not an exceptional fielder—he made 63 errors in 1910—he was a valuable member of the lineup and during an 11-year career, hit .243. The 1914 *Reach Baseball Guide* said that the 5-foot, 8-inch Barry "had no one superior in his position in the American League."

Although it didn't quite equal the standards set by the infield, the Athletics' outfield was fairly strong, too. Left fielder Rube Oldring led the way. An excellent defensive player who spent 13 years in the majors, Oldring was so good that Mack later picked him as an outfielder on his all-time team. Also known for his speed, Oldring had a career batting average of .270.

Rube Oldring played for more than 11 years with the Athletics, and was a key figure in their first three World Series winners. He hit .283 for the 1913 team.
Courtesy of Bob Warrington

Jimmy Walsh, born in Ireland, was the center fielder. The 1913 campaign was his first full season in the majors. He ultimately went on to hit .231 during six years in the majors. Eddie Murphy, who like Walsh was acquired by Mack from the International League's Baltimore Orioles late in the 1912 season, manned right field. Originally a catcher who had played at Villanova, he hit .287 during an 11-year stint in the big leagues.

The catching duties for the A's were split between three players. Jack Lapp was considered the first-string catcher while playing in 88 games. Lapp, who would hit .263 over nine years in the majors, had the edge on rookie Wally Schang, a fine defensive backstop and a good hitter who wound up hitting .284 during a 19-year career in the majors. Schang played in 77 games in 1913. Veteran backstop Ira Thomas appeared in 21 games.

As strong as they were on the field, the Athletics also had an outstanding bench, anchored by Amos Strunk. An excellent outfielder, who would hit .283 during 17 years in the majors, Strunk had been the A's regular left fielder in 1912, but injuries had restricted his play the following season and he was limited to 93 games.

Davis, a Girard College graduate and the former home run king and A's captain, joined Strunk on the bench. In 1912, Davis had become manager of the Cleveland Naps, but when that didn't work out, he returned to the A's as a coach, assistant captain, and utility first baseman.

The Athletics reserve corps also included infielders John (Doc) Lavin, a former Michigan State University player, and Billy Orr. Other outfield reserves included Tom Daley and Danny Murphy, who was in the latter stages of a splendid 16-year career during which he was the A's second baseman before being supplanted by Collins and moved to the outfield.

If the Athletics were solid in the field, they sure weren't on the mound. When the season began, pitching was considered the weak spot on the team, with only veterans Eddie Plank and Charles (Chief) Bender as reliable hurlers.

Plank, who by 1913 was thirty-seven years old, was a seven-time 20-game winner and had been 26–6 the year before. Plank, who had briefly attended Gettysburg College, was once described by Collins as "a combination of good temperment, savvy, control, and courage."

Bender had been with the Athletics since 1903, and by 1913 had won in double figures nine times. Known for his keen mind and sharp control, Bender was once called by Mack "my greatest clutch pitcher." Bender played sixteen years and posted 212 wins.

Aside from Plank and Bender, each of whom would also be used in relief during the season, the pitching staff had a lot of uncertainties. Jack Coombs was an excellent hurler, but despite winning 31, 28, and 21 games in the previous three years, he had contracted typhoid fever in spring training and would pitch in only two games in 1913. Meanwhile, Herb Pennock, a native of Kennett Square, was also waylaid by an illness in his second season with the A's and would miss much of the campaign.

Rookies Leslie "Bullet Joe" Bush and Bob Shawkey and sophomores Carroll (Boardwalk) Brown and Bryon Houck were also on the pitching staff. Although all four showed a considerable amount of promise, no one was certain of filling out the starting rotation.

Nevertheless, the Athletics, with the hunchback Louis Van Zelst as their famous mascot, got off to a quick start when they beat the Red Sox, 10–9, in the season's opener on April 10 at Fenway Park. They then took two more games at Boston before losing their first game of the year in their fourth outing.

That was one of the few A's losses of the month. They finished April with a 9–3 record, then began May with six straight wins. By the end of May, the Athletics had a 28–10 record, and except for being tied for first several times, they went into first to stay on May 30 with a 3–2 victory over the New York Yankees.

By then, Mack's team was in the midst of a fifteen-game winning streak that included four victories each over the Washington Senators, Detroit Tigers, and Yankees. On successive days on June 4 and 5, the A's clubbed the Tigers, 14–6 and 10–6. By mid-June, their lead would be up to five games over Washington, and two weeks later, the A's stretched their lead to nine games as the team posted a 20–7 record during the month.

Four straight wins over the Chicago White Sox put the A's ten up on July 18. But suddenly the team went into an unlikely slump, losing 15 of their next 20 games with their lead dropping to five and one-half games on August 17. Soon, though, the team got back on track and between September 11 and September 24, they won 10 of 12 games to clinch their fifth pennant since 1902.

The Athletics lost eight of their final nine games, but it hardly mattered. They wound up with a 96–57 record while finishing six and one-half games ahead of the second-place Senators. The A's defeated Washington in 14 of 22 games, despite the presence of Walter Johnson, who posted a 36–7 record that year. The Cleveland Naps, led by former A's player Shoeless Joe Jackson, finished a distant third, nine and one-half games back.

Collins ended up as the team's leading hitter with a .345 batting average and a league-leading 125 runs scored. Baker hit .337 while winning the home run (12) and RBI (117) titles and finishing second in runs (116). Collins and Baker placed fourth and fifth, respectively, in the batting race won by Ty Cobb with a .390 average. While winning his third of four straight home run crowns, Baker was the only batter in the American League that year to homer in double figures.

Among the other regulars, Stuffy McInnis hit .324 and was second in the league in RBI with 90. Eddie Murphy hit .295, Oldring batted .283, Barry hit .275, and Lapp averaged .227 while sharing the catching duties with Schang, who hit .266. Of the other reserves, only Danny Murphy (.322), Strunk (.305), and Daley (.255) played 40 or more games.

In the midst of a streak in which he hit over .300 in five straight years as a regular, Stuffy McInnis was one of the A's big hitters in 1913 with a .324 average.
Courtesy of Rich Westcott

On the mound, the Athletics were led by Bender, who not only posted a 21–10 record, but later was credited with recording a league-leading 13 saves while pitching in 48 games overall and compiling a 2.21 earned run average.

Plank, in his 13th season, had an 18–10 record with a 2.60 ERA and a team-high 151 strikeouts. And, as it turned out, there were no holes in the pitching staff. Unlike most staffs of the era, the Athletics used 14 different hurlers during the season with Brown (17–11), Bush (15–6), and Houck (14–6) also enjoying excellent seasons. Among the rest of the staff, Shawkey went 6–5, Weldon Wyckoff was 2–4, and the nineteen-year-old Pennock, a future Hall of Famer and general manager of the Phillies, posted a 2–1 record in 14 games.

As a team, the Athletics led the league in batting average (.280), home runs (33), and runs (794). The A's scored in double figures nineteen times. The pitching staff had a combined ERA of 3.19 with 630 strikeouts in 1,351.1 innings pitched and 17 shutouts. The A's had a 55–20 record in the first half and a 41–37 mark in the second semester. The team drew 571,896 fans to Shibe Park.

Despite their glittering record, the Athletics were not overwhelming favorites as the World Series began. The National League champion New York Giants had posted a 101–51 record during the season, finishing 13½ games ahead of the second-place Philadelphia Phillies, who two years later would win their first National League pennant.

Manager John McGraw's Giants were led by two extraordinary pitchers, Christy Mathewson (25–11) and Rube Marquard

(23–10). A third hurler, Jeff Tesreau, posted a 22–13 record during the season, while the fourth starter, Al Demaree, was 13–4.

At the plate, the Giants fielded a lineup that had the highest batting average (.273) in the league. Although no one led the league in any of the major hitting categories, and only one regular (catcher Chief Meyers) hit above .300, the Giants had a solid lineup, including first baseman Fred Merkle, captain and second baseman Larry Doyle, shortstop Art Fletcher, third baseman Buck Herzog, and outfelders Fred Snodgrass, Red Murray, and George Burns.

Outfielder Jim Thorpe, who hit .143 in 19 games that year, was among the bench players, as was Eddie Grant, a former Phillies third baseman who would later become the first major league player killed in World War I.

McGraw, of course, was a dominant force on the team. By 1913, in the midst of a 33-year career as a manager, he had won five National League pennants and one World Series. He was called brash and often nasty by sports writer Francis Richter, who wrote that McGraw was nevertheless "the greatest and most valuable asset of the New York club." Richter added, "He has absolute confidence in his own judgement, is not disposed to receive counsel or suggestions or to seek advice, is determined to always and under all circumstance run the game according to his own ideas, plans, and directions, and is rigidly insistent upon implicit obedience."

Injuries to Snodgrass (charley horse), Meyers (broken finger), and Merkle (leg) did not help the Giants' chances, and each saw little action in the Series.

But with Mathewson, on his way to becoming tied with Grover Cleveland Alexander as the third-winningest pitcher of all time, and Marquard, another future Hall of Famer, the Giants were hardly out of the running.

With eleven future Hall of Famers taking part, including umpires Bill Klem, Tommy Connolly, Cy Rigler, and Rip Egan, the first game, played ironically between two teams that many years later would be neighbors on the West Coast, was held on a dark and dreary day at the Polo Grounds in New York. Marquard was on the mound for the Giants and Bender was pitching for the Athletics. Neither was terribly effective as each team slammed 11 hits. Collins and Baker each slugged 3 hits for the A's.

The A's took a 3–1 lead in the fourth when Collins tripled and scored on Baker's single, and Shang hit a two-run triple that was misjudged in center field by the Giants' Art Shafer, who was filling in for Snodgrass. Baker followed in the fifth with a two-run homer that knocked out Marquard. A two-run single by Fletcher in the fifth sparked a three-run Giants rally, but Bender held on to finish the game with a 6–4 victory while yielding 11 hits.

Game Two played at Shibe Park had the opposite result. Old rivals Plank and Mathewson, who had been facing each other since 1905, were on the mound. Entering the bottom of the ninth, the game was still scoreless. When the A's put Barry on second and Strunk on third with no outs, another win seemed assured. But ground balls on successive plays wound up with each runner getting thrown out at the plate. A third grounder ended the inning. In the top of the 10th, the Giants scored three runs with Mathewson singling home the first run. That was followed by an error by Collins, a walk, and a bouncer over third that went for a two-run single by Fletcher. The Giants won, 3–0, as both pitchers went the distance with Mathewson allowing eight hits and Plank seven.

The third game returned the next day to New York. This time, the Athletics won, 8–2, with Bush firing a five-hitter. The A's, while tallying 12 hits, including three by Collins, wrapped up the game early, scoring five runs in the first two innings off of Tesreau. Hits by Oldring, Collins, and Baker, a triple steal, and a wild throw by Fletcher gave the A's three runs in the first. Two more runs scored with two outs in the second, then a two-run triple by Collins in the seventh and a homer in the eighth by Schang completed the A's scoring.

Bender returned to the mound in the fourth game, played back at Shibe Park. He went the distance, allowing eight hits as the A's won, 6–5, with Demaree taking the loss. The A's staked Bender to a 4–0 lead with an RBIs double by Barry in the second inning and a two-run single by Schang in the third being the key blows. Then with Marquard pitching in relief for the Giants in the fifth, the Athletics scored two more runs on an RBIs double by Barry and an RBIs single by Schang.

In the sixth, Oldring squashed a Giants threat with a sensational diving catch in center that Mack called "the greatest catch I ever saw in a World Series." The Giants scored three times in the seventh and twice in the eighth to make the score close before Bender wound up with an eight-hitter to notch his second complete game win of the Series.

Another Mathewson-Plank matchup took place in Game Five at the Polo Grounds. This time, Plank fired a sparkling two-hitter as the Athletics clinched the Series with a 3–1 win. Mathewson allowed just six hits. Baker's sacrifice fly scored the A's first run in the first inning. The A's added two more runs in the third, one on a single by Murphy and the other on McInnis's sacrifice fly.

With its original capacity of 23,000, Shibe Park had a sellout crowd at games in the 1913 World Series.
Courtesy of Bob Warrington

The win gave the Athletics their third World Series victory in four years. Baker (.450) and Collins (.421) were the big hitters in the event as the A's outhit the Giants, .264 to .201.

The Series took in a total of $325,980 and each A's player got a winner's share of $3,246.36.

Two and one-half weeks later, on October 28, the city arranged a celebration that began with the team riding in cars behind a police marching band from Shibe Park down Lehigh Avenue to Broad Street and then down to the Bellevue-Stratford Hotel in Center City. Thousands of cheering fans lined along the parade route, some with signs and shouts about their team. "Who Had No Pitchers?" said one sign.

The ever-popular Mack received a thunderous welcome as he stepped out of the first car. A joyful dinner followed with players, all but seven of whom attended the banquet, thunderously applauded. Governor John Tener was the first speaker, and he was followed by one dozen others, including Phillies president William Baker, Giants president Harry Hempstead, Brooklyn Dodgers president Charles Ebbetts, and former Philadelphia Mayor John Reyburn.

City managing director E. T. Stotesbury, filling in for the ill Mayor Rudolph Blankenburg, said that "Philadelphia is now known in places where it has never been known before, and it's all because of this wonderful ball team."

The "wonderful" ball team was back in the Fall Classic the following year after winning 99 games and finishing eight and one-half games in front of the Red Sox. But there would be no World Series victory this time. The A's were losers in four straight games to the Boston Braves, nicknamed "The Miracle Braves" because they had come from dead last in the

National League standings on July 18 to win the pennant and then the Series.

After the Series, claiming to be deeply in debt, Mack started getting rid of his top players. First to go were Coombs, Plank, Bender, Collins, and Baker. Without them in 1915, the Athletics plummeted to last place. They would finish there for seven straight years, one season posting a 36–117 record.

THE YELLOW JACKETS ARE THE CITY'S FIRST NFL CHAMPION

It is not common knowledge in this modern era, but there was a time when Philadelphia had a team in the National Football League that was not called the Eagles.

Just like the Phillies, who were not Philadelphia's first National League baseball team, and the 76ers, who were not the city's first National Basketball Association team, the Eagles were the second Philadelphia team that performed in the NFL.

The city's first NFL team was called the Frankford Yellow Jackets and they played in the 1920s and early 1930s. They even won an NFL championship. That came in 1926 when the team played in a league that was vastly different from the one that exists today.

The NFL, which had previously been called the American Professional Football Conference before changing its name in 1922, had twenty teams by 1923. They came not only from the big cities such as Chicago, St. Louis, and Cleveland, but also from places such as Racine, Wisconsin; Duluth, Minnesota; Canton, Ohio; and Hammond, Indiana. Some played more games than others, and some didn't even last through the whole season. The teams played with eighteen-player rosters.

**The Frankford Yellow Jackets (wearing dark jerseys)
were hugely popular during an era when they won the city's
first NFL championship in 1926.**
Courtesy of Rich Westcott

The Yellow Jackets, who eventually sent six members to the Football Hall of Fame, had grown out of an organization called the Frankford Athletic Association, which was formed in 1899. The association was open to the public, and members bought shares in it for $10 apiece, while also throwing in extra money to finance the club's activities. Chartered as a nonprofit organization, the group donated excess income from its football team to local charities such as Frankford Hospital and community groups including the Boy Scouts.

The association had a football team, which originally played at a place called Wister's Park at Oxford Road and Leiper Street. When Frankford High School was built on that site a few years later, the team moved down the street to a park called Brown's Field on Pratt Street.

The team was called the Yellow Jackets, and in its first season in 1899, it played its opening game against the Reading

YMCA and then against teams from other local athletic associations, plus one from Jefferson Medical College.

The Frankford Association disbanded around 1909, but a few years later, the Yellow Jackets reformed. By the early 1920s, the Jackets, with a team consisting mostly of local high school and college players, including the future Philadelphia Eagles' first coach Lud Wray, had become one of the top independent teams in the nation, often playing at least 20 games in a season.

Among others on the Frankford team were former University of Pennsylvania All-American Heinie Miller and Walter French, a West Point graduate who also played with the Philadelphia Athletics for six seasons. Lou Little, another former Penn All-American, was the coach.

In those days, baseball, as well as high school and college football, were the most popular sports in the city. Individual sports such as golf, boxing, and tennis were popular, too. Basketball was in its infancy, as was pro football. But the Yellow Jackets were known throughout the country as one of the top football teams.

In 1922, they absorbed another top local team called the Union Quakers, and that year it posted a 14–0 record and was declared the champion of Philadelphia while being labeled as the best independent team in the nation. During that and the 1923 seasons when they were 9–2–2 overall, the Yellow Jackets played teams in the NFL. Their 6–2–1 record against those teams resulted in Frankford being awarded a franchise in the NFL in 1924.

In their first season in the then eighteen-team NFL, the Yellow Jackets, coached by former Penn State star and college coach at Iowa and Dickinson Bob (Punk) Berryman, beat the Rochester Jeffersons, 21–0, in their first game. They went on to post an 11–2–1 record against NFL teams, including a 45–7 win over the Buffalo Bisons and a 27–6 victory over the New York Giants, while recording an overall mark of 17–3–1. (In those days, NFL teams were permitted to play games against nonleague teams.)

Because the NFL standings were based on winning percentage, regardless of the number of wins, the Yellow Jackets (.846) finished third, behind Cleveland (7–1–1, .875) and Chi-

In a game that vividly exhibits old-time football, the Yellow Jackets go for the tackle in a game with the New York Giants.
Courtesy of Keith Javic

cago (6–1–4, .857). Halfback Red Hamer finished second in the league in scoring with 72 points.

By then, the Yellow Jackets had moved into the new Frankford Stadium, which was built at a cost of $100,000 on

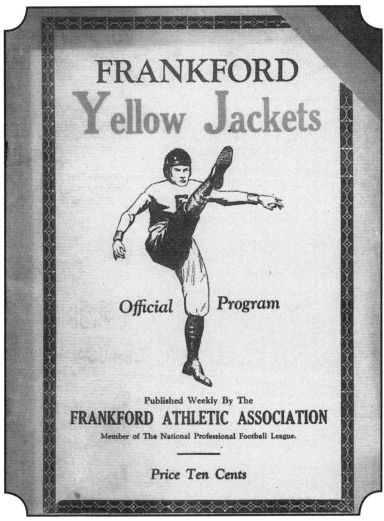

A Frankford Yellow Jackets program was always full of interesting information. It sold for 10 cents.
Courtesy of Keith Javoc

the site of an old horse racing track located at Frankford and Deveraux streets. To help finance the new stadium and the team, the Frankford Athletic Association sold $50 bonds to members, friends, and business people.

Games usually attracted crowds as large as 9,000, with stands located down both sides of the field. The Yellow Jackets even had their own all-male marching band, a team of male cheerleaders, a fight song, and a donkey for a club mascot.

Often the Yellow Jackets played two games on weekends. Due to Pennsylvania's blue laws, they were not allowed to play home games on Sundays. So home games were scheduled on Saturdays, and then the team would hop a train and travel to the other team's city, where they would meet again on Sundays.

According to Bill Hoffman, the last living Yellow Jacket, many players from the team lived in boarding houses in the neighborhood, ate at the local YMCA, and played cards at night on the front porches of people's homes, as he told Ray Didinger for an article that appeared in a 1991 edition of the *Philadelphia Daily News*. Players earned salaries usually of about $150 per game.

"The women baked us cakes," said Hoffman, a guard/tackle out of Lehigh University. "The men brought us seafood from Maryland. We'd sit outside and talk. We'd play ball with the kids. Everyone had a smile and a kind word for us. We were part of the community. That's why we were successful. We became like a family because we lived together and the people in Frankford supported us."

In their second season in the NFL, the Yellow Jackets hired Guy Chamberlain as a player-coach. A future Pro Foot ball Hall of Famer, Chamberlain had been an All-American end at the University of Nebraska and then had been a player-coach for the Canton and then Cleveland Bulldogs, leading them to three consecutive NFL championships in 1922, 1923, and 1924.

Under Chamberlain, who ran the team with no assistants, the 1925 Yellow Jackets got off to a 9–1 start, which included two victories over the Giants in the now twenty-two-team NFL.

Injuries and some dissension among key players, however, chopped the team's league record down to 13–7, which included six losses in the last 10 games and a 49–0 clobbering by the Pottsville Maroons. In another game, an estimated 35,000 fans watched in cold and rain as Red Grange led the Chicago Bears to a 14–7 win over the Yellow Jackets in a game played at Shibe Park (partly to accommodate the big crowd).

The situation changed drastically for the Yellow Jackets the following season, which they opened with a 45–0 win over the Atlantic City Roses in an exhibition game. Then the NFL season, loaded with twenty-two teams at the start, including ones from Los Angeles, Brooklyn, and Hartford, began with league president Joe Carr expressing his extreme optimism. The league, he said, "faces the best and brightest prospect in its history. With every club in the league well-financed and each with an array of past college stars, the outlook is indeed bright."

The 1926 Frankford squad consisted of numerous outstanding players. Particularly noteworthy was Harry (Two Bits) Homan, from Lebanon Valley College. At 5-feet, 4-inches and 142 pounds, Homan was the smallest player in the league,

Houston Stockton was a star fullback for the Yellow Jackets. Many years later, his grandson, John, became an NBA star with the Utah Jazz.
Courtesy of Keith Javic

but one of the best punters in NFL history, an exceptional defensive back, and a fine offensive player who excelled as a quarterback, pass receiver, and blocking back.

Fullback Houston Stockton from Gonzaga, whose grandson, John, later became a great NBA player with the Utah Jazz, was another fine player. End Les Asplundh (Swarthmore), center Bill Springsteen (Lehigh), tackle Adolph (Swede) Youngstrum (Dartmouth), and halfback Ed Weir (Nebraska) were other top players on the team.

The Yellow Jackets always tried to pave their roster with local players, and the 1926 club included backs Ned Wilcox from Swarthmore and Hamer from Penn; plus Hoffman from

Lehigh; end Rae Crowther, a former Olympic boxer out of Penn State; tackle Johhny Budd from Lafayette; and center Max Reed from Bucknell. Of all the Frankford players, no one had more than two years of experience in the pros except back Ben Jones and guard Rudy Comstock (both three years), back Wooky Roberts (four), and end Bulger Lowe and back Lou Smyth, in addition to coach Chamberlain, each with six. Nine players were rookies, and six had one year of experience.

Six days after the Atlantic City rout, the regular season began on September 25 with Frankford playing the Akron Indians to a 6–6 tie in the rain. The following week, the Yellow Jackets beat the Hartford Blues, 13–0, on Saturday at Frankford, then downed them again, 10–0, on Sunday at Hartford.

Frankford, which according to Hoffman used only 12 plays, including four or five passing plays, some running plays through the line or around the ends, and a reverse end-around, was supposed to play back-to-back games against the Buffalo Rangers the next weekend, but after beating the New York club, 30–0, at home on Saturday, they traveled to Buffalo only to have the Sunday game canceled because of wet grounds.

Another weekend series followed on October 16 and 17 with two 6–0 wins over the New York Giants at home and away. In the Jackets' Sunday win at the Polo Grounds, New York City mayor Jimmy Walker was so impressed by the team's performance that at halftime, he marched across the field to wave at the Frankford fans, who returned the gesture with what were described as "hearty cheers." After the game, the Yellow Jackets' Band and Bugle Corps led some 900 fans, most of them wearing yellow jackets, in a parade through downtown New York.

The Yellow Jackets then clubbed Jim Thorpe's Canton Bulldogs, 17–0, to stretch their winning streak to six straight games. The second game was called because of rain, and with it, the streak came to an end.

The next weekend Frankford fell to the Providence Steamrollers, 7–6, at home on Saturday. But, "fighting for revenge," as one newspaper article noted, the Jackets came back to win the next day, 6–3, in the pouring rain at Providence. With that two-game set, the Yellow Jackets' schedule of two games per weekend came to an end.

In subsequent weeks, the Jackets won eight straight games starting with a 33–7 thrashing of the Chicago Cardinals at home in a game in which Hap Moran ran for two touchdowns and drop-kicked two extra points. They then won three more games at Frankford, beating the Duluth Eskimos, starring Ernie Nevers, 10–0, and the Dayton Triangles, 35–0, behind Ben Jones's three touchdowns. Then, in what a newspaper article called "the greatest game ever played at Yellow Jacket Stadium," Frankford edged the Green Bay Packers, 20–14, before a crowd of 13,000 on Thanksgiving Day. Stockton passed to Homan for a 38-yard, game-winning touchdown as the winners overcame an early 13–0 deficit.

According to the next day's *Philadelphia Inquirer*, the win launched "a spectacle of joyful exuberance not witnessed in professional gridiron annals in this dear Quaker City of ours. Oh, what a bedlam as hats and other miscellaneous articles were tossed in the air, and the crowd threatened to break forth in its demonstration in true rabble fashion on the gridiron."

Along the way, the Yellow Jackets had also beaten the Clifton Heights (Delaware County) Orange and Black, 10–0, on the loser's field. Then they won their fourth straight league game with a 7–6 decision over the Detroit Panthers in what was billed as the first postseason game.

On December 4, the Yellow Jackets traveled the few miles back to Shibe Park where they met the undefeated Chicago Bears, a team that Frankford had never previously beaten. The Bears, who one report said were "without a doubt the greatest pro grid machine in the country," were led by their future coach George Halas, former Chicago Cardinals star Paddy Driscoll, and former All-American Hink Tyman.

Before a reported crowd of 15,000, Driscoll missed three drop-kick field goal attempts, including one at the end of the game. Meanwhile, Stockton passed to Homan on a 40-yard touchdown play in the closing minutes of the game, and Hamer kicked the extra point. With that, the Yellow Jackets captured a 7–6 victory and what was termed the league championship.

The next weekend, the Yellow Jackets, playing with "machine-like precision," beat Providence, 24–0, at Frankford, but Sunday's game in Rhode Island was cancelled because of a heavy snowstorm. By then, the Yellow Jackets had posted an eight-game winning streak.

The campaign ended on December 18 when Pottsville visited Frankford in a battle of two bitter rivals. A Philadelphia newspaper reported that the Yellow Jackets had been "practicing daily from morning until dark to be in the pink of condition both mentally and physically, and, according to Chamberlain, 'are prepared to give their all.'"

It was a wild and rough game played in freezing temperatures before a crowd of 6,000 that took just one and three-quarter hours to play. The Yellow Jackets were said to have dominated the first three quarters and the Maroons the last one. At one point, Hamer exploded on a 77-yard end run, but was tackled before reaching the end zone. The final score wound up 0–0.

The Yellow Jackets thus ended the season with a 14–1–2 record, 10 of those wins being shutouts. The 14 wins were the most for an NFL team during the regular season until the record was surpassed by the San Francisco 49ers with 15 in 1984. The Yellow Jackets also outscored their opponents, 236–49, while scoring 32 touchdowns, 7 field goals, and 24 extra points. Jones was fifth in the league in scoring with 48 points.

With their record and winning percentage of .933, the Yellow Jackets were officially declared champions of the NFL. They celebrated their title with a party at the Ben Franklin Hotel in Center City. The Bears were second with a 12–1–3 (.923) mark, followed by Pottsville (10–2–2, .833), the Kansas City Cowboys (8–3, .727), and Green Bay (7–3–3, .700).

"Coach Chamberlain and the entire squad are worthy of the highest praise for displaying the highest brand of football and clean sportsmanship ever witnessed on the local stadium, and for carrying the colors of Frankford to the top of the greatest professional football league in the United States," one local newspaper chortled.

Ironically, the rival American Football League, which had been reformed in 1926, also had a team in Philadelphia, called the Quakers. The Quakers won their league title, giving the city of Philadelphia champions in both pro leagues. An inter-league title game was proposed, but the Yellow Jackets turned down the invitation. The Quakers then played the NFL's sixth-place Giants, and lost, 31–0.

Meanwhile, Philadelphia was going crazy about the Yellow Jackets, and its players were treated like royalty everywhere they went. In addition, the Bugle Corps, which had expanded to about 60 members, was being called one of the top bands in the country and was the winner of the state championship in a contest of bands.

The honeymoon, however, didn't last long. After the season, Chamberlain announced his resignation and moved to Chicago, where he coached just one more season. He finished his coaching career in 1927 with a 58–16–6 record, including a 27–8–2 mark in two seasons with the Yellow Jackets.

Frankford Athletic Association president Theodore Holden also resigned, and was replaced by James Adams. Meanwhile, Charley Moran was hired as the new coach. Moran, however, was also a major league baseball umpire, and at the start of the 1927 season, he had to take time off to work the World Series between the New York Yankees and Pittsburgh Pirates. His son, Tom, served as interim coach in his absence.

The result was a huge letdown from the previous year. In its third game of the season, Frankford routed the Buffalo Bisons, 54–0. After that, Frankford virtually folded the tent. Using four different head coaches along the way, the Yellow Jackets finished with a 6–9–3 record, and were shut out eight times during the season. From a first-place finish the year before, the Yellow Jackets careened all the way to eighth place in what had become a twelve-team league.

Under Weir, a two-time All-American at Nebraska and a future Hall of Famer, the Yellow Jackets bounced back in 1928 with an 11–3–2 record and a second-place finish behind Providence in what was now a reduced ten-team league. Ken Mercer, as he had done the previous year, finished fifth in the league in scoring with 38 points.

Weir was replaced in 1929 by tackle/guard Bull Behman, who had played at Lebanon Valley and Dickinson. In a year when the NFL ruled that all footballs should be the same size starting with the following season, the team slipped to a 10–4–5 (.714) record, good for third place in the standings, behind the Packers (12–0–1, 1.000) and Giants (13–1–1, .929).

By 1930, the Great Depression had begun and Frankford, like all teams, was developing serious financial problems. Home games were drawing as few as 2,000–3,000 fans. As a town heavily populated with manufacturing mills, many Frankford residents had lost their jobs and were unable to pay the price of a ticket.

The financial situation got so bad that the Yellow Jackets were forced to unload most of their veteran players while stocking the team primarily with rookies. George Gibson replaced Behman as coach, and the team wound up with a 4–13–1 league record, which included 13–7 and 13–6 losses to Bronco Nagurski's Chicago Bears.

Prior to the start of the 1931 season, Frankford Stadium was badly damaged by a fire. The ballpark had also been vandalized, and having already been in a state of disrepair, it was shut down and the team was forced to find a new place to play. It wound up playing in three places—Frankford High School's field, the Phillies' Baker Bowl, and Municipal Stadium in South Philadelphia. The press began calling the team the Philadelphia Yellow Jackets. Soon afterward, Frankford Field was demolished, and the spot was later used for midget auto racing and circuses.

Because of the Depression and the distance, loyal Frankford fans were unable to travel out of their immediate area to see games, and in the two other stadiums, the Yellow Jackets were unable to pick up new fans. Adding to that was the team's miserable performance on the field and its constantly increasing financial debt. In the hopes of attracting new fans, the Yellow Jackets sent their players to social events throughout the city.

With Herb Joesting, a former Minnesota All-American, as the new coach, the Yellow Jackets lost their opener to the Brooklyn Dodgers, 20–0, drawing just 2,000 fans to the game at Municipal Stadium. In subsequent games, the crowds became so low, that in late October, the Yellow Jackets were given permission by the league to become a traveling squad.

In one game at Wrigley Field, they lost to the Bears, 13–12, but the attendance was said to be 36,000.

But by the time the Jackets had played their eighth game of the season, their record was a depressing 1–6–1, and they had been outscored by opponents 99–13. The record included seven games in which they were shut out, one being a 14–0 loss to the Portsmouth Spartans and another a 13–0 defeat by the New York Giants before 25,000 at the Polo Grounds in their last two games.

With such a bleak picture on the field, and the cost of rent at Baker Bowl far above the affordable level, the Yellow Jackets decided they'd had enough. It was time to shut down. The team suspended operations and made arrangements for its players to join other NFL teams. The once highly-esteemed Frankford Yellow Jackets would never play again.

After eight years as an NFL team, the Yellow Jackets had a 70–47–15 league record, which included more wins than any team in the NFL over that period. And they had Philadelphia's first NFL championship.

Two years after the Yellow Jackets folded, the NFL granted the defunct franchise to former Penn players Bert Bell (the head coach at Temple University) and Wray (a former Yellow Jackets player). They paid the league $2,500, and assumed $11,000 of the Frankford team's debts.

Shortly after this transaction, Bell and Wray named the team the Philadelphia Eagles. The new team played its first season in 1933. It would not be until 1948, however, when another NFL championship came to Philadelphia.

THE ATHLETICS FINALLY GO BACK ON TOP

5

The 1929 Philadelphia Athletics are generally regarded as one of the greatest teams in baseball history. It's with good reason. This is a team that won the American League pennant by eighteen games, then won the World Series in five games.

It had four future Hall of Famers on the field and two more on the bench. Five regulars and the top reserve hit above .300. It had a great pitching staff, with six hurlers earning wins in double figures and three capturing 18 or more decisions. Furthermore, the team won more games than any Athletics team had up to that point.

Few teams ever had the likes of Jimmie Foxx, Al Simmons, and Mickey Cochrane in the starting lineup or Lefty Grove, George Earnshaw, and Rube Wahlberg in the starting rotation. "They were the rulers of the game," Philadelphia sports writer Ed Pollock claimed.

But that was only part of the story. This is a team that might have been one of baseball's most colorful clubs.

Two of the Athletics' coaches were the star (Eddie Collins) and manager (Kid Gleason) of the infamous Chicago Black Sox of 1919. The manager's son (Earle Mack) was a coach. The

A's had a forty-five-year-old pitcher (Jack Quinn), a future big league umpire (Eddie Rommel), two future major league managers (Cochrane and Jimmy Dykes), and a Swarthmore College graduate (Earnshaw). They also had players nicknamed Double X, Bucketfoot Al, Bing, Mule, Moose, Rube, Camera Eye, and Black Mike.

Eddie Collins returned to the A's and wound up his playing career in 1929. Connie Mack welcomed the presence of his future Hall of Famer.
Courtesy of Rich Westcott

Of course, it was on the field that the team flourished. It posted a 104–46 record during the season, far superior to the record (88–66) of the second-place New York Yankees, winners of three of the previous American League pennants and the last two World Series, each without a loss. Indeed, the 1927 Yankees, with immortals Babe Ruth and Lou Gehrig, are usually regarded as the greatest team in baseball history, although they have considerable competition in that category from the 1929 A's.

It had been a long time since the A's had reached such a lofty level. Although they won six pennants and three World Series in the first fourteen years of the American League's existence, they had not won a fall classic since 1913 or a pennant since 1914.

After that season, Connie Mack, because of the Athletics' reported financial difficulties, had started to break up the team, selling or releasing all his good players. In 1915, the team had started a run of seven straight last-place finishes that included five seasons in which the team lost 100 or more games topped by a then-record 117 defeats in 1916.

Even Mack's long-time recognition as one of the game's leading managers had become questionable. The Tall Tactician was now in his early sixties, and his once superior skills as a manager were considered by many to have disappeared.

But in 1925, after three more second-division finishes, Mack began a rebuilding process. "The time had finally come to rebuild our team," he wrote many years later. "This meant, as it does in every line of business, heavy investments. It costs money to build a winning team."

One of his most significant investments was signing an eighteen-year-old kid named Jimmie Foxx on the recommendation of former Athletics star Frank Baker, Foxx's manager in the Eastern Shore League. Foxx's contract was purchased for $2,500.

Along the way, Mack also signed youngsters Simmons and Cochrane (who was so strongly coveted by Mack that he paid $50,000 for the controlling interest in the Pacific Coast League's Portland Beavers where Mickey played so that he could get the rights to the budding superstar). In 1925 Mack also purchased Grove from the minor league Baltimore Orioles for $100,600, an amount that was purposely designed to exceed by $600 the sum the Yankees paid the Boston Red Sox for Ruth.

The Athletics went from a sixth place finish in 1923 to second in 1925, winning 88 games but finishing eight and one-half games behind the Washington Senators. They dropped to third the following year before jumping back to second in 1927, although that season they finished 19 games behind the front-running Yankees. That year, the A's added Bing Miller, whom they had traded to the St. Louis Browns in 1926 but reacquired the next winter.

By 1928, the Athletics had the nucleus of their future winners. That year, with an outfield that included aging future Hall of Famers Ty Cobb, forty-three, and Tris Speaker, forty, the A's went 98–55, placing just two games back of the Yankees. In July, the A's had been 12 games behind the Yankees, but they rallied to take over first place on September 8. One day later, before some 82,000 at Yankee Stadium, the A's lost a doubleheader. With few opportunities left, that basically ended their pennant hopes for the season.

Cobb and Speaker departed after the 1928 campaign, leaving the A's with an outfield that consisted of Simmons in left field, Mule Haas in center, and Miller in right. Simmons, whose real name was Aloysius Szymanski, was noted for stepping toward third base when he swung, a trait otherwise known as stepping in the bucket, which resulted in his nickname.

A powerful slugger who had hit above .300 and driven in more than 100 runs each season since his rookie year in 1924 (hitting as high as .392 in 1927), Bucketfoot Al was a future Hall of Famer who would hit .334 during a 20-year career in the majors.

Foxx, who had come to the A's as a catcher but played in only 10 games in his first season in 1925 (Mack had insisted he learn the game at the major league level rather than spend time in the minors), was also headed to the Hall of Fame. Double X also played the outfield and third base before Mack wisely moved him to first base, where he replaced slugger Joe Hauser and played a full season for the first time in 1929. Foxx would wind up with twenty years in the majors, hitting .325 with 534 home runs, then the second-best behind Ruth of all time.

Cochrane, known as Black Mike because of his hot temper and aggressive attitude, had started his trip to Cooperstown in 1925. A star halfback on the football team at Boston College, he was ultimately known as one of the top five defensive catchers of all time while hitting .320 in thirteen seasons. The captain and leader of the Athletics, he also served for four years as manager of the Detroit Tigers, including the World Series winner in 1935.

Robert Moses Grove ("Lefty" Grove), who had won 109 games in the minors over five years before Baltimore owner Jack Dunn finally stopped trying to keep him for his own team and sent the pitcher to the majors, was the fourth Athletics player on his way to baseball's Valhalla. Grove, who had control and temper problems in his early years, broke in with the A's in 1925, and before his seventeen-year career was over, he had won twenty or more games in seven straight years and 300 altogether.

Right below this quartet was a distinguished group. Edmund (Bing) Miller was a noted hitter who had played in the minors for seven years before landing in Washington in 1921 at the age of twenty-seven. Traded to the A's in 1922, he spent four outstanding years in Philadelphia, hitting over .300 three times before Mack swapped him in mid-1926 to the Browns. The Browns traded him back to the A's that winter, and Miller went on to a sixteen-year big league career in which he hit .312.

Dykes was another front-liner who was especially popular because he was a native Philadelphian. Having broken in with the A's in 1918 at the age of twenty-one, he was mainly a third baseman, although he played numerous games at second base and shortstop. In twenty-two years in the majors, he hit .280. After his playing days ended, Dykes managed six different teams in the majors, including the Athletics when he succeeded Mack in 1951.

George (Mule) Haas, who joined the A's in 1928; Max (Camera Eye) Bishop, a splendid leadoff hitter and second baseman who came to Philadelphia in 1924; and Joe Boley, the shortstop and an A's rookie in 1927, completed the starting lineup. Sammy Hale, who played mostly at third base, was also a major part of the squad. Collins and catcher Cy Perkins were key utility men.

Moose Earnshaw, a rookie in 1928 who won 127 games during a nine-year career, and Rube Wahlberg, who had come to the A's in 1924 and went on to win 155 games in fifteen years in the majors, joined Grove on the mound. Mack called Grove "the fastest pitcher in baseball." Howard Ehmke, a veteran who began his big league career in 1915 and won 166 games, was a spot starter. Veteran hurlers Rommel and Quinn and rookie Bill Shores doubled as starters and relievers.

As they would do for twelve years, the Athletics spent spring training in Fort Myers, Florida. They started the season on April 17 at Washington with a 13–4 victory over the Senators. Another win over the Senators followed before the A's dropped a 2–1 decision to the New Yorkers at a seven-year-old Yankee Stadium.

Soon, however, as Philadelphia writer Sog Grauley would say, "The Athletics are back in the sun, which shunned them for the last 14 years." The point was well-taken. This was not only a team with outstanding offense, defense, and pitching, but also it was a collection of highly aggressive, highly competitive players. Some, such as Grove, who would tear apart the clubhouse after a loss, Cochrane, who was known to slam his head against the wall, and Simmons, who often showed his hatred of opposing pitchers, had fiery tempers, too.

After the Yankees series, the Athletics won 12 of their next 18 games, and on May 24, Quinn got the win in a 10–8 decision over the Tigers. The victory vaulted the A's into first place, a spot they never relinquished the rest of the season.

That run was punctuated by a notable 24–6 clobbering of the Red Sox at Fenway Park. The A's smashed 29 hits with Foxx slamming five, including two home runs. Simmons also slugged five hits with one home run, while Hale collected four safeties in a rout in which the Athletics scored eight runs in the first inning and 10 in the sixth. Grove was the easy winner while pitching just five innings before Mack decided to give his ace the rest of the day off.

After moving into first place, the Athletics won 19 of their next 22 games, with Grove and Earnshaw each collecting four wins and Wahlberg and Rommel each recording three triumphs. At one point, the A's won 11 games in a row, including a 16–2 thrashing of Boston at Shibe Park.

By the end of the run, the A's had a 31–9 record and a five and one-half game lead over the Yanks. Shortly afterward, they posted two six-game winning streaks, and by the end of June the runaway had arrived with the team holding an amazing 48–17 record and an eight-game lead.

On July 25, with a ten-game lead, the Athletics staged another memorable game when they plastered the Cleveland Indians at Shibe Park, 21–3. In a game that miraculously took just two hours to play, the A's opened with a nine-run first inning. They bashed 25 hits, three each by Bishop, Dykes,

Boley, and Grove, who collected five RBIs during six innings on the mound. Grove, Haas, and Foxx also blasted home runs. The Athletics roared through July with a 24–9 record. Shortly after a 5–3 victory over the Indians in 17 innings in a game in which Grove got the win in relief, the A's lead had exploded to 14 games by August 16. August, however, turned out to be the club's worst month of the season, as they posted only a 15–14 record. But their huge lead over the Yankees remained intact, and in early September they began a run of nine wins in 10 games to build a 16½-game pad as Earnshaw hurled a 5–0 shutout against the Chicago White Sox on September 14 to clinch the pennant for the Philadelphians.

Two weeks later, the season ended as the Athletics triumphed in eight of their final ten games, including their last two wins of the season over the Yankees, to finish with a 104–46 record and an 18-game lead over New York.

To date, it had been a glorious season. The Athletics had beaten the vaunted Yankees in 14 of 22 games, the third-place Indians 14 of 21 times, and Boston and Detroit each 18 of 22 times. A's pitchers led the league with a combined 3.44 earned run average and 573 strikeouts, while holding opponents to the fewest runs (616) in the league. The hitters finished second in team batting average at .296 and in home runs with 122, while the defense led the circuit with a .975 fielding percentage.

Simmons led the league in RBIs with 157 and total bases with 373, placed second in batting average (.365) and slugging average (.642), and was third in home runs (34) and hits (212). Foxx, who became the first batter ever to hit three balls over the left field roof at Shibe Park, was third in slugging average (.625), fourth in home runs (33), and fifth in batting average (.354) and total bases (323).

Elsewhere in the lineup, Miller batted .335 with eight homers and 93 RBIs, Cochrane went .331–7–95, Dykes was .327–13–79, and Haas recorded .313–16–82 marks. Boley batted .251 while Bishop hit .232, but led the league in walks with 128.

Jimmy Dykes hit a career-high .327 in 1929 while playing short-stop, third base, and second base. His single and double drove in three runs in a 10-run seventh inning in the memorable fourth game of the World Series.
Courtesy of Special Collections Research Center, Temple University Libraries

On the mound, Grove posted a 20–6 record while leading the league in ERA (2.81), strikeouts (170), and starts (37). Earnshaw led the league in wins while posting a 24–8 record with a 3.29 ERA. Wahlberg (18–11), Rommel (12–2), Shores (11–6), and Quinn (11–9) also won in double figures.

The Athletics attracted their second-highest crowd of all time, with 839,176 fans paying anywhere from 50 cents for a bleacher seat to two dollars to sit in a box seat. (The A's highest attendance occurred in 1925, with 869,703 people.)

The regular season, which produced a 55–21 record in the first half and a 49–25 mark in the second, was certainly scintillating, to say the least. But the World Series would take a backseat to none the A's ever played.

The opponent was the highly regarded Chicago Cubs, winners of the National League pennant with a 98–54 record and a 10½-game lead over the Pittsburgh Pirates. It was the Cubs' first pennant since 1918, when they lost the World Series to the Red Sox in six games.

The Cubs had some strong Philadelphia connections. Manager Joe McCarthy, himself a future Hall of Famer who was one of baseball's winningest managers, was a Philadelphia native from the Germantown section of the city. Center fielder Lewis (Hack) Wilson, the club's top hitter, had grown up in Leiperville in Delaware County, where he had first earned a reputation as a demolishing power hitter.

McCarthy, who as a youth was in the stands at Shibe Park in 1910 when the Athletics defeated the Cubs in the World Series, would go on to a twenty-four-year managerial career, the best of which came over the course of sixteen years starting in 1931 with the Yankees. Over that period, he won eight pennants and seven World Series.

Wilson, another future Cooperstown inductee, spent twelve years in the majors, winning four home run titles and batting .307. In 1930, he would hit 56 home runs and set an all-time record with 190 RBIs.

The Cubs had a devastating outfield. In 1929, Wilson batted .345 with 39 home runs and a league-leading 159 RBIs. Left fielder Riggs Stephenson hit .362 with 17 homers and 110 RBIs, and right fielder Hazen (Kiki) Cuyler posted a .360 batting average with 15 four-baggers and 102 RBIs.

Rogers Hornsby was the team's second baseman, and in 1929 the future Cooperstown resident and first-year Cub had one of the best seasons of his twenty-three-year career, hitting

The 1929 World Series pitted some of the game's greatest hitters, including (from left) Rogers Hornsby and Hack Wilson of the Chicago Cubs and Al Simmons and Jimmie Foxx of the A's.
Courtesy of Rich Westcott

.380 with 39 dingers and 149 RBIs. First baseman Charlie Grimm hit .298 with 10 home runs and 91 RBIs. Ned English at shortstop (.276), third baseman Norm McMillan (.271), and catcher Zack Taylor (.274) completed the starting eight.

On the mound, Pat Malone (22–10), Charlie Root (19–6), and Guy Bush (18–7) were the club's big winners. Behind them were John (Sheriff) Blake (14–13) and Hal Carlson (11–5).

Overall, the Cubs hit .303 as a team, which tied for second best in the league. They led the league in fielding average with a .975 mark and in shutouts with 14. The combined ERA of the pitching staff was 4.16.

Though loaded with outstanding players, the Cubs were about to face some bitter disappointment as the Series began on October 8 at Wrigley Field in Chicago.

After the A's had clinched the pennant, Mack had a problem. Who would be the starting pitcher in the first Series game? "I was so heavily loaded with big pitchers that I found myself in a quandary," he said many years later.

"My eyes fell on Ehmke, a grand old-timer," Mack continued. "I beckoned him to follow me. As we stood outside the locker room, I said to him, 'Howard, it looks like I'm going to have to let you go.'

"'Mr. Mack,' Ehmke replied. 'I've always wanted to pitch in a World Series, and this is as close as I'll ever get. I've got one more good game in me. How about giving me a chance?'"

That was said despite the fact that Ehmke was at the end of a fifteen-year career and had pitched in just eleven games (winning seven of nine decisions) during the 1929 season.

"I changed my mind," Mack said. "'Howard, you're going to pitch in the Series.' I asked Howard to tell no one, and he kept his pledge."

Mack told Ehmke to go on the road during the final week of the season and scout the Cubs. In between, he should work out and prepare to start the first game of the Series.

Finally, game day arrived. Still, no one but Mack and Ehmke knew who would be the A's starting pitcher. "Our opponents were eager to get this information and the newspaper men were all speculating," Mack said. "Not until shortly before game time when Howard took off his jacket and began to warm up did the secret come out."

When it finally became apparent that Ehmke would be the Athletics' starter, virtually the entire baseball world reeled in shock. But Mack knew what he was doing. He was certain that the side-arming hurler would be extremely tough on the largely righthanded Cubs lineup.

Once again, the genius of Mack rose to the top. Not only did Ehmke, who would never win another game, set an individual Series record that would stand for twenty-four years by striking out thirteen batters, he fired a complete game eight-hitter to lead the Athletics to a 3–1 victory before some 51,000 Cubs fans. Foxx's solo homer in the seventh off of Root broke a 0–0 tie, and then Miller's two-run single in the ninth clinched the win.

Ehmke had captured a heroic victory that would go down in history as one of the great World Series pitching feats. But the Cubs' penchant for whiffing continued in Game Two.

Earnshaw and Grove combined to fan 13 more Bruins in a 9–3 A's rout.

Foxx clubbed a three-run homer in the third and the Athletics added three more tallies to kayo Malone in the fourth. Earnshaw, however, was knocked out in the midst of a three-run Cubs uprising in the fifth, but Grove came in and blanked Chicago the rest of the way. Simmons's homer and four RBIs added to the A's 12-hit slugfest, with Earnshaw getting credit for the win, despite pitching less than five innings (as required today).

Two days later, the Series resumed at Shibe Park and curiously Mack picked Earnshaw to start again. Before a sellout crowd of 29,291 inside the park and several thousand more on

George Earnshaw (right), who led the league in wins in 1929 with 24, and Rube Wahlberg, who recorded 18 wins, surround their manager, Connie Mack.
Courtesy of Rich Westcott

nearby rooftops, Earnshaw hurled a complete game six-hitter and struck out 10. But the A's could score only one run against Bush, while a three-run Cubs sixth featuring a two-run single by Cuyler gave Chicago a 3–1 victory.

One day later, one of the most memorable games in World Series history occurred. Mack picked the elderly, spit-ball-throwing Quinn to start against Root. It looked like no contest as the Cubs, with the help of Grimm's two-run homer, sprinted to an 8–0 lead off Quinn, Walberg, and Rommel.

Then in the bottom of the seventh, the A's staged the all-time greatest explosion in World Series history. Simmons began the inning with a home run over the roof. Soon, an RBI single by Dykes and a two-run single by Bishop made the score 8–4 and kayoed Root. Against reliever Art Nehf, Haas hit a line drive directly at Wilson, but the Cubs center fielder lost it in the sun, and the A's hitter circled the bases for a three-run inside-the-park home run. Three batters later, Foxx singled home the tying run. Then, against Malone, the fourth Cubs pitcher of the inning, Dykes smacked a two-run double to give the A's a record 10-run inning.

Grove, who Mack had mysteriously not used as a starter, retired the final six Cubs batters and the A's went home with a 10–8 victory. "What a game that was," Mack understated.

Game Five was almost anticlimactic. With President Herbert Hoover in the stands and the fans yelling "beer, beer, we want beer" at him because of his highly unpopular prohibition edict called the Volstead Act, Mack again started Ehmke. But this time, the result was different. Ehmke gave up two runs in the fourth inning and was replaced by Walberg. The 2–0 lead held until the bottom of the ninth when the A's came to bat, having managed just two hits off Malone. With one out, Bishop singled. Then Haas tied the score with a home run over the right field wall. One out later, Simmons doubled and Foxx walked. Then Miller slammed a double to right-center and Simmons scored to give the A's a 3–2 victory and the World Championship.

The Athletics were back on top. A feeling of ecstasy engulfed the city. Dykes (.421), Cochrane (.400), Miller (.368), Foxx (.350), and Simmons (.300) had all carried big bats as the Athletics hit .281 as a team. Six A's pitchers posted a combined 2.40 ERA while holding Chicago to a .249 batting average.

Two weeks later, the joy would come crumbling back to earth when the stock market crashed on Wall Street and the nation would soon plunge into the Great Depression.

That winter, Mack received the Philadelphia Award. The award, presented by the Bok Foundation and earning the winner $10,000, was given to the citizen who contributed the greatest service to the city in 1929. Mack had certainly done that, and his contributions would continue in 1930 when the Athletics won yet another World Series.

THE A'S WIN THEIR FIFTH WORLD SERIES

6

It was a year unlike any other. And not just in baseball.

On October 29, 1929, just fifteen short days after the Philadelphia Athletics had clinched their first World Series victory in sixteen years, the United States was bludgeoned by the worst economic disaster in history when the stock market crashed. The catastrophic collapse ignited a financial plunge that would produce what became known as the Great Depression, a period that lasted for more than one decade and that produced financial ruin throughout the planet.

In the process, millions of Americans lost their jobs. In the Philadelphia area alone, nearly 20 percent of the working population lost their jobs and were relegated to lives of scraping to make a living. Men sold fruit from wagons and women scrubbed floors, all earning virtually nothing for their efforts.

The Athletics did not go unaffected. In an area surrounded by working-class people, the unemployment rate was close to 25 percent. That not only had a major effect on attendance at games, but also would ultimately play a major role in the Athletics' future success.

According to baseball historian Bob Warrington, A's owner Connie Mack did what he could to help alleviate the desperate straits of those living in the area near Shibe Park. "Neighborhood kids were hired to be sweepers or scorecard sellers at the ballpark," he said. And when there was food left over from concession stands, Mack would send it to St. Joseph's Home for Boys, a residence for needy youth at 16th Street and Allegheny Avenue. In addition, Mack hired as many men as possible to help maintain the ballpark.

Mack wasn't exactly on Easy Street himself. He had become the majority owner of the team, but carried a substantial debt. The Tall Tactician lived comfortably but not lavishly. He resided in a large, attractive house just off of Lincoln Drive on the outskirts of Germantown. It was definitely an upscale neighborhood, but not quite in a league with the posh Main Line.

Although the Athletics had an exceedingly large team payroll, Mr. Baseball, as he was also known, was not in a position to stuff extra money into the wallets of his players. In 1930, Jimmy Dykes, for instance, was paid $7,000, the same as the previous season. Jimmie Foxx drew a salary of $17,000 as part of a three-year, $50,000 contract. And Lefty Grove and Mickey Cochrane each made about $20,000 in 1930. All were far below the sums doled out to players such as Lou Gehrig and Babe Ruth, the latter being in the midst of a three-year, $160,000 contract.

The only Athletics player who commanded a substantial salary was left fielder Al Simmons, who had demanded

Jimmie Foxx (.354–33–117), Mickey Cochrane (.331–7–95), and Al Simmons (.365–34–157), all future Hall of Famers, had huge seasons for the 1929 Athletics.
Courtesy of Rich Westcott

a three-year, $100,000 contract and held out all spring before getting it just minutes before the season's first game.

With Simmons, Foxx, Grove, and Cochrane, the Athletics still had their four future Hall of Famers. Along with that quartet, the 1930 roster remained virtually the same as the previous year.

The A's also had Bing Miller in right field, Mule Haas in center, Max Bishop at second base, and Joe Boley at shortstop with Grove, George Earnshaw, and Rube Wahlberg serving as the top pitchers. The main differences on the roster were pitcher Leroy (Popeye) Mahaffey, infielders Eric (Boob) McNair, Bill (Dib) Williams, and Michael (Pinky) Higgins and outfielders Jim Moore and Roger (Doc) Cramer, a future big league star. All were young players, most of whom had been plucked from the minors, and some of whom played only part of the 1930 season in Philadelphia. The A's also brought back veteran catcher Wally Schang, who had broken in with the A's in 1913, in a trade with the St. Louis Browns for Sammy Hale, who had played much of the previous season as the team's third baseman.

Although sometimes overshadowed by his future Hall of Fame team-mates, Bing Miller was one of the A's standout players. He hit over .300 seven times in two terms with the A's, including .303 in 1930.
Courtesy of Rich Westcott

On offense, the team was still built around its future Hall of Famers—Foxx, Simmons, and Cochrane, the captain of the team and one who was noted as "the field general." Perhaps somewhat ironically for two big stars, Foxx and Simmons were roommates on the road. Like some of the other players,

Simmons lived when at home in a bedroom at 2745 North 20th Street in a house that sat behind the right field wall. Neighborhood boys usually followed him as he walked each day to the ballpark.

He might've been friendly with the boys, but he was certainly hostile when he was at bat. "They're trying to take bread and butter out of my mouth," he would say with a considerable amount of dislike for pitchers. Ty Cobb had once called Simmons "the gamest man in baseball with two strikes on him."

For Simmons, the 1930 season would turn out to be one of the best of his career. His .381 average beat Gehrig by two points and gave him the first of two straight batting titles (he hit .390 in 1931), making him the first A's player to win a batting crown since Nap Lajoie won one in 1901. Bucketfoot Al drove in 165 runs (second to Gehrig's 174), hit 36 homers, and led the league with 152 runs scored, all career highs.

Foxx, who would go on to win three straight Most Valuable Player Awards, was not far behind. He hit .335 with 156 RBIs, 127 runs, and 37 four-baggers, which ranked third in the league. Cochrane, recording the best batting average of his career, hit .357 with 10 homers and 85 RBIs, while Miller hit .303 with 100 RBIs, Dykes .301, and Haas .299. Overall, the A's hit .294 as a team, but still finished fourth as the third-place New York Yankees led with a .309 mark.

Such heavy hitting attested to the major leagues' having introduced a livelier ball that season. That, however, didn't have much of an effect on the Athletics' top pitchers as Grove racked up a 28–5 mark while leading the league in wins, earned run average (2.54), strikeouts (209), and games pitched (50). Grove was later credited with nine saves. For Grove, he would have two of the greatest back-to-back seasons in baseball history as he posted a 31–4 record in 1931 while leading the league in virtually every top pitching category and winning six straight strikeout crowns.

Earnshaw, who went 22–13 while ranking second in strikeouts (193) and games (49) and third in wins and innings pitched (296), also had a stellar season. In addition, Wahlberg registered a 13–12 mark while Bill Shores went 12–4.

Eddie Rommel and forty-six-year-old Jack Quinn served as able relievers.

As was often the case on those days, ongoing arguments raged over whether the Athletics or the Yankees were the better team. Was it Murderers' Row or the White Elephants? By the end of 1931, the A's had captured three straight pennants and two World Series. The Yankees had the same record between 1926 and 1928. In their three years, the A's had a 313–143 record (.686), while the Yanks had a 302–160 (.654) mark.

Such debates didn't matter in 1930. The Athletics were by far the best team in the American League, and they would prove to hold the same description after the World Series.

The season opened on April 15, with the Athletics downing the Yankees before an overflow crowd of 38,000 at Shibe Park, 6–2. Simmons hit a home run on the first pitch thrown to him in 1930 and Grove fired a six-hitter as the A's whipped Yanks star hurler George Pipgras.

Lefty Grove, en route to two of the greatest consecutive seasons in baseball history, posted a 28–5 record in 1930. The following year, he went 31–4.

Courtesy of Rich Westcott

Over the next month, the Washington Senators, managed by future Hall of Fame pitcher Walter Johnson, would prove to be the Athletics' main competition. In April, the A's won only six of 11 games and at one point fell as far as five games out of first place.

The A's improved considerably after that. One highlight was a 19–2 whipping of the Detroit Tigers on May 1 with Bishop, considered one of the best leadoff hitters in the game, and Foxx each smacking two home runs to lead the club's 18-hit barrage in a seven-hit effort from Grove. Then, with the help of a six-game win streak, the Mackmen climbed into first place. Although they lasted only a little more than one week there, the Athletics won 11 of 13 games through mid-May. Eventually, though, the Senators beat them seven straight times, and late in the month, the A's had fallen to as much as four games behind Washington.

Along the way, there were some very bad days. On May 11, the Cleveland Indians smashed 25 hits, including five by Bib Falk who also scored five times and drove in five runs, to annihilate the A's, 25–7. At one point, Mahaffey gave up 11 runs in three and one-third innings.

Ten days later, the Athletics and Yankees played seven straight games. The Athletics won a doubleheader on May 21 at Shibe Park, although Babe Ruth hit three homers and collected six RBIs in a 15–7 Yanks loss in the first game. The next day in another doubleheader, the New Yorkers won 10–1 and 20–13. In the second game, the two teams tied an all-time record with 10 home runs, thanks in large part to Lou Gehrig's three home runs and eight RBIs and Ruth's three more dingers, the first time in his career that he'd ever hit three homers in a regular-season game.

Two days after that, the competition resumed with a doubleheader at Yankee Stadium with the Yanks winning, 10–6 and 11–1, before an announced crowd of 61,000. Ruth homered once in each game, giving him a record eight homers and 18 RBIs in six games. The A's finally got back in the win column with a 10–3 victory on May 25. That began a streak of 10 straight wins for the A's.

That streak included two key wins over the Senators. With Washington holding a four and one-half game lead, the

Nats came to Shibe Park for a morning/afternoon double-header on Memorial Day. With the Athletics trailing 6–3 in the bottom of the ninth in the first game, Simmons smacked a three-run homer to tie the score. Ultimately, Simmons doubled, advanced to third on a hit by Dykes, and scored on McNair's single in the 13th inning to give his team a 7–6 victory.

During his trip around the bases, Simmons suffered a knee injury and was forced to sit on the bench for the second game. But, pinch-hitting in the fourth inning, he lashed a grand slam home run to give the A's an 8–7 lead. The A's went on to win the second game, 14–11.

That allowed May to finish on a positive note as the Athletics wound up winning 21 of 30 games during the month. On June 1, after a 9–6 win over the Senators, the Athletics regained the lead over Washington, which they would hold for all but two days the rest of the season.

Another big moment for the Athletics occurred on June 23, when they clobbered the Chicago White Sox, 17–9. Simmons paced a 20-hit attack with two home runs, five hits, five runs, and five RBIs. Mahaffey, who in previous years had appeared in the big leagues only briefly with the Pittsburgh Pirates, went the distance, yielding 10 hits.

In June, the A's won 13 of 16 games at one point, but they could never get more than two and one-half games ahead of the unrelenting Senators. But after slipping to second place for two days, the A's went back into first with eight straight wins in mid-July with Shores, Rommel, and Earnshaw each recording two decisions. That stretched the A's lead to three and one-half games, and it would never be that low again.

By the end of July, the White Elephants had won 23 of 32 games during the month, and were in front by eight games. Afterward, they would win 12 of 15 games, with Grove registering four victories.

The Athletics clinched the pennant on September 18 with a 14–10 victory over the White Sox at Comiskey Park in a game in which the winners slugged 20 hits, including home runs by Simmons and Foxx. Wahlberg got the win with Grove twirling three innings in relief. At that point, the A's had an eight and one-half game lead over the Senators. Three days later, they beat the St. Louis Browns, 10–4, in the second game of a doubleheader to capture their 100th win.

The season ended with the Athletics holding a 102–52 record and an eight-game lead over Washington, which finished at 94–60, but had beaten the A's 12 times in 22 games. The Yankees were a distant third, 16 games behind the A's. Incredibly, 62 of the A's games that were timed (in those days, not every game was timed) were played in less than two hours.

As an indication of the effects of the Great Depression that now engulfed the nation, the A's drew 721,663 for the season, a drop of more than 118,000 from the previous year, but by far the highest attendance the team would attract until 1947.

The World Series found the Athletics pitted against a new rival. In their previous six postseason meetings, they had never faced the St. Louis Cardinals. The Cards, however, were more than ample competition.

St. Louis was managed by the old catcher, Gabby Street, a one-time battery mate of Walter Johnson. The previous season, Street had served for two games as an interim skipper of the Cardinals, who were on their way to a fourth-place finish and a distant 20 games behind the league-leading Chicago Cubs.

En route to a 92–62 record and a two-game lead over the Cubs, the Cardinals had won 39 of their final 49 games. With a ferocious offense in which every batter in the starting lineup and three of the top utility men hit over .300, the team had a batting average of .314, which was second in the league behind the New York Giants (.319).

The lineup featured second baseman and future Hall of Famer Frankie Frisch, who had hit .346 during the season. Right fielder George Watkins (.373); left fielder Chick Hafey (.336); Philadelphia native and past and future Phillies catcher and manager Jimmie Wilson (.318); and third baseman Sparky Adams (.314) were among a host of other Cardinals big hitters.

In addition to their spectacular offense, the Redbirds had a fairly average pitching staff that had led the league in runs allowed with 1,004. The top winners were Wild Bill Hallahan (15–9), and aging future Hall of Famers Jesse Haines (13–8) and Burleigh Grimes (13–6), who was nearing the end of a nineteen-year career. The staff also included the inimitable Flint Rhem (12–8), who late in the season had disappeared after winning six games in a row. Four days later, Rhem reappeared, insisting that he had been kidnapped by gamblers.

The first Series game was played on October 1 at Shibe Park. President Herbert Hoover, attending his second of three straight World Series, threw out the first ball with a capacity crowd of 32,295 in the stands.

The attendance did not count the spectators on porch roofs and the rooftops of houses behind the right field wall along 20th Street. There, homeowners set up bleachers and sold seats at rates that ranged from 50 cents during a regular season game to $5.50 for a World Series contest and peddled beer to the fans. Some spectators reached their lofty perches on ladders, some climbed out of bedroom windows, and some even scrambled up through skylights in bathroom ceilings. Sometimes, there were as many as several thousand fans on the roofs of the line of row homes.

Once they got to the roofs, fans could peer over the 12-foot high right field wall and watch games without obstruction. The practice had been going on for a number of years, much to the chagrin of Connie Mack. In 1935, Mack, highly annoyed by the revenue he was losing, raised the height of the wall to 34 feet, effectively blocking the views of the roof-dwellers. Called "The Spite Wall" by angry fans, Mack's move eventually wound up in court with the Athletics, represented by a rising young attorney named Richardson Dilworth, a future Philadelphia mayor. They ended up winning the case over the homeowners who wanted the wall removed.

But that was five years down the road. The current issue was the World Series, and in the opener, Grove took the mound against Grimes. Because he was grandfathered following the major leagues' banning of the pitch, Grimes was the last hurler allowed to throw a spitball.

Grimes held his opponents to five hits, but each one was for extra bases, including home runs by Cochrane and Simmons, triples by Foxx and Haas, and a double by Dykes. These were enough to help the A's overcome an early 2–1 deficit and go on to a 5–2 victory as Grove got the win while allowing nine hits.

Game Two had the same size crowd with Earnshaw facing Rhem. Cochrane's homer in the first inning helped the A's jump out to a 2–0 lead. After a solo four-bagger by Watkins in the second inning, the home team added two more runs in the third and two in the fourth to knock out Rhem. With Earnshaw hurling a six-hitter and striking out eight, the A's waltzed home with a 6–1 victory.

The Series moved to St. Louis for the third game and with the home field advantage, the Cardinals slammed 10 hits and captured a 5–0 win behind the seven-hit pitching of Hallahan. Taylor Douthit homered off Wahlberg in the fourth to give the Cards a 1–0 lead and Wilson subsequently collected two RBIs. Bishop banged three hits for the A's.

With a Series-high crowd of 39,946 in attendance, the Cardinals won again in the fourth game, 3–1, with a four-hitter by Haines besting a five-hitter by Grove. Simmons singled home the lead run in the first inning, but Haines did not allow a hit after the third inning. Meanwhile, the Redbirds scored once in the third, and a Dykes throwing error led to two more runs in the fourth.

The teams were now tied in the Series, and Game Five in Sportsman's Park became a pivotal match. "The fifth game is the big one," Foxx exclaimed. "If you win it, you're over the hump and coasting. If you lose it—well—that's not good at all."

The A's answered the call with a 2–0 victory, although they managed just five hits off Grimes. With Earnshaw on the mound for the Mackmen, each team had only two hits through the first seven innings and neither club scored through the first eight frames, although the visitors loaded the bases in the eighth. Taken out for a pinch-hitter that inning, Earnshaw had allowed just two hits. The Athletics finally won in the ninth when Cochrane walked and Foxx smashed a two-run homer. Grove pitched the final two innings in relief to get the win.

Two days later on October 8, the Series resumed in Philadelphia. Mack chose Earnshaw to make his third start of the Series. The A's got off to a 2–0 lead in the first inning against Hallahan, with Cochrane and Miller each doubling in runs. An upper deck solo homer by Simmons in the third and a two-run blast by Dykes in the fourth gave the A's a 5–0 pad, and the Philly team went on to win, 7–1, despite collecting only seven hits—all for extra bases. Earnshaw again went the distance and gave up only five hits while pitching in his third game in six days.

The Athletics had done it again. By a four games to two count, they were winners of their second straight World Series. Earnshaw had hurled 25 innings, won two games, and allowed just 13 hits and two runs. "He's an iron man if there ever was one," Cardinals catcher Wilson told the *Inquirer.* Grove won the other two games (and lost one) while yielding 15 hits in 19 innings.

Although they hit just .197 as a team (the Cards hit .200), Simmons (.364) and Foxx (.333) were the Athletics' batting leaders. Charley Gelbert (.353) was the only Cardinals' batter to hit over .300. Hafey, with a .273 mark, came next.

After the Series, Mack was ecstatic. "Our teams are world-beaters," he said. "We had a magnificent pitching staff in Lefty Grove, George Earnshaw, and Rube Wahlberg. And

Fans sat on roofs of homes along 20th Street while others jammed the street as they got ready to watch the Athletics and Cardinals play in the 1930 World Series.
Courtesy of Rich Westcott

what an aggregation of power hitters—Jimmie Foxx, Al Simmons, Mickey Cochrane, Bing Miller."

Continuing their spectacular success, the Mackmen would win the American League pennant again in 1931, setting an all-time Athletics record with 107 wins. But they would lose the World Series in seven games to the Cardinals.

Soon afterward, the good years of the Athletics came to an end. Attendance continued to plummet, with Athletics crowds tumbling to as low as 233,173 in 1935. Meanwhile, Mack was forced to sell or trade his key players in what would be an unsuccessful attempt to help his devastating financial problems.

"We were caught in a financial earthquake," Mack said many years later, "and like most business houses, we were forced to retrench. With our heavy investment and the expenses of building Shibe Park and operating the costliest team in our national game, we had to borrow $700,000 from one of our banks."

By the time the depression arrived, the A's were still $400,000 in debt. When the bank demanded payment, Mack and his associates had no choice. They were forced to break up their once-great team, which by then included five players earning a combined lofty total of $100,000 and was, according to Mack, the highest-paid team in baseball history up to that point.

By the end of 1934, Grove, Cochrane, Simmons, Miller, Dykes, Bishop, Earnshaw, and Wahlberg had all been dealt away. Foxx, who during his years in Philadelphia had hit

28 home runs over the left field roof at Shibe Park, became the final Athletics star to go when he was sent in 1935 to the Boston Red Sox, whose general manager was former A's star Eddie Collins.

Unfortunately, after 1932, the Athletics were never again serious pennant contenders, finishing in the first division only three times (1932, 1933, and 1948) after their last World Series appearance. In 1954, the Athletics played their final season in Philadelphia. They would move to Kansas City and later Oakland. And Philadelphia baseball would never again be quite the same.

WARRIORS BECOME PRO BASKETBALL'S FIRST CHAMPS

7 Like most sports in their early years, professional basketball endured a period when it was not considered a major sport. In its infancy and for a number of years thereafter, pro hoops was a game that attracted only the most avid fans and was played in second-rate arenas.

Professionally, the game was played mostly in the East and Midwest, sometimes in cities that ranked somewhat below the country's top metropolises. The teams received little coverage, seldom had African-American players, a tall player was one who stood at six feet, and in many cases, both players and fans were Jewish. College basketball was a more popular segment of the game, and had been since James Naismith invented the sport in 1891.

While independent teams and a few leagues had existed and in some cases thrived beginning in the early 1900s, professional basketball didn't really exist until the 1930s. By then, a team called the Philadelphia SPHAS (South Philadelphia Hebrew Association), which had originally been organized by a young schoolteacher named Eddie Gottlieb in 1918, had not only risen to a high level of popularity in their city, mostly among the Jewish community, but had become one of the country's foremost teams. Ultimately, paying players five to ten dollars per game, the SPHAS operated in several professional leagues over the years, and were famous for their games followed by dances on Saturday nights at the Broadwood Hotel on Broad Street.

Pro basketball, however, was still well below big-time college basketball in terms of public recognition. A league called the National Basketball League was formed in 1937, but while purporting to be a major league, it consisted mostly of mid-western cities and was not well known in the East.

In 1946, a major step in bringing big-time pro basketball to the East was taken when Gottlieb and several other noted basketball figures formed the Basketball Association of America. There were eleven teams, including ones in Philadelphia, New York, Boston, and Washington and their rosters consisted of many of the top college and pro basketball players in the country. Each team would play a sixty-game schedule.

The BAA had numerous ups and downs during its first season of 1946–47, but it prevailed and quickly climbed to a spot as the top pro league in the nation. And in that first season, the Philadelphia Warriors became pro basketball's first true major league champions.

The team played most of its games at a place called the Arena, which stood at 45th and Market Streets in West Philadelphia and had a maximum seating capacity of 7,800. Built in 1920, the Arena was originally noted as an ice hockey venue; in fact, it was the home rink that year for the Yale University hockey team, which lacked a suitable place to play in New Haven.

Eventually, the Arena was used for the Ice Capades when they came to Philadelphia, or by various pro and college ice hockey teams, wrestling and boxing matches, rodeos, swimming shows, concerts, dancing matches, bicycle races, weddings, and auto shows. When the building was being used by others, the Warriors played at Convention Hall near 34th and Locust Streets. One game was even played at Trenton High School. The team practiced either on a court on Boathouse Row along the Schuykill River or at the Palestra.

The principal owner of the Warriors was Pete Tyrell, a former manager of the Arena who had become one of its owners. Gottlieb was the coach and ran the basketball side of the operation.

The team was run out of a two-room office located on the second floor of a movie theater at 1537 Chestnut Street. Aside from Gottlieb, the only other full-time member of the staff was Mike Iannarella, the ticket manager. Dave Zinkoff was the public address announcer and edited the game program, called *The Wigwam*. *Evening Bulletin* sportswriter Harvey Pollack handled the publicity with the help of *Inquirer* sportswriter Herb Good.

"Everything about Gotty was centered behind his desk or in his pocket," said Bill Campbell, the team's play-by-play broadcaster during its early years. "I don't know how he kept track of all those notes he kept in his pocket. It was amazing.

But Eddie was one of the most intuitively bright guys I've ever been around."

Gottlieb had been involved with basketball since his days as a teenager and had become among other things a sports promoter, part owner of a sporting goods business, and an entrepreneur at several levels. He also still ran the SPHAS, which he would do until the team folded in 1954. By the time the BAA was formed, Gottlieb was one of the leading figures in pro basketball, and as one of the league's principal founders, he was largely responsible for making pro basketball what it is today. Along the way, he would also serve for the next forty years as the league's schedule-maker and for twenty-five years as the chairman of the rules committee.

The first job of "The Mogul," as he was known, was, of course, to line up a team. A firm believer in filling the roster with local players because he felt that they would draw bigger crowds, he quickly picked Angelo Musi and Jerry Rullo from Temple; Matt Guokas, George Senesky, and Petey Rosenberg, who had played at St. Joseph's; and Howie Dallmar, a Penn graduate. Rosenberg, also a Philadelphia native, Guokas, and Senesky, plus other squad members Art Hillhouse, Ralph Kaplowitz, and Jerry Fleishman, all had played with the SPHAS.

"I felt we should get as many local players as possible to help the box office," Gottlieb wrote in a guest column in 1971 in *Inside Basketball.* "I didn't want to use all SPHAS players because we were stepping up from a representative club to major league status representing the entire city."

Gottlieb's biggest pick was a player from little-known Murray State College in Kentucky. His name was Joe Fulks, and he would go on to become not only the BAA's first star, but also become known as the "father of the jump shot."

Fulks was from the backwoods town of Birmingham, Kentucky, where drunkenness, shootouts, and other forms of lawless behavior were common. The town, located along the Tennessee River, was a major supplier of bootleg whiskey to Chicago speakeasies operated by mobster Al Capone.

After a sparkling high school career in the late 1930s where he began using a revolutionary technique called a "jump shot," Fulks enrolled at Murray State. He played three years there, then entered the Marine Corps during World War II. While he was stationed in the Far East, Fulks perfected the jump shot playing in a league with other troops.

Eventually, Gottlieb found out about Fulks when Rosenberg gave him a glowing report after seeing Fulks play service ball. After his discharge from the Marines, Fulks signed with the Warriors for $8,000.

"He said he would come if the price was right," Gottlieb recalled years later, "so I offered him $5,000. We had a salary limit of $55,000 for a ten-man team, so that was about the average salary. He said he would like to play, but wouldn't consider less than $8,000. It seemed very high, but I was in no mood to lose him."

Gotty signed the 6-foot, 5-inch Fulks for the player's asking price. And as the coach said, "Without Joe, I don't think the team would've lasted in Philly, and the league might not have existed, either. He was the biggest star, the biggest attraction, and he carried the league."

That he did. With his jump shot, Fulks became the most widely discussed person in basketball. "He revolutionized basketball with that shot," said Campbell. "He just electrified everybody with it."

"People saw that shot, and they'd say, 'What the hell was that?'" recalled basketball Hall of Famer Dolph Schayes, who played with the Syracuse Nats through most of Fulks's career. "The shot was so different, and most people had never seen it before."

Joe Fulks, the father of the jump shot, was big league pro basketball's first superstar. Jumpin' Joe was the BAA's first scoring champion with a 23.2 average (1,389 points) in 1946–47.
Courtesy of Rich Westcott

Fulks's shot drew quick attention when he scored 25 points as the Warriors won their opening game, 81–75, over the Pittsburgh Ironmen at the Arena. Then in the seventh game of the season, Fulks scored 36 points, but the Warriors lost, 64–60, to the New York Knicks. In the next game, Fulks scored 37 to lead his team to a 76–68 victory over the Providence Steamrollers.

Fulks, of course, wasn't the only talented player on the Warriors, a team that focused on passing and defense. Musi and Senesky had been standout guards in college, and were key starters in the backcourt. Dallmar, who had originally attended Stanford, and Fulks were the forwards, and Hillhouse, the tallest player on the team at 6-feet, 7-inches,

The Warriors had a star-studded team that included (from left) Joe Fulks, George Senesky, Angelo Musi, Jerry Fleishman, and Johnny Murphy.
Courtesy of Rich Westcott

was the center. Fleishmen, Rosenberg, Rullo, Guokas, and Kaplowitz (who joined the team during the season) were the top reserves.

"We all got along well with each other," Rullo, the last surviving member of the team, recalled in 2014. "Everybody was in good shape, and we all played well together. We always went out together for dinner on the road. It helped that a lot of us were local guys and we already knew each other or had played with or against each other before we came to the pros. It was really a very good time for all of us."

Despite that, the Warriors did not get off to a glittering start. With low-scoring games dominating play—teams often scored in the 60s and even the 50s, and in one game the locals beat the Pittsburgh Ironmen by the unbelievable score of 53–46 —the Warriors played pretty close to .500 ball through the first half of the season. On January 14, they registered their biggest win of the year with a 104–74 clobbering of the Toronto Huskies in a game in which the Warriors not only recorded a season's high in scoring, but Fulks set a season's high with 41 points. The win gave the Warriors a 15–13 record.

Two games later, the Warriors beat the Boston Celtics, 59–43. They then lost, 57–55, to the Washington Capitols before bouncing back one night later to down the Cleveland Rebels, 83–79.

While playing at the Arena on a court that sat atop ice for the skating rink and was often slippery, the Warriors always drew an avid crowd of followers. Crowds often exceeded the venue's seating capacity. Some fans showed their loyalty by constantly banging folding chairs on the floor. And, of course, with smoking then permitted in all playing sites, the air was always thick with smoke. It was so thick, in fact, the fans seated at the rear of the stands sometimes had trouble seeing the action on the court, not to mention breathing.

On January 30, the Warriors beat the Knicks, 65–58, to launch a run in which they won five straight games. After a 79–61 victory over Toronto for their fifth win in a row, the Warriors had a 23–16 record.

The record jumped to 28–20 with a 75–65 win over the St. Louis Bombers on February 26. Then on March 22, the Warriors posted their second and last 100-point game of the season with a 103–82 victory over Providence.

The season ended on March 30 as the Warriors downed New York, 76–72, to finish with a 35–25 record. That placed them a distant second behind coach Red Auerbach's Capitols (49–11) in the six-team Eastern Division. The Warriors finished just two games ahead of the third-place Knicks (33–27).

With his jump shot attracting attention throughout the league and many players trying to imitate it, Fulks became the league's first scoring champion, with 1,389 points. His 23.2 points-per-game scoring average was particularly amazing because most teams in the league usually scored in the 60–70 point range. The Warriors averaged 68.6 points per game, which ranked fifth in the league, while also placing fifth with 65.2 points allowed per game.

Fulks's average was nearly seven points per game higher than the second-leading scorer, Bob Feerick of Washington,

Warriors teammates Ralph Kaplowitz, Art Hillhouse, and Jerry Rullo (from left) congratulate Joe Fulks after he scored his 1,000th point of the season.
Courtesy of Jim Rosin

who managed a 16.8 mark with 926 points. Suggesting that he missed a lot of shots, Jumpin' Joe, as he was called, had a 30.5 percent field goal percentage.

Dallmar was fourth in the league with 104 assists, 98 behind leader Ernie Calverley of Providence. No other Warrior, however, finished in the top five of the other major statistical categories. Musi was the second-leading scorer on the Warriors with 562 points (9.4 ppg), followed by Dallmar with 528 (8.8), Senesky with 368 (6.3), and Hillhouse with 360 (6.1).

The Warriors wound up outscoring their opponents 4,118–3,909. They had a 25–7 record at home and a 10–18 mark on the road.

By no means expected to make a run at the BAA title, especially with two teams in the Western Division (Chicago and St. Louis) holding better records, the Warriors opened the best-of-three quarterfinals with a 73–68 victory over St. Louis. The Bombers decisively won the next battle, 73–51, but the Warriors came back to win the series with a 75–59 victory at St. Louis.

Advancing to the semifinals, the Warriors swept the Knicks in two games, winning the first match, 82–70, at the Arena, and 72–53 at Madison Square Garden. That put them in the best-of-seven finals against the Chicago Stags.

Chicago had stunned BAA followers by scalding what was regarded as the league's best team, the Washington Caps, four games to two, in the semifinals. With backcourt ace Max Zaslofsky and center Chuck Halbert leading the Stags, Chicago was a heavy favorite to win the championship.

Gottlieb and his plucky crew, which included former SPHAS legend Cy Kaselman as assistant coach, had other ideas, though. With Fulks, Musi, and Dallmar leading the way, the Warriors squashed the Stags four games to one, winning the first two games in Philadelphia. Fulks scored 37 points and Musi tallied 19 as the Warriors won the opener, 84–71.

They won the second game, 85–75, behind 18 points by Dallmar and 13 by Fulks. In Game Three, the score was tied 31–31 at halftime, but the Warriors outscored the Stags, 28–26, in the fourth quarter to get the verdict at Chicago Stadium, 75–72, as Fulks scored 26 points. The Warriors nearly overcame a 65–52 deficit after three quarters by outscoring the Stags 21–9 in the final period, but lost the fourth game, 74–73, despite 24 points by Senesky and 21 by Fulks, who fouled out.

Returning home, the Warriors faced the Stags at the Arena in the fifth game before a sellout crowd of 8,221 with another 5,000 turned away at the gate.

The Warriors led, 22–7, after the first quarter, but held just a 40–38 edge at halftime. The Stags moved into a 68–63 lead by the end of the third period. But with Fulks heating up, the Warriors rallied to tie the score at 78–78 with 1:20 left in the fourth quarter.

Although he was playing with calluses on his left foot, Dallmar sank a 15-foot set shot to put the Warriors in the lead. Kaplowitz followed with a foul shot on a play that went down as one of the most memorable blown calls by a referee in history. It was actually Rosenberg who was fouled, but when he walked to one side, the deadly accurate Kaplowitz stepped to the foul line. Referees Pat Kennedy and Eddie Boyle didn't catch the switch, and Kaplowitz made the shot to put the game away.

The final score was 83–80, and the Warriors had become the BAA's first champion. Fulks finished with 34, while Musi scored 13 and Senesky 11. Tony Jaros led Chicago with 21 points, while Zaslofsky was held to five and Halbert to eight. Ironically, Hillhouse fouled out of each of the five games.

The winning team received $14,000 for its victory, and the losers got $10,000. With the Warriors having won $10,000 from their previous two series, each player walked away with $2,150, nearly one-half of the season's pay for most of them.

"They are a great team," Stags coach Harold Olsen said of the Warriors. "There is not a team in the league that I would rather have lost to."

Gottlieb was as happy as he'd ever been. "I have never coached a finer group of boys," he told the assembled writers. "They were easy to handle, and I never had to fine a single one. We never had a bit of dissension. The fellows never thought of anything but winning games.

"Another thing," Gotty added. "I've never been connected with a team that was as popular all around the league as this one. They are a credit to the game of basketball."

Gottlieb revealed that the Warriors practiced fewer times than any team in the league. "We held one scrimmage during the entire playoffs," he said. "Daily workouts weren't necessary with these kids. They always were in perfect physical condition. That's why I say a better group of athletes can't be found."

Eddie Gottlieb, one of the creators of big league basketball, was the first coach of the Warriors and later the team's owner. A member of the Basketball Hall of Fame, he led the Warriors to the newly formed BAA's first championship.

Courtesy of Jim Rosin

To celebrate their victory, the Warriors flocked to Sam Framo's seafood restaurant at 23rd Street and Allegheny Avenue, a place where Gottlieb often threw sometimes wild affairs. A raucous party took place, with the participants not leaving until nearly sunrise.

As the first champion of a major basketball league, the Warriors were the toast of the basketball world. "We started pro basketball on its way to being a popular sport for everybody," Rullo said. "That was especially true in Philadelphia where college basketball had always been more popular. We became so popular that throughout the offseason different players were frequently invited to banquets and other events throughout the city."

No one, though, was more widely saluted than Fulks. By the time the playoffs had begun, Fulks was already the biggest name in pro basketball. His popularity increased considerably after the playoffs.

"Joe Fulks was the man who focused the attention of the world on professional basketball," reported *The Modern Encyclopedia of Basketball*, edited by Zander Hollander. "He was the link between the pre-war days and the modern era of basketball."

"We felt he brought great popularity to the game," remembered Rullo. "People went crazy when he made a jump shot. And sometimes he did it with two or three guys on him."

It was not entirely a one-man team, though. Senesky was an outstanding point guard, a term not then used. Dallmar was a fine set-up man, who it was said "could move like a scared kangaroo," and the 5-foot, 9-inch Musi, the team captain, was a speedy little fellow with a good shooting touch. The 6-foot, 3-inch Guokas was a strong rebounder known for his rugged performance under the boards.

Over the entire season, the Warriors drew a paid attendance of 128,950, the highest in the BAA and an average of more than 4,000 per game, a figure some 1,000 higher than the next closest team. Net receipts for the year were $191,117, second best in the league behind the Knicks.

As the first professional sports team in Philadelphia to win a title since the 1930 Athletics won the World Series, the Warriors were determined to keep their good record alive.

The BAA had a vastly different look in 1947–48 with four teams—Detroit, Cleveland, Pittsburgh, and Toronto—folding. With seven teams left and an unbalanced schedule, the BAA added the Baltimore Bullets of the American Basketball League to the circuit. Also, to help teams cut travel expenses, the schedule was dropped from 60 to 48 games.

The Warriors won the Eastern Division title with a 27–21 record, one game ahead of the second-place Knicks. With a bye in the quarterfinals, the Warriors then beat St. Louis, four games to three in the semifinals. Although Baltimore had been considered a far inferior team, the Bullets downed the Warriors in the finals, four games to two.

The BAA was struggling financially, though, and in 1949–50 it merged with the National Basketball League to form a seventeen-team National Basketball Association.

Meanwhile, the players from the championship Warriors wound up going in many different directions. Fulks, who finished second in scoring in each of the next two years after the title season and set a record with 63 points in one game in 1949, played through the 1954–55 campaign. While battling a drinking problem, he moved back to Kentucky, where he jumped from one job to another. In 1976, drunk and forlorn, he was shot and killed by the son of his girlfriend following an argument at a trailer park. He was fifty-four years old. One year later, he was elected into the Naismith Basketball Hall of Fame.

Senesky later became the coach of the Warriors, leading them to their second league championship in 1955–56. Dallmar went on to become the head coach at Penn for six years and then Stanford for 21 seasons. For many years, Musi ran the 24-second clock at Warriors and then 76ers games. Rullo became a teacher and prominent referee.

After the 1946–47 season, Guokas was involved in an automobile accident that required the amputation of one leg. Becoming a broadcaster, Guokas ultimately served as the public address announcer at Philadelphia Eagles home games for more than three decades.

For most of the players—and, for that matter, an entire city—the 1946–47 season provided an unforgettable year. It not only gave the city its first major league basketball championship, it also began to make pro basketball a popular sport throughout the area.

THE EAGLES WIN THE NFL TITLE IN A BLIZZARD

8 It was the kind of day that is a rarity on the Philadelphia weather charts. The snow had been coming down so hard all night that hardly a creature was stirring. By noon, the accumulation was nearly one foot. By any standards, the city was being hit by a blizzard, one of the worst blizzards in Philadelphia history.

The date was December 19, 1948, and the Philadelphia Eagles were scheduled to meet the Chicago Cardinals at Shibe Park for the National Football League championship. But that morning there was a huge degree of uncertainty. Some thought the game would be postponed.

One of those who did was Steve Van Buren, the Eagles' star running back. There was no sense trying to get to the ballpark, Van Buren surmised. The game wasn't going to be played. Besides, he couldn't even get his car out of the driveway of his Lansdowne home.

"I didn't think there was any way we could play," Van Buren said many years later. "So I stayed home. Then Greasy Neale (the Eagles coach) called. 'Where the hell are you?' he said. He told me to get right down there because we were going to play."

As it turned out, because of the snow, Neale did not want to play the game "after working all year for one big climactic game," but Commissioner Bert Bell, a native Philadelphian, did. The game was a sellout, Bell determined, and network radio rights had been sold. It was a no-brainer. The game should be played.

But Neale felt strongly that the decision should be made by the two teams. Accordingly, he went to the Chicago locker room to confer with Cards coach Jimmy Conzelman. The Cardinals wanted to play, and when Neale returned to the Eagles' locker room, he learned that his team had taken a vote, and by a 13–12 count, the players had elected to play.

So the game was on. But the Eagles' best player was nowhere to be found. That's when Neale called Van Buren's home in Delaware County.

"I ran out of the house, down a few blocks, and got a trolley to 69th Street," Van Buren remembered in an interview before he died. "Then I got the El down Market Street to City Hall, and finally the subway up Broad Street."

Van Buren rode the subway to Lehigh Avenue. But Shibe Park was still seven blocks away. So he walked those seven blocks through blinding snow to the ballpark. "I got there about a half hour before the start of the game, which had been delayed about one hour," he said.

During the delay, workers had tried to clear the playing field of snow. Some of the players even helped shovel. Large mounds of snow lined the edges of the field. But it continued to snow throughout the game. The snow came down so hard that spectators could hardly see the field.

"It was so bad I couldn't even see the Cardinals' safety man," said Van Buren, who had come out of Louisiana State University and joined the Eagles in 1944. "And you couldn't see when you were out of bounds because the lines on the field were covered. But at least, the footing was okay. The ground wasn't frozen."

Ultimately, as blizzard conditions continued, snowbanks formed all around the field, and ropes had to be hung on stakes to mark the out-of-bounds lines. Van Buren would score the game's only touchdown and the Eagles would capture a 7–0 decision and their first NFL championship. It was a game that ranks as one of the most unusual and most memorable in Philadelphia sports history.

Until the previous season, the Eagles had never come close to winning a title. The team, formed in 1933, had suffered through ten straight losing seasons in its early years. Although they had winning records after that, the Birds didn't play in the postseason until 1947. After opening the campaign with an inconceivable 45–42 victory over the Washington Redskins, the Eagles went on to tie the Pittsburgh Steelers during the regular season for first place with an 8–4 record.

The Birds beat the Steelers, 21–0, in the division playoffs. They then advanced to the championship game, but lost, 28–21 to the Cardinals in a game played on an ice-covered field in freezing temperatures at Chicago's Comiskey Park. In that game, Eagles quarterback Tommy Thompson set a playoff record with 44 passes, of which 27 were completions for 357 yards.

That game, though, inspired the Eagles to put a major effort into going for the championship again. And in 1948, everything fell into place for the team, whose owner, Alexis (Lex) Thompson (no relation to Tommy), a millionaire playboy from New York, had purchased it for $165,000 in 1940.

The 1948 Eagles had a roster bulging with outstanding players. Many had served in World War II. Others were young players with limited experience. They all got along, however, and often were spotted playing cards together in the team's clubhouse or on the train as they rode to an away game. Bookbinder's—a high-class, center city restaurant—had a standing policy that whenever the Eagles shut out an opponent, players and their wives and children could come for a free meal.

Van Buren, regarded even today as the greatest running back in Eagles history, led the squad to such victories. Van Buren was as good as Jim Thorpe, according to Neale. A rookie in 1944, he had led the NFL in rushing yardage in 1945 and 1947, when he gained 1,008 yards.

There were several others who joined Van Buren in creating a standout Eagles offense. Thompson, a Tulsa alumnus and one of the top quarterbacks of the era, was an outstanding passer, and he had a band of excellent receivers, led by Pete Pihos, a clever pass-catcher who was one of the league's leading receivers, and Jack Ferrante, who grew up in South Philadelphia and many years later became a successful head football coach at Monsignor Bonner High School. Bosh Pritchard, a strong and shifty ball-carrier, was also a top running back, as was fullback Joe Muha, also the team's punter.

Al Wistert; Vic Lindskog; Al Wojciechowicz, the oldest veteran with eleven years in the NFL; Bucko Kilroy, a product of Temple University; Vic Sears; George Savitsky, who played at the University of Pennsylvania; and Jay MacDowell were the top lineman. In an era when players performed on offense and defense, many of them played both ways, as did Van Buren, Pihos, Thompson, Pritchard, and various others. Russ Craft was one of the first players who specialized in being a defensive back.

"We had a great offense and a defense that was stronger than most other teams," Wistert, one of the few living members of the team, recalled decades later. "The players on this team were a band of guys who looked forward to excelling. We made no bones about it. We all loved to play. Many of us played 60 minutes. From my standpoint, I didn't mind that at all. I rather enjoyed it."

The Eagles' defense was the creative design of Neale. It featured a five-man line, two linebackers, and four backs. Sometimes, one of the linemen would drop back and play linebacker. Because it was new and different, opposing offenses were often foiled by the unusual configuration.

"Van Buren was as tough as they come," said Wistert, a product of the University of Michigan. "He was the greatest running back there ever was. He was just so good. Thompson was an outstanding passer. Nothing fazed him. He could get knocked down, and it didn't bother him a bit. He'd get right up."

Wistert, called by Neale one of the greatest tackles who ever played, was also the team's captain. His teammates looked up to what he did and said, and tried to follow the example he set. "I gave them a lot of pep talks," he remembered. "During the season, I often told them what it would take to win. They listened to what I said."

Eagles coach Earle (Greasy) Neale discusses tactics with captain and star tackle Al Wistert. Neale, a one-time big league baseball player, won two championships with the Eagles. Wistert was one of the team's greatest tackles.
Courtesy of Rich Westcott

The Eagles held their training camp in 1948 at Saranac Lake High School in upstate New York near Lake Placid. Along with Neale, the team's coaches included Charles Ewart (backfield), Larry Cabrelli (ends), and John Kellison (lineman).

The season opened after the Eagles split four exhibition games. In the year's opener, the Eagles played at Comiskey

Park against the Cardinals. And for the second time in a row (having lost an exhibition game there), the Eagles lost to the Cardinals, this time by a 21–14 count. Thompson threw touchdown passes to Pritchard and Pihos, but Chicago broke a 14–14 tie when Charlie Trippi connected with Mal Kutner on a game-winning, 64-yard TD pass in the fourth quarter. The game was marked by a particular tragedy as Cardinals' tackle Stan Maudlin collapsed on the field with a heart attack and died shortly afterward in the locker room.

One week later, the Eagles could manage only a 28–28 tie with the Los Angeles Rams, a team that a few years earlier had been the Cleveland Rams. Thompson completed 11 of 15 passes for 133 yards in the first half and pitched two touchdown passes to Pihos and one to Neill Armstrong, and Pitchard ran for another to give the Eagles a 28–0 lead in the third quarter. But the Rams rallied with four touchdown throws by Bob Waterfield, including three in the fourth quarter, to earn the tie.

The situation changed dramatically in the third week of the season when the Eagles captured their first win with a 45–0 rout of the New York Giants, the worst defeat in that club's history. Thompson ran for one touchdown and passed for two more to Pihos and Ernie Steele, while Van Buren, Ben Kish, and Jim Parmer all ran for TDs. Cliff Patton kicked a field goal and six extra points as the Eagles finished with a 21-point fourth quarter.

That victory launched a six-game winning streak for the Eagles. Amazingly, the Eagles won their second straight 45–0 game the following week as they trounced the Washington Redskins, with Van Buren rushing for three touchdowns, Pritchard and Steele each running for one, and Thompson passing for Pihos for another. Again, Patton booted six extra points and a field goal. The Eagles' 28 first downs set an NFL record.

During the season, the Eagles often held practice across the street from Shibe Park on a field that was part of a city-owned park. "Sometimes during practice we'd play touch football," remembered Jack Myers, one of the team's many good running backs. "That was always a lot of fun, but so was playing with this team. The morale was great and everybody liked everybody else."

On October 24, with Thompson out for a week with a torn muscle and Bill Mackrides taking over at quarterback, the Eagles recorded a 12–7 win over the Chicago Bears, with the Birds scoring on a Van Buren touchdown, a Patton field goal, and a safety on an end zone tackle of Sid Luckman by Walt (Piggy) Barnes. That was followed by a 34–7 trouncing of the Steelers, with Pritchard scoring on a 55-yard punt return and an 18-yard fumble return, Patton booting two field goals, and Van Buren rushing for one TD and Ferrante snaring a Thompson pass for another.

Next came a 35–14 decision over the New York Giants with Van Buren rushing for 143 yards and two TDs, Pihos catching two Thompson touchdown passes, and Pritchard racing 65 yards for another TD. The Eagles' third 45–0 victory of the season was a whitewash of the Boston Yanks with Thompson passing for 197 yards and connecting on TD passes to Craft, Ferrante, Pihos, and Pritchard. Backup quarterback Mackrides hit Armstrong for another touchdown, while Parmer rushed for the final TD of the game. Van Buren rushed for 154 yards on 16 carries.

Another high-scoring match came next with the Birds foiling the Redskins, 42–21, before 36,254, the largest home crowd of the season. Van Buren, who picked up 171 yards on 29 carries, and Myers ran for TDs, Thompson passed to Armstrong, Craft, and Pihos for three more scores, and Ferrante snatched a Mackrides throw for the game's final touchdown. The Eagles then downed Pittsburgh, 17–0, on a six-point run by Pritchard, a scoring pass from Thompson to Pihos, and a Patton field goal in a game that clinched the Eastern Division title.

Three of the stars of the 1948 Eagles were known as "The Three Ps."
They were (from left) halfback Bosh Pritchard, place-kicker Cliff
Patton, and end Pete Pihos.
Courtesy of Rich Westcott

After they had clinched the title, the Eagles made a marvelously classy gesture by proclaiming that if the Cardinals failed to make the NFL championship game, the team would award a full share of their earnings in the title game to Mauldin's wife.

The Eagles' winning streak finally ended on December 5 at Fenway Park when the lowly Yanks (3–9), trounced the Birds, 37–14. With Van Buren and some of the other starters resting on the bench, the Eagles could score only twice in the first half on touchdown passes from Thompson to Ferrante and Muha. Then in the final game of the regular season, the Eagles got back on track by going over 40 points for the fifth time with a 45–21 bashing of the Lions. Ferrante scored three times on passes from Thompson, who also tossed to Pihos for another TD. Van Buren and Parmer both ran for six-pointers.

The win gave the Eagles a final record of 9–2–1, which up to that point was their best mark in club history. Washington was second in the Eastern division with a 7–5 log. The Eagles were second in the league in points scored with 376, while allowing just 156 points. They were also second in team passing with a 52.8 percentage on 159 completions out of 301 attempts for 2,241 yards, and third in rushing yardage with 2,378 yards on 528 carries.

Van Buren, who it was said developed his running skills by chasing pigs as a youth, led the league in rushing with 945 yards (10 touchdowns) for the third time in five years. Thompson was first in passing with 1,965 yards on 141 completions in 246 attempts for 25 TDs. Pihos was second in the league with 46 receptions for 766 yards (and 11 TDs). Muha led the league in punting with a 47.3 average, and Patton was tied for first in points as a kicker with the Cardinals' Pat Harder (74 points).

The Cardinals had a highly rated team that had posted an 11–1 record, finishing ahead of their crosstown rivals, the Bears, owners of a 10–2 mark. The Cards, later to become the St. Louis and then the Arizona Cardinals, had scored the most points in the league (395) with what was then being called the "dream backfield."

Running back Trippi (690 yards) and Elmer Angsman (638) ranked second and third in the NFL behind Van Buren in rushing yardage. Ray Mallouf—who had replaced the injured Cards quarterback, Paul Christman—was second in the league to Thompson in passing, and Harder, with 110 points overall, was the league's leading scorer. Teammate Mal Kutner was second, with 90 points.

Because a division playoff to break a tie in the standings was unnecessary this year, the Eagles and Cardinals went right into the championship game just seven days after the end of the regular season. It was a game that none of those who were there—whether on the field or in the stands—can ever forget.

That was certainly true of Mackrides, who many years later was the highly regarded head football coach at Springfield (Delco) High. At the time a resident of West Philadelphia, he left his home with the intention of walking to Shibe

Park. "After a while, I got a ride, so I didn't have to walk the whole way," he recalled.

The field at Shibe Park had been covered with giant tarpaulins during the night, but as game-time approached, some ninety workers and players from both teams were needed to remove the now incredibly heavy tarps. The snow underneath the tarps was still deep enough that the yard-markers couldn't be seen, and the teams agreed that head referee Ron Gibbs would make the final decision on first downs.

As the game began, the snow continued to cascade down on the field and the 28,864 (36,309 tickets had been sold) in the stands. Many of the fans wore boots and caps with earmuffs while carrying blankets to their seats. In addition, more than 200 writers and a 46-station radio and television network were there to cover the game.

"The snow was coming down so hard, it was really difficult to play in," said Wistert. "You tried to make due the best you could, but you really had to rely on your basic talent to get the job done."

The players could barely see where they were going, although the stadium lights were on throughout the game. Along with many others who angrily criticized the league for not postponing the game, sports columnist Jimmy Cannon later called it "a parody of a football game."

"It was terrible. As far as execution of plays goes, it was absolutely terrible," Myers said. "At times, you could hardly see anything. That was not only true of the players, but also the referees. They couldn't see anything either. The one good thing was, a lot of us played both ways. That was good because you didn't have to go back and forth off the field all the time. You could save a little energy."

On the Eagles' first play of the game, as part of a special plan devised by Neale to catch the Cardinals off-guard, Thompson passed to Ferrante, who went all the way to the end zone to score on a 65-yard play. The touchdown, however, was nullified when officials called an offside penalty against Ferrante.

Thereafter, neither team could score as snow continued to pelt the ballpark, which the Eagles had called home since 1940 and where the baseball Athletics and Phillies both played. The Cardinals' Harder missed a 37-yard field goal attempt, but Chicago got as far as the Eagles' 10-yard line once in the second quarter before getting stopped by the fierce Eagles defense.

Late in the third quarter, Kilroy and Wojciechowicz hit Mallouf, causing the Cardinals' quarterback to fumble. Kilroy recovered the loose ball on the Cardinals' 17-yard line.

After the recovery, Pritchard gained six yards just before the quarter ended. Then, after the teams walked through snow to the other end of the field, Muha ran for another three, and Thompson got three more on a quarterback sneak. Then, with just 1:05 gone in the fourth quarter, Van Buren took a handoff from Thompson at the five-yard line and behind blocks by Kilroy and Muha, rumbled through a big hole into the end zone. With Cardinals' defensemen barely touching him, Van Buren called it "one of the easiest touchdowns I ever scored."

Patton, who had missed two field goal attempts, scraped a pile of snow away and then kicked the extra point to give the Eagles a 7–0 lead.

In one of the most famous plays in Eagles history, Steve Van Buren (#15) plows through the snow and Cardinals' line to score the game's only touchdown in blizzard conditions at Shibe Park.
Courtesy of Rich Westcott

The lead held up as the Eagles defense stymied the Cardinals for the rest of the game. While the Eagles were stopping the Cards' offense, Van Buren and Thompson ate up big time on the clock by controlling the ball on offense for the Eagles.

The Cards had one last chance, but were stopped by the Eagles in the fourth quarter. The Eagles then started a drive from their own seven-yard line with ten minutes left to play. With Van Buren, Pritchard, and Thompson running for long gains, the Eagles drove to the Cardinals' 23-yard line, but had to settle for a 30-yard field goal attempt by Patton, which failed. Subsequently, Chicago was pushed back to the Eagles' 8, after which the Birds took the ball and ran out the clock.

As the final gun went off, in the absence of much passing, the game had taken just two hours and two minutes to play. And the Eagles had walked away with a 7–0 victory and their first championship. Fans rushed onto the field and carried Van Buren and Thompson on their shoulders. "We got it," screamed Thompson.

In the post-game celebration, coach Greasy Neale celebrates with his team, including Tommy Thompson (left), Ben Kish (#44), and Steve Van Buren (#15) following the Eagles' 7–0 victory.
Courtesy of Rich Westcott

According to an article in the *Philadelphia Inquirer* by Art Morrow, "the din was deafening as the Eagles stampeded like elephants into the locker room and circled around as though engaged in a game of musical chairs. Forgotten were the snow-soaked uniforms, pounds heavier than they'd been at the start of the day, and no one thought of frost-bitten fingers."

"You played a good game, boys," Neale told the new champs.

"You couldn't put a value on winning that title," Wistert remembered. "It was just a wonderful feeling. We had guys who loved to play the game. To be on that kind of team and to win a championship was a thrill that words can hardly describe."

Van Buren, who had no competition as the star of the game, finished with 98 yards on 26 carries. Trippi and Angsman totaled 59 yards together, and Chicago finished with just 139 total yards and seven first downs. The Eagles had 16 first downs and led in rushing yardage (225–96) and in offensive plays (232–107). With neither team passing, the Eagles had a net yardage of seven, while the Cardinals were plus 11 yards.

"When you're drawing up a lineup for next season," said Thompson, "list me as a ball-carrier."

The Eagles got $1,540 apiece as the winners' share, while the losing Cardinals each received $874.

After the season, Van Buren was named the NFL's Most Valuable Player and along with Wistert, Thompson, and Pihos was named first team All-Pro. Those were just rewards for a team that had just staged an incredible season.

EAGLES REPEAT AS CHAMPIONS IN THE RAIN

9 By the time the 1949 season began, the Eagles had become noteworthy examples of the old saying, "nothing ever stays the same." Maybe some teams would have rested on their laurels after winning a championship, but not the Eagles. During the off-season, some major changes had occurred.

Foremost was the change in ownership. Alexis (Lex) Thompson had owned the team since 1940 when he bought it for $165,000. But despite the Eagles championship season in 1948, he had incurred severe financial problems. Incredibly, he had lost $88,000 during the season, and in the final week, he was so broke that he had to borrow money from the NFL just to pay the players' salaries.

Thompson's millions had disappeared, and he wanted out. Fortunately for him, a group headed by James P. Clark, a wealthy national trucking company owner, a major stockholder in Liberty Bell Race Track, and an active Democrat who later played a large role in John F. Kennedy's election as president, was interested in buying the team. Ultimately, the group known as the "100 Brothers," which reportedly included such notables as singer Frankie Laine and comedian Bob Hope, purchased the team for $300,000, with each member paying a reported $3,000. Vince McNally was named general manager.

Just three weeks before the sale, another major event had occurred, which would have an unparalleled effect on the Eagles' fortunes for the next dozen years. Although, as defending champions, they would normally have had the last pick in each round of the college draft, the Eagles had won what was called a Lottery Bonus Pick, which gave them the first choice in the entire draft.

In a draft that included Doak Walker, Norm Van Brocklin, and George Blanda, the Eagles picked the University of Pennsylvania's All-American center, Chuck Bednarik. Concrete Charlie, as he was known later, would go on to become one of the greatest Eagles players of all time during a 14-year

Former Penn All-American and number one draft pick Chuck Bednarik (left) takes off after intercepting a pass from Bob Waterfield during a game with the Los Angeles Rams. Defensive halfback Pat McHugh (right) gets ready to throw a block.
Courtesy of Rich Westcott

career with the Birds, and along with teammates Pete Pihos, Al Wojciechowicz, and Steve Van Buren, a member of the football Hall of Fame.

Pihos was an All-American from Indiana University who would play for the Eagles for nine years while winning plaudits as one of the best pass-catchers in the NFL. Wojciechowicz was a New Jersey native who came out of Fordham, breaking in with the Detroit Lions in 1938 before going on to a thirteen-year NFL career, including five seasons with the Eagles.

Bednarik would play both center and linebacker—indeed, he was the last sixty-minute player in pro football—while joining a solid group of linemen from the previous year's team, led by Al Wistert, Bucko Kilroy, Wojciechowicz, Vic Lindskog, Jay MacDowell, and Vic Sears. Added to that group, the Eagles had acquired in a trade with the New York Bulldogs lineman Mike Jarmoluk, a Philadelphian who, like Kilroy, came out of Temple University.

"We had pretty much the same team as we did in 1948," Wistert recalled. "And we had talented players at every position."

The Eagles had two other noteworthy rookies in running backs Clyde (Smackover) Scott from Arkansas and Frank Ziegler from George Tech. In addition, running backs Jack Myers and Jim Parmer, guards Mario Giannelli, John Magee, and Walt Barnes, and tackle George Savitsky were only in their second years in the NFL, giving the Eagles a youthful flavor.

"We were mostly a bunch of young guys," Bednarik recalled. "Many went to small schools and had worked their way up to the top. But we were tough. And we all hit it off nicely together."

Put together largely by general manager Vince McNally, the team also had a strong local attachment with Kilroy; Jarmokuk; three former Penn players, Bednarik, Savitsky, and Frank Reagan, who joined the club prior to the season; and Jack Ferrante and Bill Mackrides, all of whom had either grown up in Philadelphia or gone to college there. Ironically, Ferrante, who grew up in South Philadelphia, and Mackrides, a native of West Philadelphia, would both become highly successful high school football coaches in neighboring towns in Delaware County.

"From top to bottom, we had one of the great teams in football," recalled Myers. "We had strength at every position. We had youth. We had a phenomenal quarterback in Tommy Thompson. Van Buren could run through anything. Bednarik was a helluva great player. Pihos was one of the best receivers in football. And we had an outstanding defensive team that carried us many times. Truly, this was a team that was so good that it was quite a joy to play for it.

"About half of our players went the whole 60 minutes," Myers added. "You had to stay healthy to do that. A lot of guys played with injuries. But if you weren't tough, you didn't stay in the lineup."

The Eagles were also blessed with a brilliant leader. Earle (Greasy) Neale had an amazing career as both a player and a coach. He had been a three-sport star at West Virginia Wesleyan College, and while there he also played under an assumed name with Jim Thorpe on the professional football team, the Canton Bulldogs.

After college, Neale signed with the Cincinnati Reds, and ultimately spent seven full seasons starting in 1916 as an outfielder in the major leagues. In the infamous 1919 World Series when the Reds defeated the Chicago White Sox, who were later called the Black Sox and charged with throwing the Series, with eight players subsequently banned from baseball for life, Neale hit .357 for the highest batting average in the Series. Neale played in 22 games with the Philadelphia Phillies in 1921 before returning to the Reds and finishing his baseball career in 1924 with a .259 career average in 768 games.

While still playing baseball, Neale had begun a career as a football coach. Between 1915 and 1922, he served not only as head coach of the professional Dayton Triangles, but also as a college head coach at Muskingum University, West Virginia Wesleyan College, Marietta College, and Washington and Jefferson College, which in 1921 he led to the Rose Bowl, where it played California to a scoreless tie. Later, he was head coach at the University of Virginia (1923–28) and West Virginia University before moving to Yale as an assistant, serving there from 1934–40. Along the way, Neale was also the head coach in basketball at Marietta, and in baseball at Virginia.

Neale, who posted an 82–54–11 record as a college football coach, became the Eagles' head coach in 1941. Ultimately, he would go on to a 66–44–5 record in 10 seasons with the Eagles, and later be inducted into both the college and pro football halls of fame.

Greasy, a name that was given to him by a boyhood friend while joking about nicknames, was regarded as a brilliant coach who was one of the pioneers of the T formation and the creator of the 5–2–4 defensive alignment. Although he was known to chastise his players, screaming and swearing and using foul language, he was friendly off the field with his players and often played cards with them as they traveled on trains to different cities.

"He was the greatest coach there ever was," said Wistert. "He was highly intelligent, and he put everything out front. He had good talent, and he had a real good knowledge of the background of these guys. He could swear. Oh, could he swear. But for the most part, we got along tremendously well. He was like a father to me."

Neale was far ahead of his time in many ways off the field, too. He put together a team of scouts and kept detailed records on potential college draft choices. He also closely followed opposing teams, having his scouts put together reports on their strengths and weaknesses.

"He was a great coach and a wonderful man, but his system was hard to learn and he didn't take any crap from anybody," Myers said. "And when Sunday came, you'd better be ready to play. He'd say, 'You better shape up and be ready to play or you won't be here much longer.' He was a coach who could be very psychological. He made sure you played your best."

"When he spoke, you listened to everything he said," Mackrides added. "He had everybody's attention. He was a leader, and playing under him helped me a lot when I later became a coach."

In his first two years with the Eagles, Neale's teams won only two games each season. Then, after the 1943 season when the Birds merged with the Pittsburgh Steelers to form the Steagles, the Eagles improved tremendously. Neale never had another losing season. By 1949, after going to two straight championship games and winning one of them, the Birds were on top of the football world.

The Eagles launched the 1949 season with training camp at UM North Central Agriculture School in Grand Rapids, Minnesota. They posted a 5–0–1 record in preseason games, including a 38–0 victory at Comiskey Park over the College All-Stars, a team coached by Bud Wilkinson and that included Bednarik and future Eagles coach Jerry Williams. They also recorded a 51–14 trouncing of the Chicago Cardinals during the preseason.

Looking ahead to the real season, Neale told his players, "A team does not prove it is great until it can repeat."

When the real season began, according to Mackrides, the Eagles usually practiced across the street from Shibe Park in an open, city-owned recreation park. "The ground was hard and sometimes muddy, and once Van Buren slid on the dirt and really got hurt," he said. Often, players dressed in their practice gear at home and then drove to the site. Strangely, fans seldom stopped to watch the team go through its drills.

In their season's opener, the Eagles' mastery of their opponents continued when they edged the newly franchised New

Often, the Eagles worked out in a recreation park across
Lehigh Avenue from Shibe Park. Here Tommy Thompson gets
set to handoff to Jack Myers (far right) as Jim Parmer (with hood)
prepares to run interference.
Courtesy of Rich Westcott

York Bulldogs, formerly the Boston Yanks, 7–0, with Bosh
Pritchard scoring on a 16-yard run. Incredibly, a crowd of just
8,426 showed up for the game.

In their second straight away game, the Eagles rallied
from a 14–5 third quarter deficit to beat the Detroit Lions,
22–14, with Van Buren scoring two touchdowns and Cliff Patton kicking a field goal in the final period. Van Buren finished
with 135 yards, enough to set a new NFL record with 3,951
career yards.

In their Shibe Park opener the following week, the
Eagles met their championship game opponent of the last

two years. It was no contest, as Van Buren and Parmer each scored two touchdowns to lead the Birds to a 28–3 victory over the Cards.

The Eagles' three-game winning streak came to an end the next week when they were whipped by the Chicago Bears, 38–21, before a crowd of 50,129 at Wrigley Field, despite touchdown passes by Tommy Thompson to Pihos, Van Buren, and Ferrante. The Eagles would not lose another game all season.

The following week, they launched an eight-game winning streak with a 49–14 rout of the Washington Redskins. Pritchard caught a pass from Thompson to score on a 74-yard play, and then ran 77 yards for another TD to pace a victory that also saw Van Buren, Thompson, Mackrides, and Ziegler run for touchdowns and Thompson pass to Neill Armstrong for another. Patton kicked seven extra points to set a new NFL record with 77 straight extra points, breaking the old mark of 72 owned by the Bears' Jack Manders.

The Eagles took over first place with a 38–7 clobbering of the Steelers with Scott, the Eagles' first pick in the regular draft and a former Olympic hurdler and world record-holder, returning a punt for an Eagles record 70-yard return and a touchdown, and Van Buren scoring twice. Thompson scored from scrimmage and Mackrides hit Pihos with another six-point pass. After booting a 48-yard field goal, Patton had to leave the game with a bruised leg, and punter Joe Muha took over and banged through five extra points. Van Buren wound up rushing for 205 yards, an Eagles record that would stand for 64 years until broken by LeSean McCoy in 2013.

Next came the Los Angeles Rams, and before what Mack-rides said were typical "loud and boisterous" fans, a record crowd of 38,230 at Shibe Park watched the Eagles slam the league's only undefeated team, 38–14. Russ Craft scored on an interception, Thompson hurled TD passes to Pritchard and Pihos, and Myers and Parmer each ran for touchdowns. The Eagles held the Rams to just 27 yards rushing.

A 44–21 thrashing of the Redskins followed, during which Thompson threw two TD passes to Ferrante, one to Scott, and one to Pihos. Van Buren and Pritchard both scored from the ground, and Patton kicked a field goal and five extra points.

In their ninth game of the season, the Eagles scored 38 or more points for the fifth straight time as they clubbed the Bulldogs, 42–0. Van Buren scored twice and ran for 174 yards on 35 carries. Scott ran for one touchdown, Pat McHugh returned an interception for another, Thompson passed to Ferrante for one, and Mackrides found Armstrong for another TD.

Van Buren was the main show in the next tilt, running for 205 yards and setting an NFL record with his 225th carry of the season as the Eagles downed the Steelers, 34–17. Thompson passed to Armstrong and Ferrante for touchdowns, Parmer ran for two six-pointers, and Patton booted two field goals and four extra points.

In their next game, the Eagles slugged the Giants, 24–3, as Thompson's pass to Armstrong, Reagan's run, and Muha's interception accounted for the Eagles' six-pointers. Van Buren pushed his rushing yardage to 1,050 for the season, breaking his old NFL mark of 1,008 set in 1947.

The Eagles' explosive backfield included (from left) Bosh Pritchard, Tommy Thompson, Joe Muha, and Steve Van Buren.
Courtesy of Rich Westcott

The Eagles ended their season on December 11 with a 17–3 victory over the Giants as Thompson passed to Armstrong and Van Buren scored on a run for the Birds' two touchdowns. The win gave the Eagles a final 11–1 record and a .917 winning percentage, a team record that still stands.

For the season, Van Buren won his fourth rushing title in the last six years with an NFL record 1,146 yards, a record 263 carries, and a league-leading 11 touchdowns rushing. Thompson completed 116 of 214 passes for 1,727 yards and 11 touchdowns, and Patton ran his record of consecutive extra points to 82, while finishing with 109 points altogether. Ferrante (508 yards, 34 receptions, and five touchdowns) and Pihos (484–34–4) were the top receivers. Van Buren, Thompson, Ferrante, Pihos, Kilroy, Sears, Wistert, and Patton were all named to the All-Pro team.

The Eagles led the league with 364 points while their defense yielded just 134 points, the fewest in the league and 80 points lower than the next closest team (Pittsburgh).

For the Eagles, it was on to the championship game against the Rams, a team that in 1946 had moved to Los Angeles from Cleveland. The Rams had led the Western Division with an 8–2–2 record.

Clark Shaughnessy, who was in his second and last year with LA, coached the Rams, the first major league sports team to play in California. The Rams' main weapon was its offense, which focused on a passing game with veteran Bob Waterfield, an outstanding passer who was married to the gorgeous actress Jane Russell, and rookie Van Brocklin, a future Eagles hero, sharing time at quarterback. Once, when asked why he rotated the two quarterbacks, Shaughnessy said that he used Waterfield "to test out the opposition" and Van Brocklin "to make the big play." The main targets of the two were Tom Fears, the NFL leader in touchdown receptions with nine, and Elroy (Crazy Legs) Hirsch.

The game was scheduled for December 18 at Los Angeles Memorial Coliseum. It was heard only on the West Coast, and Harry Wismer and Red Grange were the announcers.

The Eagles traveled by train to Los Angeles, a trip that took three days. Along the way, Neale stopped the train so the team could work out in Albuquerque, New Mexico. Once they reached California, the Eagles held a practice session at UCLA.

Like the previous year, the weather played a major role in the game. Although the weather prediction, as is often the case, erroneously called for a light rain that would stop before game time, a driving rain pounded the area throughout the night, leaving some one and one-half inches of water on the ultra muddy playing field.

Both teams wanted Commissioner Bert Bell to postpone the game until the following Sunday, which would be Christmas Day. But, despite a fierce argument by Rams owner Dan Reeves, Bell, back home in suburban Philadelphia because he was ill, refused, claiming the league had a contract with Mutual Broadcasting Network to broadcast the game, and it couldn't be broken.

With that decision governing play, the game began. The field was a big puddle of mud, and players slipped and slid throughout while coaches huddled under umbrellas on the sidelines. Some spots on the field had mud that was ankle deep.

"The rain came down really hard throughout the game," Scott remembered some sixty-five years later. "You couldn't play your regular game. The whole time, you were trying to keep from slipping. The Rams were very good, so we were fortunate to have been able to beat them at their place and in the heavy rain."

Meanwhile, although 40,000 advance tickets had been sold and a crowd of at least 75,000 was expected to attend the game, a tiny gathering of just 22,245 spectators were scattered throughout a stadium that could hold up to 101,000. The

Rams, playing host to the first pro championship game ever held in California, had averaged 51,555 during the season.

"Before the game, I told everybody, we're going to have 100,000 there," said Myers. "Tell your wife she can have a whole new outfit. But hardly anybody showed up. It was awful."

Neither team could do much throughout the game as the defenses dominated the action. The only offensive player with a substantial amount of success was Van Buren, who gained 196 yards on 31 carries, a playoff game record that stood for 38 years.

Right from the start, the game featured each team's defense with Bednarik leading the favored Eagles' attack. The Eagles took the lead early in the second quarter, driving down the field as Thompson completed 11- and 16-yard passes to Ferrante before hitting a wide-open Pihos on a 31-yard pass for a touchdown. Patton added the extra point.

In the third period, the Birds scored again when rookie defensive end Leo Skladany, who had just joined the team near midseason and whose son would later play with the Eagles, blocked a Waterfield punt after a high snap from center. Skladany scooped up the ball on the two-yard line, and then rolled into the end zone for a touchdown. Patton again kicked the extra point, and the Eagles had a 14–0 lead.

The Eagles had missed two other scoring opportunities. One came when Thompson teamed with Van Buren on a 49-yard pass deep into Ram territory only to see the Eagles lose the ball on a fumble by Parmer on the LA seven-yard line. Another time came after a Thompson interception deep in Rams territory.

For most of the game, though, with both teams playing cautiously but as one sports writer described, "sluggishly," the Eagles controlled the ball on offense while the defense stymied the vaunted Rams attack. LA advanced once to the Eagles 25 yard line and another time to their 37, but could never get closer, despite tackle Dick Huffman, eligible to catch passes on two plays, grabbing throws good for 18 and eight yards on successive plays in one Rams drive.

At the final gun, the Eagles held a 14–0 lead and had gained their second straight NFL championship with their second straight shutout. No team in NFL history had or to date, would ever win two straight titles with shutouts.

For the game, the Eagles rushed for 274 yards to the Rams' 21, an all-time NFL low. Thompson completed 5 of 19 passes for 68 yards, while Waterfield and Van Brocklin connected on 10 of 27 throws for 98 yards. The Eagles had 17 first downs to LA's seven.

"To win the championship two straight times was a thrill that's hard to imagine," Wistert recalled. "We knew we had talent, but we played against a very good team. It was something that to us back then was the biggest thing that would ever happen to us."

After the game, Eagles owners staged a party at the swanky Bel Air Hotel where the team had stayed. Hollywood celebrities such as Clark Gable, Bob Hope, and Johnny Weissmuller attended the party and mingled with the players.

The Eagles celebrated in a hotel in Westwood, California, after their championship victory over the Rams. Taking part were (from left) Pete Pihos, Greasy Neale, Steve Van Buren, club president Jim Clark, Leo Skladany, and Tommy Thompson.

Courtesy of Rich Westcott

Later, the team got on the train and headed home. "Some guys celebrated more than others," Mackrides recalled. "But everybody was having fun." There was no big citywide celebration once the team arrived back in Philadelphia. Players and their families went to a downtown restaurant and had their own party.

The winner's share turned out to be $1,094.68 per person. The losers got $739.66 each, but they would substantially better that sum when they went to the championship game in each of the next two years against the Cleveland Browns, losing in 1950 and winning the following season.

For the Eagles, it was the end of a glorious run. The team slipped to a 6–6 record in 1950, and Neale was dismissed and replaced by Bo McMillin, who left after two games and was replaced by Wayne Millner as the Birds tumbled to a 4–8 record in 1951. It would be more than a decade before the Eagles won another championship. Until then, the 1948 and 1949 seasons stood as the two greatest in Eagles history.

LOCAL BOYS MAKE GOOD FOR THE WARRIORS

10 Throughout his years with the Philadelphia Warriors, Eddie Gottlieb always tried to keep his teams well-stocked with local players. Gottlieb believed that homegrown talent attracted local fans, and the more local players there were on the roster, the more fans would turn out to watch games.

Gottlieb's theory was never more evident than in 1955 when he put together a team that included seven local players. Paul Arizin and Larry Hennessy had played at Villanova, Tom Gola, Jack George, and Jackie Moore came from La Salle, Ernie Beck had gone to Penn, and George Dempsey was a native of Merchantville, New Jersey. The only nonlocal players on the roster were Neil Johnston, Joe Grabowski, and Walter Davis.

The roster, though, was not just one that had a special appeal to local fans. It was one that in 1955–56 formed the best team in the National Basketball Association, posting by far the best regular season record in the league, and then waltzing through the playoffs to easily win the league championship.

Coached by George Senesky, another local guy who had played at St. Joseph's, the Warriors ran away with the

Eastern Division title, compiling a 45–27 record and finishing six games ahead of the second-place Boston Celtics. In the playoffs, the Warriors, drawing a bye until the division finals, beat the Syracuse Nationals, three games to two, and then whipped the Fort Wayne Pistons, four games to one, in the championship finals.

It was a spectacular season for the Warriors, who the previous year, despite the fact that Johnston and Arizin ranked first and second in the league in scoring, had finished dead last in their division and in the three seasons before that had never finished above fourth place. In 1955–56, Arizin and Johnston finished second and third behind Bob Pettit of the St. Louis Hawks in scoring, and Jack George was second behind the Boston Celtics' Bob Cousy in assists.

Paul Arizin was the Warriors' leading scorer with 1,741 points (24.2 average), which ranked second in the league. A future Hall of Famer, Arizin led the NBA in scoring twice during his NBA career.
Courtesy of Rich Westcott

Naturally, the Warriors' outstanding achievements played the key role in attracting local fans. In addition, though, the roster amply supported Gotty's theory about a team heavily stacked with local players being a good attraction at the gate. Counting playoffs, the team averaged 6,200 fans per game at Convention Hall and drew a total of 210,777 for the season. That was more than double the attendance of the previous season.

So anxious were fans to see the Warriors that on Thanksgiving night, 8,537 fans climbed into the 9,000-seat Convention Hall. On December 9, 5,238 loyal supporters showed up at Convention Hall on a snowy night when the temperature had dropped below freezing, and there was an ice hockey game at the Arena, a basketball doubleheader at the Palestra, and Sugar Ray Robinson was defending his middleweight boxing title on television.

By the mid-1950s, of course, basketball had begun to command a major place not only in the Philadelphia sports scene but across the nation. New York had once been considered the capital of the basketball world, but betting scandals in the early 1950s that involved several of the city's colleges and top players had a large effect on reducing the elevated status of that area.

Meanwhile, basketball in Philadelphia was becoming increasingly popular. The formation of the Big Five in 1954, an increasing number of standout large and small college teams, and the emergence of many nationally prominent local players and coaches all contributed to an expanding interest in the sport.

A major contributor to this interest was the fact that Philadelphia had a professional basketball team that was not only good and well stocked with local players, but that possessed the kind of character and personality that appealed strongly to those who followed the game.

"Everybody did his job, and did it well," recalled Beck, still a resident of the area and a long-time teacher and coach at Bok Vocational High School in Philadelphia after his retirement as a player. "Since a lot of us were local guys, we had played against each other in high school or college. We all blended together and everybody got along with each other. We always felt that we could win every game. It was a real team effort."

Many of the players had fascinating backgrounds. Three—Johnston, Arizin, and Gola—would later earn places in the Naismith Basketball Hall of Fame.

Johnston, a native of Chillicothe, Ohio, played basketball and baseball at Ohio State. His favorite sport was baseball, and after his sophomore year, he signed as a pitcher with the Philadelphia Phillies. Johnston played three years in the Phillies farm system, including two years with the Class B Wilmington (Delaware) Blue Rocks. After the 1951 season, Johnston quit baseball. "I decided I was going nowhere," he said. "So, from then on, I put all my athletic apples in the peach basket." Johnston joined the Warriors, and before his career ended in 1959, "Gabby," as he was called, led the NBA in scoring three straight times and was named to six All-Star teams despite standing just 6-feet, 8-inches as a center.

Neil Johnston (6), demonstrating his famous hook shot, was a three-time NBA scoring champ who finished third in the league in 1955–56 in scoring with 1,547 points (22.1 ppg). Ernie Beck (left) awaits a possible rebound.
Courtesy of Rich Westcott

Arizin was another player with an interesting background. Raised in South Philadelphia, he was cut three times from his La Salle High School basketball team. As a sophomore at Villanova, coach Al Severance spotted him playing in a gym, and persuaded him to try out for the Wildcats team. Arizin made it with flying colors. During his three years as a player, he led Villanova to the Final Four, scored 85 points in one game, led the nation in scoring while becoming the first Wildcat ever to score 1,000 career points, and was named an All-American and college Player of the Year. The 6-foot, 4-inch Pitchin' Paul went on to win two NBA scoring titles and a Most Valuable Player Award, was named to ten All-Star teams, and eventually wound up in the Basketball Hall of Fame.

Gola grew up in Olney and also graduated from La Salle High before enrolling at La Salle College. There he became a three-time All-American and led the Explorers to both the NIT and NCAA championships. For many years, Gola was La Salle's all-time scoring leader. A 6-foot, 6-inch rookie in the NBA during the Warriors' championship year, he became an outstanding pro scorer, rebounder, and defensive player during a ten-year NBA career, and was a five-time All-Star. Later, he became a highly successful coach of the Explorers basketball team.

As a former standout catcher who had spent one year in the minors, Jack Edwin George, the man with three first names, might have had catches with Johnston under the grandstands. But they focused on basketball, with George holding the role of playmaker and ballhawk with the Warriors. A native of Washington, DC, the 6-foot, 2½-inch George bypassed a baseball career to attend Notre Dame, but then transferred to La Salle. Called one of the "hardest drivers" in the league, he was in his third year with the Warriors in 1955–56.

A starting forward, the 6-foot, 8-inch Graboski had joined the pros in 1948 with no college experience. A Chicago native, who as a teenager had served as a waterboy for his hometown Stags team, Grabbo was noted for his two-hand shots from the corner. He joined the Warriors in 1953 and was the club's third-highest scorer during the 1955–56 season. Graboski played thirteen seasons in the NBA, including eight with the Warriors.

Beck was the club's standout sixth man from Penn where he broke every scoring record in the school's history and is still its all-time scoring leader. The 6-foot, 4-inch All-American was a graduate of West Catholic High School near where he grew up. An outstanding shooter and rebounder, Beck broke in with the Warriors in 1953, but missed a year while serving in the military, and was actually still in the Navy when the season began.

The team's other key reserve was the 6-foot, 3-inch Dempsey, who came out of Merchantville High School and Kings College, where he was one of the nation's leading small college scorers. A fine ball-handler, he had originally played with the South Philadelphia Hebrew Association (SPHAS) team before breaking into the NBA with the Warriors in 1954.

The other three players on the team were not as frequently used, but all contributed to the champion Warriors. Moore went to La Salle College and starred on the school's 1952 NIT champions after leading Overbrook High to three straight Public League titles. The Warriors' first African-American player, the 6-foot, 5-inch forward was a top rebounder. Hennesy was a 6-foot, 3-inch guard from New Rochelle, New York. A Villanova star who broke Arizin's career scoring record, he was in his rookie season in 1955–56 after serving two years in the Army. Davis was holder of the world's high jump record and a gold medal winner in the 1952 Olympics. At 6-foot, 8-inches, the former Texas A & M star from Nederland, Texas, was an outstanding rebounder and one of the game's early dunk shot-makers.

Early in the season, the Warriors' roster also included Philadelphian Bob Schafer from Villanova University, who on December 3 was sold to the St. Louis Hawks. Jim Mooney from Villanova and Mike Kearns from Princeton were also on the club's preseason roster.

Although he had spent his entire eight-year pro playing career as a play-making guard with the Warriors, Senesky was a newcomer to the coaching ranks. In his first year after retiring as a player in 1954–55, he was the team's assistant

Coach George Senesky (kneeling) and owner Eddie Gottlieb pose with their team (from left) Jack George, Larry Hennessy, George Dempsey, Ernie Beck, Paul Arizin, Jackie Moore, Tom Gola, Neil Johnston, Joe Graboski, and Walter Davis.
Courtesy of Rich Westcott

coach. But when Gottlieb came down with a stomach ailment during the season, Senesky in effect became the head coach. He was officially named to that position the following season.

Senesky was the coach, but Gottlieb was never too far from the action. Usually sitting near the Warriors' bench, he often badgered referees and yelled instructions to his players. Sometimes after the Warriors lost a game, he would tromp into the clubhouse to berate his players.

Gottlieb had become the team's chief owner in 1952 when he (with friends and local businessmen Jules Trumper and Lou Glazer) bought the team for $25,000.

With the help of ticket manager Mike Iannarella and jack-of-all-trades Dave Zinkoff, Gottlieb ran the team from a tiny center city office at the Essex Hotel at 13th and Filbert Streets.

Zinkoff, of course, was the ubiquitous public address announcer whose booming voice would dazzle the audience with his clever calls. "Gola goooooal," he would shout. Or "two minutes left in the quwaartah." The Zink, who also gave away salamis during games, was unchallenged when it came to his unique style behind the mike.

"The whole atmosphere...Zink, Gotty, the crowds, good teams, good players...was electrifying," Arizin once said. "I don't think there was anything like it anywhere else in the NBA."

The Warriors also had an outstanding radio team. Bill Campbell, who would go on to a legendary seventy-year career in Philadelphia, calling not only the Warriors games, but also those of the Philadelphia Eagles, 76ers, and Phillies, was the play-by-play announcer. Chuck Thompson, a former Phillies broadcaster who later became a prominent Hall of Fame announcer with the Baltimore Orioles, handled the color.

Adding to the dynamics was the fact that doubleheaders were often played, allowing fans to see two pro games for the price of one. Two other NBA teams or the Harlem Globetrotters would play in the first game. Then the Warriors would take the floor in the nightcap. Often players from one game sat in the stands behind one of the backboards to watch the other game. And even when there weren't pro teams involved in the opener, games between teams from local leagues would usually precede Warriors battles.

Although the Warriors' home court was Convention Hall, their home games were not always played there due to other events taking precedence. Sometimes, the team played at the Arena, its former home court at 45th and Market Streets. The team also played an early-season game at Hershey. Indeed, the Warriors home opener on November 9 was played at Lincoln High School in Northeast Philly.

Seven games in eight nights wasn't unusual. Travel, though, was another issue. Most of the time, the team traveled by bus or train. One night, the team drove in cars to Allentown to catch a train to Syracuse. Another time, the team's plane to Rochester was grounded in Newark, and the squad had to ride the remaining 336 miles in taxis at a cost of $360. When the team was on the road, sometimes on Sundays, Senesky called a cab and took the players to church.

The Warriors trained in Hershey and played fourteen exhibition games before the season. In the second exhibition game, played in Houlton, Maine, Gola, who in a stunning move for a rookie had held out for a salary of $15,000 before eventually signing for a reported $12,500, broke his hand. Nevertheless, the Warriors were still picked to win the NBA title.

"We were very, very good," said Arizin. "In earlier days, George Mikan (and the Minneapolis Lakers) had ruled the league. Then the Syracuse Nationals came along and were the league's top team. Then we put everything together and became an excellent team that was rarely stopped."

Before the season even began, the Warriors had already made major headlines.

That spring, Gottlieb had persuaded the other NBA owners to institute a change in the territorial draft rule. In addition to being able to select college players from a team's local area, Gottlieb had the rule changed so that high school players could be similarly drafted. And thus, in 1955 Wilt Chamberlain became a future Warrior. Ironically, the next Philadelphia pro basketball team to win an NBA title would be the 1966–67 76ers led by Chamberlain.

But that was still more than a decade down the road. In 1955–56, in the second year of the 24-second clock, the Warriors were still Philadelphia's team.

After losing their opener, 98–87, to the Boston Celtics, the Warriors met the Lakers at Lincoln High and romped to a 117 106 victory. The following night in the first game of a doubleheader at Madison Square Garden before a crowd of 18,245, the Warriors downed the Rochester Royals, 89–84. Two nights later, the Warriors played in Hershey, where they conked Minneapolis, 100–89.

Gola returned to the lineup on November 17 as the Warriors blew away the Celtics, 106–92. The Warriors then beat the defending champion Nationals two games in a row, with Johnston scoring 37 points in a 102–94 verdict. Two more wins followed as the Warriors' winning streak reached eight straight games.

The streak ended on November 27 with a 99–94 loss to the Lakers. Then, after losing to the St. Louis Hawks, the Warriors came back to beat them, 115–98, with Johnston scoring 31 points and grabbing 25 rebounds. After finishing the month of November with an 8–3 record, the Warriors went through December with an 8–5 mark. Hennessy's last-minute set shot beat the Celtics in one game, 109–108, and Beck's nine-point fourth quarter led his team to an 80–73 win over the Ft. Wayne Pistons in another.

The Warriors ended the 1955 part of the season with a 112–83 thrashing of the defending champion Nats with a record crowd of 11,236 jamming Convention Hall despite rain and sleet covering area streets.

January began with the Warriors playing on six straight nights in five different cities. Starting on New Year's Day, they played the Celtics at Boston, the Royals at New Haven, the Pistons at home, the Nats at Syracuse, the Pistons at New York, and the Knicks at home. After a day off, the Warriors then played six more games in seven nights, three at home, including one at Lincoln High School, and ones at New York, Rochester, and St. Louis. The Warriors won nine of those 12 games. Graboski sank a 50-foot shot to win one game, and the Warriors overcame 12- and 13-point fourth quarter deficits in two others, during one of which they sank 43 of 49 foul shots to beat Rochester, 97–94.

After playing eight games in the final eleven days of the month, the Warriors finished January with a 29–16 record. Then they began February with a 105–104 double overtime loss to the Knicks in a game in which George played all 58 minutes. In their fifth game of the month, on February 7, Johnston poured in 41 points in a 128–95 trouncing of Syracuse. Later in the month, in the midst of an eight-game winning

Rookie Tom Gola (15) turned out to be an invaluable addition to the Warriors starting lineup. A skillful scorer, rebounder, passer, and defensive player, he played a major role for the team.
Courtesy of Jim Rosin

streak, the Warriors scored a league-high 135 points in a six-point victory over Boston with Gola showing his great versatility by hitting a triple-double with 20 points, 17 rebounds, and 10 assists.

"Gotty told me that first year that he didn't need me for my shooting, but for others things," Gola told broadcaster Skip Clayton many years later. "They needed me to rebound, play defense, and pass the ball. But if I got myself in a position where I thought I could score, I'd shoot."

With a 41–21 record at the end of February, the Warriors had strongly demonstrated their position as the top team in the league. And whether it was Johnston, Arizin, Gola, or any of the other members of the team, everyone played an important part in the Warriors' success.

"We had everything," Dempsey recalled. "It was a well-balanced team, and everybody did what he had to do. We had good unity, a deep bench. Everything seemed to gel, and that year, there wasn't anybody who was going to stop us."

Winning wasn't everything, though. It seemed as though almost every game was marked by some unusual occurrence. In one game, Celtics coach Red Auerbach loudly complained about Senesky kneeling in front of the bench. Gola said that the coach was actually praying.

On Neil Johnston Night, the player credited with having the best hook shot in the league received $7,000 in gifts, including a car and a basket of vegetables, and he was given an off-season job with a cleaning firm in Delaware County. Mikan came out of retirement just so he could play against the Warriors. Referees Mendy Rudolph and Arnie Heft were pelted with raw eggs after one game at Convention Hall, and Sid Borgia had to be escorted from the court after another. Pettit scored 46 points in a game for St. Louis, and Rookie of the Year Maurice Stokes scored 29 points and grabbed 26 rebounds in another.

Evening Bulletin sports writer Bill Dallas called Arizin "Popskull Paul." After one game, he wrote that "Gola did everything but comb Gotty's hair." Allen Lewis of the *Inquirer* called Beck "Senesky's special fireman." Fans often yelled "Let George do it," in support of the Warriors' guard.

All the while, Senesky was earning plaudits for his coaching skills. "He was a good coach," said Beck. "He really knew the game. He wasn't a screamer or a hollerer. Gotty did that from the stands."

The Warriors began March losing three of their first four games. Then they split their final six games, ending the season with a six-game lead over the second-place Celtics in the Eastern Division. The Nationals and Knicks tied for third place, finishing ten games behind the Warriors.

After drawing a bye in the first round, the Warriors faced Syracuse for the division crown. The Nats, led by Dolph Schayes and coached by the volatile Al Cervi, had beaten the Knicks in a one-game special playoff before downing the Celtics in the best-of-three semifinals.

Arizin's 29 points and Johnston's 24 rebounds led the Warriors to a 109–87 victory in the opener of the division finals. Alternating home courts, the Warriors lost the second game, 122–118, at Syracuse, then won Game Three, 119–96, with 11,292 packing Convention Hall. Then after a 108–104 loss, the Warriors won the best-of-five playoffs with a 109–104 verdict on their home court with Arizin hitting 10 of his first 12 shots. Ironically, eight years later, the Nats would move to Philadelphia to become the 76ers.

Two days later, the championship series against the Pistons began at Convention Hall. Ft. Wayne, a team that two years later would move to Detroit, had won the Western Division with a 37–35 record, the only winning mark in the division. Coached by Charley Eckman, a former NBA referee, Detroit had lost the first two games of the division finals, then won three games in a row to defeat St. Louis.

Beck came off the bench to score 23 points as the Warriors overcame a 15-point deficit to win Game One, 98–94, at Convention Hall. Ft. Wayne, which featured high-scoring forwards Mel Hutchins and George Yardley, Philadelphia native and La Salle College graduate Larry Foust at center, and former Warriors star Andy Phillip at guard, won the second game, 84–83, on Yardley's two foul shots with 42 seconds left in the game.

Back in Philadelphia, the Warriors toppled the Pistons, 100–96, with Arizin scoring 27 points and Johnston scoring 20, and an all-time record crowd of 11,698 jammed into every available space. Moving to Ft. Wayne, the Warriors won again, this time by a 107–105 count as Arizin scored 30, George 20, and Gola 19. Referees ruled that a field goal by the Pistons' Corky

Devlin came after time had run out, thereby giving Philadelphia its first win in Ft. Wayne in four years.

Now leading the best-of-seven series three games to one, the Warriors returned to Convention Hall where on April 7, they beat the Pistons, 99–88. With 11,194 watching, Graboski scored 29 points and grabbed 16 rebounds, while Arizin scored 26 to lead the Warriors to their first championship since 1947.

In ten playoff games, Arizin had scored 289 points, a figure topped in the NBA only by Mikan. During the regular season, Arizin scored 1,741 points (24.2 points per game average) while Johnston tallied 1,547 (22.1). Among the G-men, Graboski registered 1,034 points, George scored an even 1,000 with 457 assists (6.3 per game), and Gola, who would spend the following year in the military, bagged 732.

Senesky said winning the title was "quite an achievement. I thought we had a tougher time with Syracuse than with Ft. Wayne," he added.

Following the game, the Warriors flocked to Sam Fraimo's restaurant at 28th Street and Allegheny Avenue. Gottlieb's girlfriend, Alicia Trejo, a Spanish-born singer-dancer, sang, everyone drank, and the party spilled long into the early morning hours. Most players didn't get home until at least 4 a.m.

"We thought all along that this was going to be our year," Beck recalled. "Going in, we felt we were the best team in the league. We thought we could win every game."

Each Warriors player received $1,500 for winning the title. Gottlieb also added some money to the players' wallets, giving them bonuses of $400 to $1,000

A few days after the final whistle, the city and the Chamber of Commerce co-sponsored a special banquet at the Bellevue-Stratford Hotel to celebrate the championship. Tickets cost $10 each and a sold-out crowd of more than 500 people showed up, including Mayor Richardson Dilworth and City Council president and future mayor James H. J.Tate.

"This shows that basketball has arrived as a big league sport in a big league city," Gottlieb told an ecstatic audience. The thunderous applause that followed showed full support of that statement.

EAGLES WIN THE TITLE WITH A STORIED FINISH

11

It is a scene that is forever etched in the minds of those who were there.

December 26, 1960. Franklin Field. A crowd of 67,325 hysterical fans jammed into every possible inch of the stadium. The Green Bay Packers versus the Philadelphia Eagles.

And there was the Eagles' Chuck Bednarik, Concrete Charlie as they called him, perched atop the Packers' Jim Taylor, pinning him to the ground on the nine yard line as the final seconds of the game ticked off the clock.

Game over. Eagles win, 17–13. And with that they became champions of the National Football League, the first title for the team since 1949 and the last time the Eagles have worn the crown to date.

Bednarik, the former All-American from the University of Pennsylvania, at thirty-five, the oldest player on the team, an All-Pro selection eight times, and the last player to play both ways, had hit Taylor high while defensive back Bobby Jackson hit him low following a short pass to the Packers' fullback. Bednarik slammed Taylor to the ground, then sat on top of him, making sure Green Bay's great running back couldn't get up and his team couldn't run another play.

It was a play that ranks as one of the most memorable in Philadelphia sports history, and to this day no Eagles play was ever larger.

When the clock finally expired, Bednarik, having played 58 of the game's 60 minutes, got up and stood over Taylor. "You can get up now, you SOB," he screamed. "This [expletive] game is over."

More than one-half a century later, Bednarik, by then a Hall of Famer, recalled the play. "When you're that close to a championship, you play a different game," he said. "You want to knock the crap out of somebody. And we did."

With that came the end of a season that few except the Eagles themselves had believed could be possible. This was a team that had posted a highly mediocre 7–5 record in 1959. The year before that, the Birds had won just two games out of 12.

"Going into the 1960 season, we were a better team than a lot of people thought," said defensive tackle Eddie Khayat. "We knew after the 1959 season, that we would get better. We had a really smart team. It was very well coached, and we had great leadership among the players."

Head coach Buck Shaw, one of the most respected and popular coaches in the game, was in his third season with the Eagles. A star tackle at Notre Dame, Shaw had been coaching since 1922, mostly at the college level. He was the San Francisco 49ers' head coach from 1946 to 1954, registering a 71–39–4 record, but then had returned to the college ranks as the first head coach at the Air Force Academy. After two years there, he joined the Eagles.

"Shaw let his assistants do much of the work," tight end Pete Retzlaff recalled. "He set things up, but he expected them to be responsible for their particular areas once we went onto the field. But he was the leader. I remember in his second year with the club, we had a meeting. He said, 'Guess what? We're going to have three teams. One playing, one coming, and one going. You guys decide where you want to be.'"

Shaw had surrounded himself with an outstanding staff in which two of his assistants—Jerry Williams and Nick Skorich—would go on to become head coaches in the NFL, and

Four of the key players in the Eagles' offense are joined by coach Buck Shaw during a practice session at Franklin Field. They include (from left) Norm Van Brocklin, Tommy McDonald, Pete Retzlaff, and Bobby Walston.
Courtesy of Rich Westcott

one other—Bucko Kilroy—would become an NFL general manager. Players Khayat, Marion Campbell, and Norm Van Brocklin also became head coaches. Skorich, Khayat, and Campbell would all become Eagles head coaches.

"We were a very smart team and we stuck together," said running back Billy Ray Barnes, also an outstanding baseball player who was considered a sure bet to make the majors as a third baseman. "We had a lot of very good football players. We knew we were good, but we also had good leadership both on and off the field. On the field, nobody was smarter than Van Brocklin. He was not only the best, but the smartest quarterback I ever played with. On the field, he was the boss. He was our leader. If you made a mistake, you didn't want to go back into the huddle because he'd really let you have it."

Van Brocklin was also in his third season with the Eagles, having arrived in Philadelphia in a trade with the Los Angeles Rams. In eleven seasons in the pros, he had set several passing records while leading the league in passing three times and compiling an amazing completion percentage of 53.6.

"Dutch," as he was called, was the perfect quarterback for this team. He was the unchallenged leader on the field, a tough guy who took nothing lightly. He was also a masterful passer. "The ball would be in the air before you made your final move," Retzlaff recalled. " He'd throw it where you were going to end up. If you broke the pattern, you'd hear about it back in the huddle. But we had a very good relationship with both him and Sonny Jurgenson. In fact, Sonny was a better passer, one of the best I ever played with."

The rest of the Eagles offense was outstanding, too. Along with Barnes, Clarence Peaks, Ted Dean, Timmy Brown, and Theron Sapp were called "the best set of five backs in the league," by *Evening Bulletin* writer Hugh Brown. Retzlaff, Tommy McDonald, and Bobby Walston were all brilliant receivers. On the interior line, Bednarik at center anchored a superb group that over the course of a game included J. D.

Billy Barnes (33) slams his way through a gang of Pittsburgh Steelers in a game played in the snow at Forbes Field. Barnes was a major part of the Eagles' running game.
Courtesy of Rich Westcott

Smith, Jim McCusker, Stan Campbell, Riley Gunnels, John Wittenborn, Gene Gossage, Gerry Huff, and Howard Keys.

On defense, the Eagles also had a collection of highly skilled performers with Marion Campbell, Joe Robb, and Bob Freeman as ends. Jesse Richardson and Khayat were successful tackles playing virtually all the time; Bednarik, Maxie Baughan, Bob Pellegrini, and Chuck Weber were standout linebackers, and Tom Brookshier, Don Burroughs, Jimmy Carr, Gene Johnson, and Jackson did solid jobs manning the secondary.

"We got turnovers all over the place," Khayat recalled. "Interceptions, fumbles, we were always getting them. Our attitude on defense was, if we can get the ball back to Dutch (Van Brocklin), he'd figure out a way to score."

The Eagles had numerous other assets. "We had a lot of people who were very good players and knew how to play the game," Baughan, a first round draft pick, recalled. "And the backup quarterback, Jurgenson, was a future Hall of Famer. What's that tell you about how good this team was?"

The Eagles, owned by a group for which Jim Clark served as chairman of the board and Philadelphia Fire Commissioner Frank McNamee was the team's president, played as a team should play. "We stuck together," said Brown. "We all had confidence in each other. We were a very cohesive unit. Everybody was on the same page. We had good leadership, too. And as the season went on, our confidence kept building."

"It was a family from top to bottom," Gunnels added. "We had a lot of camaraderie. We had a great relationship with each other. We went out together. We enjoyed each other's company. Plus, we had the best fans in the country. They made it very enjoyable to play in Philadelphia."

The Eagles roster was not loaded with veteran players. Dean, Brown, Baughan, Jackson, Gunnels, and Gossage were playing in their first full seasons. Smith, Robb, and Sapp were among those playing in their second seasons, and McCusker, Huth, end Dick Lucas, and Wittenborn were in their third years. Conversely, Van Brocklin and Bednarik were both in their twelfth seasons, Walston was in his tenth, and Richardson was in his eighth.

Van Brocklin was the highest-paid player with a salary of $25,000. Bednarik earned $15,000. The average salary on the team was $13,000, with Brown the lowest-paid player at $7,500. Many of the players had full-time jobs in the off-season. During the season, a lot of players lived in West Philadelphia, many in a big apartment building at 63rd and Walnut Streets. Across the street was a bar where they hung out together.

"Back in those days, neither the players nor the team had a lot of money," recalled long-time Eagles pubic relations director Jim Gallagher, who in that era served as the team's personnel director. "We had a little office at 15th and Locust. We rode buses or trains to the games in nearby cities. And we didn't have a lot of scouts. Often, if he lived in that area, you'd call one of your former players to go look at a college player."

Despite some obvious talent, twelve of the Eagles' twenty-two starting players were castoff from other teams. Three starters were natives of the Philadelphia area and attended local high schools—Dean at Radnor, Richardson at Roxborough, and Weber at Abington.

When the season began, the team wasn't favored to win the NFL's Eastern Conference championship. That honor went to the Baltimore Colts, winners in 1958 over the New

York Giants in one of the most famous games in football history, and NFL champs again in 1959.

"We were a better team than a lot of people thought we were," said Khayat. "Vince McNally, the general manager, and his staff had done a great job putting this team together, and Van Brocklin brought out the best of everybody on the field, so we were pretty confident."

That confidence was bolstered as the Eagles held their training camp at Hershey, Pennsylvania, then launched a six-game exhibition schedule. In their first outing, they downed the Rams, 20–7, at Los Angeles. One week later, at San Francisco, they were bashed by the 49ers, 45–28. The Eagles bounced back with a 24–6 win over the Washington Redskins at Norfolk, Virginia, and a 40–10 rout of the Detroit Lions at Norman, Oklahoma. They then lost, 34–13, to the host Cardinals in their first year in St. Louis. But the preseason campaign ended on a high note when the Birds whipped the Colts, 35–21 at Hershey.

"After that game, we thought we had a real good chance to win the championship," Gunnels said. "That game gave us some confidence, and the feeling that we might be pretty good."

That confidence was rudely interrupted as the season began. Having left Shibe Park—their home since they moved out of Baker Bowl in 1940—after the 1957 season, the Birds were now flying at Franklin Field, owned by the University of Pennsylvania. Located on the Penn campus at 34th and Walnut Streets, it was a true football stadium with stands surrounding the playing field that normally held crowds as big as 60,000.

In their first game of the season, with the largest crowd (56,303) ever to watch a pro game in Philadelphia, the Eagles were routed by the Cleveland Browns, 41–25, at Franklin Field. It was a devastating loss, which Khayat said, "brought us back to reality." But it had a positive effect.

"That game did a lot to straighten us out," said Gunnels. "After that, we started working a lot harder. We knew we had a good team, and we felt that we could come together. That game put us on the right track."

Herb Good, who covered the team for the *Philadelphia Inquirer*, expounded on that theory. "It was the fires of adversity fanned by a 41–24 thumping at the hands of the Browns in the 1960 opener," he wrote, "that welded the Eagles into a solid unyielding unit and forged the relentless determination and drive that was to produce a club record of nine straight victories."

In their next game, Freeman, a newly acquired defensive end, amazingly blocked two extra point attempts, Barnes ran for two touchdowns, and the Eagles beat the host Dallas Cowboys, 27–25. The victory launched a nine-game winning streak.

The following week, Van Brocklin threw two touchdown passes to Retzlaff and one to McDonald as the Eagles edged the Cardinals, 31–27, at home. Then the Eagles whipped the Detroit Lions, 28–10, in another home game with Peaks running for two touchdowns and Van Brocklin passing for two more. The Birds intercepted four passes and Baughan had a magnificent game on defense with 15 tackles while breaking up three pass plays.

Walston was the star of the next game as he kicked four extra points, caught a touchdown pass, and booted a game-winning 38-yard field goal with 10 seconds left to play as the Eagles got revenge with a 31–29 victory over the Browns at Cleveland. Barnes scored twice, and Peaks racked up 102 yards on 13 carries.

"After that," Good wrote, "the Eagles were convinced they could beat anyone under any circumstances, and that's what they proceeded to do, coming from behind time after time to win game after game until the pennant was clinched."

In the sixth game of the season, before 58,324 at Franklin Field, Van Brocklin threw three touchdown passes to McDonald to lead the Eagles into first place with a 34–7 rout of the Pittsburgh Steelers. One week later, the Birds nipped the Redskins, 19–13, with Van Brocklin firing two touchdown passes and Walston's second field goal of the day clinching the victory. The Eagles, however, suffered a critical loss when Peaks went down with a fractured leg. Dean replaced him for the rest of the year.

Game Seven of the season belonged to the defense. Carr scored a touchdown on a recovered fumble, Brookshier made 15 tackles, and Robb, Baughan, and Weber also stood out as the Eagles came back from a 10–0 deficit to edge the Giants, 17–10, at Yankee Stadium. In a play that drew widespread attention, Bednarik leveled Frank Gifford with a smashing tackle that not only knocked out the Giants' stellar running back, but caused a serious concussion. As Gifford fumbled the ball while the Giants were driving deep into Eagles territory, Bednarik danced over the stricken halfback. "I was jumping up and down like a cheerleader," he recalled.

In curiously back-to-back games pitting the same teams, the Eagles edged the Giants again the following week, 31–23, with Van Brocklin tossing two touchdown passes to Dean and one to Barnes as the Eagles overcame a 17–0 deficit with the help of four fumble recoveries at Franklin Field. One week later, the Eagles clinched the Eastern Division title with Van Brocklin throwing six-pointers to Retzlaff and McDonald in a 20–6 road win over the Cardinals.

The Eagles streak came to an end in the next game at Pittsburgh with the Steelers taking a 27–21 decision. The Eagles nearly overcame a 27–0 deficit in the fourth quarter with Jurgensen getting some rare playing time and throwing two touchdown passes, one to Brown, who also scored on a run.

The season finally came to an end as the Eagles downed the Redskins, 38–28, in their third straight road game. Brown scored twice and Van Brocklin fired two TD passes to McDonald as the Eagles ended the season with a 10–2 record, their best mark since the 1949 team went 12–1.

Walston wound up second in the league in scoring with 105 points. Van Brocklin was runner-up to the Colts' Johnny Unitas in passing with 24 touchdowns with 153 completions in 294 attempts for 2,471 yards. Retzlaff was fifth in receiving with 46 catches for 826 yards. The Eagles were second in their division in points scored (321) and the second lowest in points allowed (246).

"Winning the division was a wonderful feeling," remembered Khayat. "The team hadn't won in such a long time and it was great to give the city something to cheer about. But we still had some work to do. The season wasn't over yet."

The Green Bay Packers under coach Vince Lombardi posed one more obstacle. Lombardi, in his second year with the Packers, would go on to win five championships over the next seven years, including the first two Super Bowls, and become known as one of the greatest football coaches of all time. But after going 7–5 and tying for third place in the Western Conference in 1959, the Packers weren't there yet.

The team from the icy cold little town in Wisconsin, which hadn't won a title since 1944, finished the regular season with a division-leading 8–4 record. The Packers had many outstanding players led by quarterback Bart Starr, running backs Paul Hornung (who finished first in the league in scoring) and Jim Taylor (who was second to Jimmy Brown in the league in rushing yardage), center Jim Ringo, tackle Forrest Gregg, and linebacker Ray Nitschke, all future Hall of Famers. In addition, Jerry Kramer and Henry Jordan led a stellar offensive line, while Ron Kramer, Max McGee, and Boyd Dowler were top-level receivers. The defense, which had held opponents to just 209 points during the season, was anchored on the line by Willie Davis with Radnor High graduate Emlen Tunnell at safety.

"I remember they used to say, 'You mess up, and you're going to be sent to Green Bay,'" Barnes remembered. "But they were a lot like us. They hadn't been too good for a long time. But like us, they finally had a good season. All of the sudden, things came together."

The Packers were slight favorites to win. But that hardly mattered to the Eagles. "We thought we had the talent to come out on top," said Retzlaff. "The one trouble as far as I was concerned was that most of our practice sessions were held indoors. I had the feeling that since we were limited by that, we might not be prepared as well as we should be."

To add to the uncertainty, the game was going to be played on Monday afternoon because the previous day was Christmas and games were never played on that holiday. Long before television took over, games were not played on Mondays either. The starting time was at noon, set that early in case the game had to go into overtime. There were no lights at Franklin Field.

Nevertheless, the teams lined up at Franklin Field and with 7,000 temporary bleachers added, a record 67,325 fans packed the stands. The game was not televised locally, but it was aired on radio with Bill Campbell, a fixture in Philadelphia broadcasting circles for more than sixty years, making one of the most exhilarating broadcasts ever called. Game-time temperature was 48 degrees Fahrenheit, but there were frozen spots on the playing field that had thawed and turned into mud puddles.

The game started auspiciously for the Eagles. On the first play of the game, Van Brocklin threw a short pass to Barnes, but the ball bounced off the receiver's fingertips and was intercepted by Bill Quinlan at the Eagles' 14-yard line. Although they got down to the six-yard line, the Packers couldn't score. But three plays later, Barnes fumbled and Green Bay regained possession at the Eagles' 22-yard line. Two runs by Hornung put the ball on the 12, but that's as far as the Packers got, and Hornung kicked a 20-yard field goal.

Hornung booted a 23-yard field goal early in the second quarter, but the Eagles recovered to score on a 35-yard touchdown pass to McDonald. Walston kicked the extra point to give the Birds a 7–6 lead.

Shortly afterward, Van Brocklin completed a 41-yard pass to Retzlaff and a 22-yarder to Dean to put the ball on the Packers' eight-yard line. But after three incomplete passes, the Eagles had to settle for a Walston field goal. Then, after a missed field goal attempt by Hornung, the Eagles held a 10–6 lead at halftime.

Early in the third quarter, Hornung went out with a shoulder injury (but returned later in the game). Soon afterward, Green Bay's John Symank intercepted a Van Brocklin pass in the end zone. Late in the quarter, McGee ran 35 yards to the Eagles 45-yard line on a fake punt. The quarter ended with no scoring.

But the Packers still had the ball as the fourth period began, and after a drive deep into Eagles territory, Starr flipped a seven-yard pass to McGee for a touchdown. Hornung's extra point gave Green Bay a 13–10 lead.

On the ensuing kickoff, Dean raced 58 yards to the Green Bay 39-yard line. Soon afterward, he raced into the end zone from the five-yard line, achieving the first rushing touchdown in his pro career. Walston's extra point gave the Eagles a 17–13 lead with 5:21 left to play.

Ted Dean scored the game-winning touchdown in the Eagles' 17–13 victory over the Green Bay Packers. Dean scored from the five-yard line shortly after returning a kickoff 58 yards.
Courtesy of Jim Gallagher

After the ball exchanged hands, Green Bay went on the attack, plowing 43 yards down the field and reaching the Eagles 22-yard line with eight seconds left to play. The Packers had one play left. With his receivers covered, Starr flipped the ball to Taylor. The Packers' ace fullback plowed his way through Eagles defenders. Taylor "ducked his head like a charging bull and bolted like an enraged beer truck into Philadelphia's congested secondary," wrote noted columnist Red Smith of the *New York Herald Tribune.*

But Taylor was surrounded by Eagles. Burroughs hit him, then Baughan banged into him. Both got shoved aside. Then Taylor ran into Jackson and Bednarik.

Concrete Charlie wrestled him to the ground and held him there while the final seconds ran off the clock.

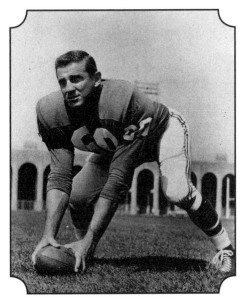

Chuck Bednarik made the most famous tackle in Eagles history when he grounded the Green Bay Packers' Jimmy Taylor as time ran out in the championship game.
Courtesy of Jim Gallagher

And when they did, the Eagles were the NFL champions. Franklin Field as well as the whole city of Philadelphia went wild.

"Thousands of fans ran out onto the field and some of them tore down the goalpost, and it almost hit Burroughs," recalled Baughan. "If it had, it might have killed him. I was only a rookie and I knew very little about the Eagles when they drafted me, but I can tell you, that game was easily the highlight of my (eleven-year) career and a lot of other guys who played that day, too."

Among the final figures, the Eagles were outgained by the Packers, 401 yards to 296 and trailed in first downs, 22–13. Van Brocklin, in what turned out to be the final game of his career, completed nine of 20 passes with one touchdown and one interception and was named the game's Most Valuable Player. The Eagles earned a winners' share of $5,116 apiece.

While Shaw would announce his retirement after the game, the outcome would mark the first and only loss for Lombardi in 10 playoff games. The Eagles, on the other hand, would play in two Super Bowls (1981, 2005), but up to the present would win no more championships.

"I'll never forget what happened after the game," Brown said 54 years later. "Lombardi was on the Packers bus waiting to leave. People were all around trying to get autographs. Lombardi made the bus wait, and he got off and went over to the entrance where some of us were standing. He congratulated us and said what a great game we played."

That is was. A great game to end a great season for one of the great teams in Philadelphia sports history.

76ERS BECOME ONE OF BASKETBALL'S GREATEST TEAMS

12 In Philadelphia, as well as the rest of the world, there had never been a team like the 1966–67 Philadelphia 76ers. From one end of the court to the other, and from every other possible direction, the 76ers were a team that even today is still remembered for its history-making season.

The team had a 7-foot, one-inch center who was arguably the best player in basketball history. The others in the starting five were all outstanding players who did exactly what their specific roles demanded. The team had an excellent bench, and it had one of the most respected coaches in the game.

Put all these together and what do you get? A team that up to that point had the best single-season record in pro basketball history and that easily won the championship of the National Basketball Association. Now, nearly fifty years after the 76ers demolished the rest of the league, they are still regarded as one of the greatest teams that ever performed in the NBA.

With Wilt Chamberlain at center; Chet Walker and Luke Jackson as forwards; Hal Greer and Wali Jones as guards; Billy Cunningham, Larry Costello, Matty Guokas, Bill Melchionni,

Dave Gambee, and later Bobby Weiss forming a superb group of reserves; and Alex Hannum serving as coach, the 76ers raced through the regular season with a 68–13 record. Then they romped through the playoffs, winning 11 of the 15 games they played, to give Philadelphia its first NBA championship in eleven years.

Wali Jones (24) was one of the league's top playmakers and a capable scorer while starring as a point guard for the 76ers. To the right is Luke Jackson (54), a power forward and outstanding rebounder.
Courtesy of the Philadelphia 76ers

It had been just four years since the 76ers came to town. After former Warriors owner Eddie Gottlieb had persuaded Nats owner Danny Biasone to sell the club previously known as the Syracuse Nationals to businessman Irv Kosloff and attorney Ike Richman in May 1963, Kosloff and Richman quickly moved the franchise to Philadelphia and it was named the 76ers. The name was the winning entry in a contest in which nearly 500 names were submitted.

Philadelphia's new team played poorly in its first year, but made the playoffs in its second season before losing in seven games in the Eastern Division Finals to the Boston Celtics. The following season, the Sixers won the division title during the regular season, but got blasted out of the division finals in five games by the Celtics.

After the season, the 76ers hired legendary St. Joseph's College coach and athletic director Jack Ramsay as general manager. Head coach Dolph Schayes was dismissed and replaced by Hannum, a forty-three-year-old who had played nine years in the NBA and had been a head coach for the previous seven and one-half seasons. Hannum had led the St. Louis Hawks to victory over Boston to win the NBA title in 1957–58, and then later coached the Nats and San Francisco Warriors.

He was a hard-nosed coach who believed that basketball was a team game and should be played the right way and not as an individual piece of showmanship. Although highly respected by his players because he treated them fairly, he would not hesitate to confront them if he wasn't pleased with the way they were playing. Indeed, he had a famous locker-room confrontation with Chamberlain in which the two had to be separated by other players. Ironically, Chamberlain had played under Hannum when they were at San Francisco.

"Sometimes, Wilt was a little dysfunctional," recalled Walker many years later, "and Alex would have to keep him in line. Alex was a player's coach. But he didn't take any stuff from anybody. He was an old-fashioned kind of coach, and he would lay down the law. You had to do it his way, although sometimes he would do it the players' way."

Those players were all magnificently talented. Walker, a 6-foot, 6½-inch forward playing in his fifth season, had been an outstanding baseball player as a teenager, but was hit in the head, ruining his ambition to be a big league player. Instead, he went to Bradley University, where he led his team to the NIT championship. Once he got to the NBA, he became an exquisite scorer, his specialties being driving layups and one-handed shots from the corner.

Jackson, the team's 6-foot, 9-inch, 265-pound power forward, played at Pan American University and was the hero of the United States' victory over Russia in the 1964 Olympics. Voted NBA Rookie of the Year in 1965, he was a strong rebounder who could score and block shots. In his third year with the Sixers, he was known for his forceful play under the boards.

Greer, a 6-foot, 3-inch product of Marshall College, was considered one of the league's top middle-distance shooters. Owner of an outstanding jump shot, he was known for his quickness and skill on fast breaks, and as a fine defensive player. In his ninth year in the NBA, Greer had been annually among the league's leading scorers and had already scored 10,000 points.

Jones (his first name was then spelled "Wally"), in his third year in the league, came out of Overbrook High School and Villanova University to become the Sixers' top playmaker and ball-handler, often registering assists in double figures. He was also one of the team's top defensive players. The 6-foot, 2-inch guard could also score when necessary.

The 76ers' bench featured Cunningham as their sixth man, a 6-foot, 6-inch high-scorer and rebounder in his second season after playing at the University of North Carolina. Guokas, whose father Matt had played with the Warriors, was a 6-foot, 6-inch skilled playmaker from St. Joseph's. Both he and the 6-foot, 1-inch Melchionni, a crack outside shooter from Villanova, were rookies. The bench also included 6-foot, 6 ½-inch Gambee, a defensive standout from Oregon State, and Costello, a 6-foot, 1-inch veteran of eleven pro seasons from Niagara University, who was hurt in midseason and missed the rest of the campaign. Weiss, a 6-foot, 2-inch backcourt player from Penn State, took Costello's place on the roster.

Walker, Greer, Gambee, and Costello (who, at thirty-five years old, was by far the oldest player on the team) had all played with the Nats before they moved to Philadelphia.

And then there was Wilt. Once, he had scored 90 points in a thirty-two-minute high school game for Overbrook High. He scored 100 points in an NBA game. In between he went to the University of Kansas, then played one year with the Harlem Globetrotters. Now in his eighth year in the NBA, he had become the greatest player of his or any other generation, a two-time Most Valuable Player, the league's scoring leader in each of his seven previous seasons, and at the time, the league's all-time scoring leader, who would go on to score 50 or more points in a game 118 times.

"Wilt was dominant," Walker said. "He could score, rebound, block shots, and, as we learned, he was a good passer. He was a great all-around player. He was certainly the star of our team. But we had a lot of great players. And on any given night any one of us could score thirty points. We had few close games all season. We always pushed hard to score a lot of points because that's what people came to see."

Although, as Chamberlain once said, "no team ever had a superstar cast like this one," the 76ers were by no means a herd of prima donnas playing for the benefit of their own egos.

"The most important thing was camaraderie and fellowship," said Jones. "Hannum preached the importance of family, and that's what this was. A family. We stayed together, we went out a lot together, and we worked hard together. This was a very intelligent group, and we were very visible in the community. Every player on that team took part in community activities, and we traveled to all parts of the city."

Jones pointed out that there was another important part of the 76ers' makeup. "Our team was made up of a lot of different ethnic groups," he said. "And this was the height of the civil rights era. Having come from different cultures, the relationships we built with each other were very important. It was very appropriate that we played in the City of Brotherly Love."

It was also very appropriate that when they were on the court, the Sixers played virtually every phase of the game well. No matter which end of the court they were on, whether it was scoring, rebounding, or defense, the team excelled. "When you were on the court, you wanted to have the respect of your peers," Jones said.

"We had all the pieces," Jackson remembered. "We had power with Wilt, Chet, and me up front. We had speed and guys who could really shoot and handle the ball in Hal, Wali, and Matty. And we had very good defense. It gave you a really good feeling playing with that team.

"Alex always said, 'You do what you want to do. Just remember, you have to play tomorrow, and you better be ready.' We bled together. We cried together. And we enjoyed each other tremendously. It was a real pleasure to be part of that team."

Training camp was held for the third straight year at the Greater Atlantic City Jewish Community Center in Margate, New Jersey, where intra-squad games were held in a dinky little gym. The team stayed at a nearby hotel in Longport. After a thirteen-game exhibition schedule with games as far away as Nevada, California, New Mexico, Louisiana, and West Virginia, the team was set to go.

"We all felt we were ready to play," said Jackson. "We were all in great condition, and when you're in good shape, you can do a lot of good things."

The 76ers played their home games at both the Arena at 45th and Market Streets and at Convention Hall on 34th Street right down the street from the Palestra and Franklin Field. With a capacity of only 6,500 and virtually no parking facilities, the Arena was far less desirable. In both places, though, the building reverberated with the loud and colorful pronouncements of legendary public address announcer Dave Zinkoff, a fixture at Philadelphia basketball games since the 1930s.

"I loved to play at Convention Hall," said Walker. "It had a great atmosphere. People were close to the court. And they were really into the game. We definitely had the home court advantage when we played there."

During the season, the 76ers also played six games at Pittsburgh, and other games at Syracuse; Memphis, Tennessee; Evansville and Ft. Wayne, Indiana; and Cleveland, Ohio.

The season opened on October 15 with the 76ers pulling away from a 61–59 halftime lead to down the New York Knicks, 128–112. Chamberlain scored 28 points and Walker added 25. The Sixers went on to win their first seven games, including a 138–96 lacing of the defending champion Boston Celtics in a game in which Greer's 26 points led a group of seven 76ers in double figures.

As it would soon become apparent, Wilt, who had been traded back to Philadelphia by San Francisco during the 1964–65 season, was not being counted on to carry the full offensive load. Hannum had convinced him to shoot less and pass the ball more often. Although it was the kind of game he'd never played before, nor had he ever played with this kind of multitalented team, Chamberlain became one of the top passers in the league, and, in fact, placed third in assists that year behind Guy Rodgers and Oscar Robertson.

Wilt Chamberlain (13) was arguably the most dominant player in NBA history. He led the NBA in scoring seven times and in rebounding 11 times and is the only player in league history to average 30 points and 20 rebounds per game over his entire career.
Courtesy of Rich Westcott

"Not only was I shooting less, I was shooting more selectively," said Chamberlain in his book *Wilt*. "We had the players and we had the coach, and there was no reason we shouldn't go all the way if I was willing to sacrifice my image as a prolific scorer." As a result, Chamberlain took only 1,150 shots that year, less than half of what he'd been averaging since he came into the league.

In their seventh win of the season, the 76ers edged the Warriors (a team they would meet again that season in more critical circumstances), 134–129, despite 46 points by Rick Barry. Then, after losing 105–87 to the Celtics, the Sixers launched an eight-game winning streak, due in part to Chamberlain's 30 points in a 118–100 win over the Detroit Pistons, the first game of a doubleheader at New York's Madison Square Garden.

As November ended, the Sixers, now ensconced in an eleven-game winning streak, had a 20–2 record. By December 10, the mark had stretched to 26–2 as Greer's 39 points paced his team to a 133–123 victory over the St. Louis Hawks. A 117–103 loss to Boston followed, and then the Philly team went out and posted another eleven-game winning streak. Included in that run was a 148–142 overtime victory over the Knicks on January 3, with Cunningham scoring 36 and Chamberlain 35. With that win, the 76ers had begun the New Year with a 36–3 record. They were a team that was virtually unstoppable.

"At first, we didn't know how good we really were," Walker recalled. "The year before, we were good, but then we turned into something special. We knew we could beat anybody. We had become an absolutely great team that had all the elements needed to win."

And win they continued to do. After a 112–105 decision over St. Louis on January 23 at Memphis, the 76ers' record stood at a phenomenal 46–4, the best start of any team in pro basketball history. Starting the next day, though, the 76ers encountered their only slump of the season, losing four of the next five games before stopping the skid with a 140–127 win over the Warriors, with Jones scoring 33 points.

From there, the Sixers won eleven of their next thirteen games. This included a 149–118 clobbering of the Baltimore Bullets in which they tallied a season-high total number of points (with Chamberlain tallying 42 points and Greer 36). One game later, the 76ers ended February with a 58–10 record. Slightly less than three weeks afterward, they finished the season beating the Bullets, 132–129, for their sixteenth win in the last nineteen games and a season-ending mark of 68–13. That record would stand as the best in NBA history until broken in 1971–72 by the Chamberlain-led Los Angeles Lakers with a 69–13 mark.

As could be expected, while winning the Eastern Division title, the 76ers dominated the 1966–67 season statistics. Chamberlain led the league in rebounds (1,957) and field goal percentage (.683), was third in assists (630) while setting a record for centers by averaging eight assists per game, and third behind Barry and Robertson in scoring with 1,956 (24.1 ppg) points, ending his string of seven straight scoring titles.

Greer was sixth in scoring with 1,765 points. Walker scored 1,567 (19.3), Cunningham tallied 1,495 (18.5), Jones had 1,069 (13.2) with 303 assists, and Jackson recorded 970 (12.0) with 724 rebounds. Chamberlain was named the NBA's Most Valuable Player and was a first team selection on the league All-Star squad, with Greer being named to the second team.

Hal Greer (15), one of the best guards in 76ers history, was an outstanding shooter who placed sixth in the league in scoring in 1965–66 with 1,765 points (22.1).

Courtesy of the Philadelphia 76ers

As a team, the 76ers led the league in points per game (125.2), assists (2,138), and field goal percentage (.483), and were third in rebounds (5,701) behind San Francisco and Boston. During the regular season, the Sixers drew a total home crowd of 246,275 fans, an average of 8,224 per game.

A tragic spot on the team's otherwise magnificent season was the death of co-owner Richman after he was stricken with a heart attack while attending a 76ers-Celtics game at Convention Hall. Richman had been a key figure in Philadelphia pro basketball for many years, having once been Gottlieb's attorney and later Chamberlain's first lawyer.

The NBA playoffs began that year on March 21. In the semifinal round, the 76ers were pitted against the Cincinnati

Royals, third-place finishers in the Eastern Division with a 39–42 record.

In the first game at Convention Hall before a sparse crowd of 5,097, the Royals, behind Robertson's 33 points, unexpectedly captured a 120–116 decision, despite Chamberlain's 41 points. That was it for the Royals. The 76ers roared back to take three straight verdicts, starting with a 123–102 win at Cincinnati, with Chamberlain netting 37 and Greer 28. Then they captured a 121–106 victory at Philadelphia as Greer scored 33 and Walker scored 24. They clinched the match back in Ohio with a 112–95 victory with Greer (30) and Walker (23) leading the way before an astonishingly paltry crowd of 2,624.

Victory in the division semifinals brought the 76ers face-to-face with the Celtics, who had finished second during the regular season, eight games behind Philadelphia with a 60–21 record.

The Celtics, with a team that featured Bill Russell, Sam Jones, John Havlicek, Bailey Howell, and a parade of other top players under coach Red Auerbach, were not only the defending champions, but the winners of the last eight NBA titles. They had beaten the Knicks in the semifinals, three games to one. Unquestionably, the 76ers had a tough road ahead of them.

"We believed we could beat them," Walker remembered. "Nobody else believed they were beatable. But we felt we were better than them. We had a very positive attitude, and when you have that, you are most likely to get the job done."

And so they did. Playing in the best-of-seven Eastern Division finals, the Sixers knocked off Boston in five games.

Starting in Philly, they went from a 66–49 halftime lead to a 127–113 victory with Greer scoring 39 points and Chamberlain and Jones each bagging 24. On to Boston, the Sixers won again, 107–102, after overcoming a 58–55 halftime deficit with Walker (23) and Jones (22) leading the way. Greer's 30 points led the team to a 115–104 triumph in Game Three at Convention Hall before a crowd of 13,007, despite Havlicek's 30 for the Celtics. Boston interrupted the streak four days later with a home 121–117 win as Sam Jones (32) and Havlicek (31) topped Jackson (29) and Greer (28).

Game Five was back in Philadelphia. With five players in double figures, led by Greer (32), Chamberlain (29), and

Chet Walker (right) is about to receive a pass from Wilt Chamberlain during a game at Convention Hall. Walker, an extremely versatile offensive player, was the 76ers' third highest scorer.
Courtesy of Rich Westcott

Walker (26), the Sixers overcame a 37–26 first quarter deficit to win going away, 140–116, with another crowd of 13,007 filling every corner of the stands. The win gave the 76ers the Eastern Division championship.

"Everybody was so glad we stopped the dynasty," Jones remembered. "People had been saying, 'Who's ever going to beat these guys?' It had been a long season, and we didn't rest until it was over, but I honestly believe that we were ready for Boston. And we proved that was right."

The win sent the Sixers to the finals against the Warriors, once a storied Philadelphia team that had been sold after the 1961–62 season by Gottlieb to a group headquartered in San Francisco.

The Warriors, later to become the Golden State Warriors, featured Rick Barry, one of the superstars of the league, and a great center in NateThurmond. That season, they had romped through the Western Division, finishing with a 44–37 record and a five-game lead over St. Louis during the regular season, then erasing both the Chicago Bulls and the Lakers in three games each in the Western Division playoffs.

The Warriors were certainly a superb team with loads of talents. But the 76ers were unfazed. "Just like Boston, we knew San Francisco was going to be tough," Jackson said. "But again, we knew we were the better team."

The first two games were played in Philadelphia, and the 76ers won both of them. Greer's 32 points and Jones's 30 led them to a 141–135 victory in a wild overtime game in which Barry scored 37 points for the losers, who had overcome a

43–30 first quarter deficit. Game Two was no contest, as the Sixers trounced San Francisco, 126–95, with Greer scoring 30 and Cunningham 28.

Traveling to San Francisco, Barry scored a phenomenal 55 points to lead the Warriors to a 130–124 victory. Then in Game Four, Barry continued his sensational series with 43 points, but the 76ers prevailed with a 122–108 win behind the scoring of Greer (38) and Walker (33).

Back to Philadelphia, the Sixers missed an opportunity to clinch the title as the Warriors gained a 117–109 decision, with Barry exploding this time for 36 points in a game in which the 76ers squandered a 96–84 lead at the end of the third period.

"I felt we should've won it," Hannum said in the locker room afterward. "It was a tough one for us to lose. But all the credit should go to the Warriors. [Tom] Meshery [a Warrior when they were in Philadelphia who scored 17 points] hurt us at the end. Now, we'll get some rest, fire back, and get the job done."

And so they did. As Chamberlain had said, "tomorrow's another day." Back in the city of the Golden Gate, the Sixers finished off the series with a 125–122 victory after overcoming a 102–96 third quarter deficit and despite 44 points by Barry. Jones scored 27 and Chamberlain 24 to lead the Sixers to their first NBA championship.

"It was a year I'll never forget," said Jackson. "It was a season filled with great achievements by some of the game's greatest players."

There was a small celebration in the clubhouse after the game, and then the team flew home to Philadelphia where hundreds of fans assembled at the airport to greet the plane as it landed. As they disembarked, players waved joyfully to the cheering crowd.

A few days after their arrival back in Philadelphia, the 76ers were saluted at a ceremony at City Hall. And then the players departed for their homes around the country.

The Sixers would win the Eastern Division title again in 1967–68, but after beating the Knicks in a six-game series, they lost to the Celtics, four games to three in the Eastern Division finals. After that, the team's makeup began to change.

Hannum, who after the championship season had been denied the coach of the Year Award—it went instead to the Bulls' Johnny Kerr, who led his expansion team to 33 wins in its first season—resigned from the Sixers after the 1967–68 season and joined the American Basketball Association's Oakland Oaks. With Barry as its star player, the Oaks would capture the league championship in 1968–69.

Ramsay was appointed as head coach, where he stayed for four seasons before moving on, first to the Buffalo Braves and then to the Portland Trailblazers, whom he led to the NBA championship in 1976–77, when they beat the 76ers in the finals. Meanwhile, Chamberlain was traded to the Lakers after the 1967–68 season in what was the start of the breakup of the championship team.

In 1980, the 35th anniversary of the league, the 1966–67 76ers were chosen as the greatest NBA team in league history

up to that point. Ultimately, Chamberlain, Greer, Cunningham, Hannum, and Ramsay were inducted into the Naismith
Basketball Hall of Fame.

FLYERS DELIVER THE CITY'S FIRST STANLEY CUP

13 They were known as the Broad Street Bullies, a belligerent bunch who played tough and who would fight at the drop of a puck. Their coach was a brilliant but aloof taskmaster who searched through libraries for inspirational quotes. An aging singer was their good luck charm. And every player on the club came from Canada, most of them from small towns far from the shining lights of the big cities.

But, oh, could they play ice hockey.

The Flyers gave Philadelphia is first look at real ice hockey, and then the 1973–74 team provided the city with its first sip from the Stanley Cup. The fact that another Cup arrived the following year solidified the Flyers as one of Philadelphia's most unforgettable teams.

Ice hockey, of course, wasn't new to Philadelphia when the Flyers first took the ice for the 1966–67 National Hockey League season. Prior to the Flyers' arrival, the city had been the home of ten professional ice hockey squads, starting with a team in 1927 called the Arrows that competed in the Canadian-American Hockey League and including the Quakers, a team that played one year in the NHL in 1930.

The Flyers had originally arrived in Philadelphia as an expansion team in 1966. That season, playing in a West Division made up of the NHL's six new teams, the Flyers finished first in the division during the regular season before getting eliminated in the playoffs in the first round.

In subsequent years, the Flyers reached the playoffs three more times, but got past the quarterfinals only once—in 1972–73 when they lost four out of five games to the Montreal Canadiens in the semifinals.

It was a different story, though, the following year. With a highly talented team and coach Fred Shero now in his third season with the Flyers, an air of confidence hung over the

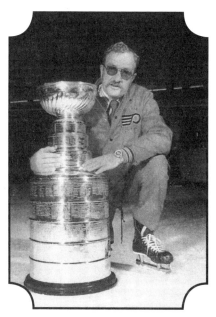

Coach Fred Shero was in his third season with the Flyers when he led them to their first Stanley Cup.
Courtesy of the Philadelphia Flyers

team as it began training at the University of Pennsylvania's Class of '23 rink.

"After the previous season, we knew that summer that we had a real good chance of making a strong run at the title," recalled Bill Barber. "We had all the elements it takes to win—ruggedness, hard-nosed, hard-working [players]. We could score, we could shut the other team down, and we had a great group of guys who blended together and wanted to win."

That group featured a combination of veterans and youngsters. Thirteen players were twenty-four years old or younger. Most of them had no idea where Philadelphia was located. Only seven players were thirty or above.

Bobby Clarke, drafted as a skinny twenty-year-old out of Flin Flon, Manitoba, in 1969, was the team's top scorer and team leader. Despite being burdened with diabetes, he played with limitless skill and energy, and had won the coveted Hart Trophy the previous season.

Bernie Parent was a magnificent goalie who had originally been drafted by the Flyers in 1967, was traded to the Toronto Maple Leafs in 1971, and then had been dealt back to the Flyers for goalie Doug Favell and a first-round draft choice in 1973. In effect, when the Flyers got him back, Parent was the final piece of the puzzle in the team's lineup.

The team was loaded with other stellar players. Standout scorers included Clarke, Rick MacLeish, Orest Kindrachuk, Bill Clement, and Terry Crisp. Barber, Dave Schultz, Don Saleski, Bob Kelly, Gary Dornhoefer, Simon Nolet, Bill Flett, and

Ross Lonsberry took their shifts as wingers. Joe Watson, Ed Van Impe, Andre Dupont, Barry Ashbee, Jimmy Watson, and Tom Bladon manned their lines as defensemen. Bobby Taylor was the backup goalie.

"We had two or three superstars," recalled Watson, "but basically we were guys who brought our lunch pails and went to work. We were a bunch of plumbers, and we had to work hard for everything we achieved."

As head coach, Shero never left anything to chance. Shero was the special pick of general manager Keith Allen, the former coach who had guided the Flyers through their first two years in the NHL. After spending thirteen years as a minor-league coach, Shero had been hired by the Flyers in 1971 to replace Vic Stasiuk and would go on to a seven-year career with the team.

Noted for an obsession with the fundamentals of the game, his innovative techniques, masterful ability at handling players, and his sometimes unusual ways of dealing with people, Shero was held in high regard by his players. Shero would go on to win the first Jack Adams Award as coach of the year in 1973–74.

"He was an outstanding coach who wanted us to play every minute of the game properly," said Clarke, who at the age of twenty-three was the youngest team captain in NHL history. "We had really talented and aggressive players, and we all made sacrifices for each other. Fred taught us that every minute of the game was important, and that we could win every game we played."

Under Shero, a loner who away from the ice often kept to himself, each player had a specific duty. The Flyers had four players who would score more than 30 goals during the season—Clarke (35), Barber (34), Lonsberry (32), and MacLeish (32). They also had a defense that was virtually impassible.

"Our strongest point," said Crisp, "is that we were balanced. It was like having the best quarterback, the best pitcher, and the best goaltender. That's what it takes to win a championship, and that's what we had. We had young players and veterans. Everybody was really enthusiastic, and everybody had a specific role. "

One of these roles became the calling card of the team, although in a way it tended to overlook some of its other strengths. During their sixth year of operation, veteran sports writer Jack Chevalier had called the team the "Broad Street Bullies" in an article he wrote for the *Philadelphia Evening Bulletin*. The name was meant to describe the Flyers' willingness to play rough and tough and to fight whenever the opportunity arose.

No one fought harder and more often than Schultz, whose nickname was "The Hammer." Schultz would start a fight at the slightest opportunity. His fights were often bloody and nasty, and he would become known as the fiercest enforcer and intimidator in the league.

"People think I was a lot tougher than I was," said Schultz. "On the other hand, if somebody picked on one of my teammates, he had to deal with me or somebody else. We all protected one another. I never had a fight until I was twenty

Dave Schultz (8) was nicknamed "The Hammer" and was the leader of a defense that was called "The Broad Street Bullies."
Courtesy of the Philadelphia Flyers

years old. I always hated fighting. Then all of a sudden fighting became expected of me and I focused on it. If somebody took a cheap shot, I was going after him."

"The Flyers were originally a small team and other teams took advantage of us," recalled Van Impe, the team's first pick in the expansion draft. "Then Schultz came along and he gave us courage. That was a vital part of our team. On defense, we played like it was better to give than to receive."

Schultz, a fifth round draft pick in 1969 whose accumulation of time in the penalty box usually reached high levels, including 348 minutes in 1973–74, was joined by a rugged constituency that included Saleski and Kindrachuk on the third line. Those three were especially known as checkers, agitators, penalty-killers, and body-bashers who showed no mercy when the other team had the puck.

"When we went into a building," Saleski remembered, "people on the other side knew they were going to get hit. We had a really tough team, and we got under the opposing team's skin. We always knew we had Schultzie to finish things off. He was the lead character. And there was no better agitator than Dornhoefer. Overall, we had a very tough, very physical team, and everybody contributed."

Saleski exemplified the small town upbringing of practically every Flyers player.

"As a kid growing up in Saskatchewan, it was always in my dreams that someday I'd win a Stanley Cup," he said. "Then I grew up and did."

Watson had a similar childhood. "Growing up in British Columbia near Alaska, I figured my way out was through sports," he said. "When I was sixteen, I went to a camp where they had 104 kids trying out for five positions on a Junior A team. I made it, and went from there."

Despite the varied paths the players took to reach the big time and the club's reputation as the king of fisticuffs, there was a unity on the team the level of which few teams enjoy.

"This was a family," Parent said. "Not just a hockey team, but a family. We had good ownership [the principal and still owner was Ed Snider and local businessman Joe Scott was the team president], good coaching, good scouting, and, of course, you have to have good players. Plus, we had 20,000 people rooting for us. We had the right combination of everything, and we knew what we had to do. It was a heckuva journey."

The journey began inauspiciously when the Flyers lost their first exhibition game of the 1973–74 season by a 10–3 score to the New York Rangers at the Spectrum, a venue in South Philadelphia that had been opened in 1966. Parent, in his initial outing since his trade back to the Flyers, was slammed for four goals in the first period and seven overall before Shero yanked him off the ice.

On October 11, the Flyers opened the regular season with a 2–0 victory over the Toronto Maple Leafs at the Spectrum. The game was significant in several ways, not the least of which is that it marked the first live performance at a Flyers' game of Kate Smith singing "God Bless America."

The Flyers had played a tape of Smith, a powerful radio, television, and Broadway singer, belting out the song many times at the start of games in previous seasons. The song, written by Irving Berlin who had given Smith the exclusive rights to sing it, had in effect become the team's theme song. In the first three years that the Flyers played it before a game, they had produced a 19–1–1 record. But before the start of the 1973–74 season, Smith had never appeared in person at the Spectrum.

Persuaded by Flyers vice president Lou Scheinfeld to appear in person, Smith was paid a reported $5,000 for her pregame performance. She rocked the house with her first live rendition. In was the start of a long relationship during which she would appear live on numerous occasions at Flyers home games before her passing in 1986.

After their opening game, the Flyers came back to take a 6–0 decision from the New York Rangers at Madison Square

Garden. They went on to win their first four games, outscoring opponents 18–3, before losing three in a row. That was followed by a run of eight wins in 10 games, which included 6–0 and 7–0 triumphs over the Pittsburgh Penguins.

By the end of November, the Flyers had a 13–6–2 record. They then reeled off 14 wins, including a 9–3 tromping of the Vancouver Canucks, in their next 20 games, which by mid-January had given them a 27–9–3 record, including a 4–2 victory over the Rangers with Schultz scoring three goals.

"It wasn't like I couldn't play," said Schultz. "I could do a lot of other things besides fight. But once the media gave me the nickname of 'The Hammer,' it was a matter of once you get labeled, that's what you're known as."

In the next home game, Schultz recorded another hat trick in a 7–4 win over the Minnesota North Stars. Shortly afterward, Clarke, Parent, Joe Watson, and Van Impe were named to play in the All-Star Game.

In early February, the Flyers crushed the Detroit Red Wings, 12–2. Then they won eight straight, including two victories over the Buffalo Sabres. Along the way, they posted the team's 200th win with a 2–1 victory over the Islanders. Ultimately, a 5–3 victory over the Bruins, in a game in which the Flyers topped Boston for the first time since 1969, and a 6–2 decision over the North Stars gave the team six wins and one tie in its final eight games.

The season ended with the Flyers holding a 50–16–12 record, placing them well ahead of the second-place Chicago Blacks Hawks (41–14–23) and the third-place Los Angeles Kings (33–33–12) in what was called the West Division. During the campaign, the Flyers had beaten the St. Louis Blues six times in six games, while posting 5–0 records against the Sabres, Blues, Red Wings, New York Islanders, and California Golden Seals.

"We knew we could do it," recalled MacLeish. "We all played together as a team. We were underdogs all season, but we were strong and eager, we had a lot of guts, and we had a will to win."

The Flyers wound up outscoring opponents, 723–164. Clarke, who the previous season had become the first Flyer and ninth player in NHL history to score 100 points in one season while winning the Hart Trophy as the league's Most Valuable Player, not only led the team in goals (35), which ranked fifth in the league, but also in assists with 52. It was a magnificent season for the Flyers' young captain and team leader.

"My role was never very complicated," Clarke said forty years later. "We had lots of guys who could score, so I never based my results on the number of goals I scored. My goal was to always play hockey as hard as I possibly could, and to help the team win. I just tried to play to the best of my ability."

Parent also etched his name in Flyers history books by setting a then-record of 47 wins while playing in all but five games during the regular season. He posted a 47–13–12 record, including 12 shutouts, and a 1.89 goals-per-game average, allowing 136 goals on 2,038 shots. After the season, he became co-winner with the Black Hawks' Tony Esposito as the winner of the Vezina Trophy, which goes to goaltenders who played 25 or more games and allowed the fewest goals.

"Bernie was the best goalie in the business," Van Impe said. "He never gave up an easy goal. He always came through with big saves whenever we needed one."

The Flyers wound up drawing an average crowd of 17,007 at the Spectrum. The club's fans, usually packing the stands with a sea of orange and black clothing and screaming at the tops of their lungs, certainly played a role in the team's 28–6–5 home record (their road record was 22–10–7).

When the playoffs began, the Flyers were decided underdogs. "The Rangers and Bruins were supposedly the two best teams in the league," said Clarke. "But we felt we could beat either one of them. We had a better team and a better coach."

"We were very confident. Very focused," Saleski added. "There wasn't a guy on the team who didn't believe we couldn't win the title. It didn't matter who we played. We knew we were going to beat them."

That view came into sight in the first round of the playoffs when the Flyers met the fourth-place Atlanta Flames (30–34–14), the only team to win two games that season at the Spectrum. In a best-of-seven quarterfinals, it took the Flyers just four games to move to the next round.

They won the first game, 4–1, with Kindrachuk scoring twice. MacLeish took center stage in the second game as his hat trick led the Flyers to a 5–1 victory. Moving to Atlanta, the Flyers captured Game Three with a 2–1 decision in a contest marked by a bloody brawl between Schultz and much of the

Flames' bench. Later that night, Shero was mugged by someone outside of the hotel as he began his customary late-night walk. Allen sent him back to Philadelphia and put assistant coach Mike Nykoluk in charge of the next game.

The next night, after falling behind 3–0 in the second period, the Flyers rallied on goals by Dupont, Dornhoefer, and Blandon to tie the score and send the game into overtime. Then, at the 5:40 mark, Schultz snagged a pass from Clarke and scored to give the Flyers a 4–3 victory and a trip to the semifinals.

Two days later, the Flyers met the Rangers at the Spectrum in Game One of the semifinals. The Rangers, who had upset defending champion Montreal in six games, were no match for the gang from Philadelphia.

A goal by Lonsberry, two by MacLeish, and one more by Barber gave the Flyers a 4–0 win. That was followed by a 5–2 Flyers win in a game in which goals by Lonsberry and MacLeish gave the victors a lead they never relinquished.

Perhaps a bit overconfident, the Flyers lost the next two games in New York, blowing a 3–1 lead to lose Game Three, 5–3, and dropping a 2–1 decision in overtime in a game in which Parent registered 37 saves. The game had a disastrous moment when Ashbee was hit in the eye with a puck, and carried off the ice. Because of extensive retinal damage, he never played in another game.

With Dupont and Clement also out of action because of knee injuries, the Flyers returned home and skated to a 4–1 victory in Game Five on goals by Bladon, Simon Nolet, Kelly, and MacLeish. Back at Madison Square Garden two days later, the Flyers fell to the Rangers, 4–1, to return the series to the Spectrum for the deciding game.

The Rangers scored first on a goal by Bill Fairbairn. Less than one minute later, MacLeish tied the score. Then the Flyers snatched a 3–1 lead in the second period on goals by Kindrachuk and Dornhoefer. Another goal by Fairbairn narrowed the Flyers lead to 3–2 with less than nine minutes to play. Dornhoefer and the Rangers' Pete Stemkowski traded goals, but with a 4–3 lead, with Schultz reaching the heights of his intimidation game, and with five and one-half minutes left to play, the Flyers held on to clinch the series.

That sent the Flyers up against the Bruins, Stanley Cup winners in 1970 and 1972 and winners over the Black Hawks in six games in their semifinals. Boston, led by all-time great Bobby Orr, was a heavy favorite to win the Cup.

"Fred [Shero] said to us, we're going to win this series," Watson recalled. "He said we're going to control all six corners, block the middle, score points, and Bernie will stop everything from all angles. As it turned out, Bernie was our salvation. We wouldn't have won without him."

In the first game, played at Boston Garden, the Flyers quickly fell behind, 2–0, but a goal by Kindrachuk in the second period and one by Clarke in the third produced a 2–2 tie. Orr's shot with 22 seconds left in regulation gave Boston a 3–2 win.

In Game Two, the Flyers again fell behind, 2–0, in the first period. Clarke scored in the second period, but the Flyers still trailed as the final minutes ticked off the clock. With 52 seconds left, Dupont rammed in a goal to tie the score. Then in overtime, after a sensational save by Parent, Clarke lifted a rebound shot into the net at 12:01 of overtime to give the Flyers their first win in Boston in six and one-half years.

Back at the Spectrum for Game Three and the first Stanley Cup game ever held in Philadelphia, the Flyers captured a 4–1 decision. Again, they overcame an early Boston lead to win, with Blandon's goal tying the score and Crisp's shot proving to be the winner margin.

Game Four in Philadelphia saw goals by MacLeish and Schultz, which gave the Flyers an early lead. Boston came back to tie the score before the first period ended. It took until the third period before there was another goal, with Barber slamming home a shot with six minutes left. Dupont added another goal to give the Flyers a 4–2 victory.

Returning to Boston, the Bruins scored in the opening 24 seconds, and after Clement's goal produced a 1–1 tie, the Bruins went back ahead to stay, grabbing a 5–1 victory in a penalty-ridden game.

The series then returned to the Spectrum. In the first period, not long after Kate Smith's widely celebrated appearance, MacLeish slapped in a shot off Dupont's stick to give the Flyers a 1–0 lead. It would be the only goal of the game as defensive heroics by Van Impe, Nolet, and Jimmy Watson repeatedly foiled the Bruins' attack.

At 5:01 p.m. on an unforgettable Sunday, May 19, the Flyers became the first expansion team ever to win the Stanley Cup. "The Flyers win the Stanley Cup! The Flyers win the

Players and fans celebrate after the Flyers' 1–0 victory over the Boston Bruins in the Stanley Cup clincher at the Spectrum.
Photo courtesy of the Philadelphia Flyers

Stanley Cup! The Flyers Win the Stanley Cup!" the popular Flyers broadcaster Gene Hart screamed into the microphone.

Fans poured from the stands down onto the ice. Players erupted with unbridled joy, streamers flew, people screamed. Bedlam reigned as NHL commissioner Clarence Campbell battled to present the Flyers with their Stanley Cup.

"Scoring that goal was certainly the high point of my career," MacLeish recounted many years later. "It came in the first period, so I never thought it would stand up.

"But it did. And we won."

MacLeish wound up as the Flyers' top scorer in the pay-offs with 13 goals and 9 assists for 22 points. Clarke recorded 5 goals and 11 assists, while Lonsberry had 4 goals and 9 assists. Parent, who allowed just 36 goals in 17 games, won the Conn Smythe Trophy as the Playoff MVP.

Soon after the final buzzer, the whole Philadelphia area erupted in celebration of the first pro sports championship in seven years. People danced in the streets. Many got drunk. Strangers kissed each other. Vandals smashed windows. Some 10,000 people jammed the intersection of Frankford and Cottman Avenues. And riding in the back of a pickup truck, five naked men threw their underwear into the crowd at Broad and Dickinson Streets.

The next day, players boarded convertibles at Veterans Stadium to prepare for a parade up Broad Street to a cere-

Bobby Clarke (left) and Bernie Parent hoist the Stanley Cup after the clinching victory over the Boston Bruins. Both players have been inducted into the Hockey Hall of Fame.
Courtesy of the Philadelphia Flyers

mony at City Hall. An estimated crowd of two million lined the parade route.

"It was almost incomprehensible," Clarke remembered of the event. "It was so crowded, we almost couldn't get out of the parking lot to get started. We wondered where all the people had come from."

Actually, Clarke's car didn't get far from the parking lot. The one in which he and Van Impe were riding became surrounded by so many people that it never made it up Broad Street.

Saleski almost didn't, either. "Three blocks up Broad Street," he recalled, "the engine overheated. A couple of guys dressed in Mummer's costumes came along and pushed us all the way to City Hall."

Once they got there, though, they became part of an event that showed how a city that just nine years earlier had no major league ice hockey team could react to a winner.

FLYERS CAPTURE SECOND STRAIGHT STANLEY CUP

14 Whenever a team wins a championship, it usually thinks it can do it again the following season. There's nothing unusual about that. It's called confidence.

The Flyers had plenty of that after winning the Stanley Cup the previous season. This was a team that was certain it would win it again.

The Broad Street Bullies may have been the underdog going into the 1974 playoffs. But one year later, they were the heavy favorites.

They were also the favorites of Philadelphia sports fans. The Phillies were coming off a dreary decade and were rebuilding. The Eagles were in the midst of a long losing period and would go 4–10 in 1975. And the 76ers were not far removed from their atrocious 9–73 season of 1972–73. Nobody had won a championship since 1967. The Flyers were easily the best game in town, and in 1974–75 they played before a then-record 683,080 (average 17,077) fans, including sellout crowds in all 40 home games.

Much of the team's roster was the same as the year before, but the Flyers had made a few key additions, the best of which was acquiring right wing Reggie Leach in a trade with the California Golden Seals. Leach was a solid performer who came in exchange for little-used Al MacAdam and a first-round draft pick. He would go on to become one of the Flyers' leading scorers.

"When I first came, I had to learn to become a team player, how to perform on the ice with everybody," Leach recalled. "That's what they were taught by Fred Shero. That's what his system was all about—being a team player. We never quit. We never gave up. We kept plugging away until the game was over. Overall, these guys were incredible, but I learned to mesh with them and everything turned out perfectly."

The Flyers also landed defenseman Ted Harris, who had previously played for four Stanley Cup winners, and backup goalie Wayne Stephenson in separate deals with the St. Louis Blues. Bill Flett and Simon Nolet were two Flyers from the previous year who departed, while Barry Ashbee's career had ended the previous season when he was hit in the eye with a puck. In 1974, he became an assistant coach with the Flyers.

The squad was otherwise basically the same group that had been put together starting at the end of the 1960s, by coach (and by 1969 the general manager, a position he held for fourteen years) Keith Allen. Center Bobby Clarke and goalie Bernie Parent were the top guns on a squad that included a stellar collection of other star players.

"There wasn't a lot of difference between the two clubs," Bill Barber said. "Maybe there was a little more talent the second year, but we still played the same way. We had a very committed group, and we always knew we were going to get the opportunity to win if we played well."

**Bill Barber was one of the Flyers' leading scorers while earning
a place as one of the top players in the team's history.**
Courtesy of the Philadelphia Flyers

The Flyers were still the toughest guys on the ice. They were so tough, in fact, that Dave Schultz set an NHL record that season with 472 penalty minutes. And again, Don Saleski, Orest Kindrachuk, Joe Watson, Moose Dupont, Ed Van Impe, Jimmy Watson, and Harris formed the best defense in the league.

"We kicked the crap out of people," said Parent, who inspired the saying, "Only the Lord saves more than Bernie Parent." "We didn't give anybody a break. We had a good hitting team, and we just went out there every game and got very physical."

"Today, they would call it physicality," Saleski said. "We played hard the previous year, and with this team, we played just as hard. We were tough. And when we got Harris, we were even tougher."

Clarke, Leach, Barber, Rick MacLeish, Ross Lonsberry, and Gary Dornhoefer were the top scorers on an offense that was the best and most explosive in the league. But of all their assets, none was bigger than the Flyers' unity as a team. It was one for all and all for one. Clarke, of course, was the team's premier player.

"My role was never complicated," said Clarke, the team's captain. "We had a lot of guys who could score. My job was to play hockey to the best of my ability and always play as hard as I possibly could to help the team win. I never based my results on goals. It was whether or not we won."

"We played together, we worked hard together," said Leach. "It was something that Allen, Ed Snider, and the coaches taught. Everybody had a job to do, and once you got on the ice, you did what you were supposed to do. I can recall many times when going into the third period, we were a couple of goals down. Clarkie didn't say much, but in these situations, he'd talk to us, and say, 'It's time to go to work.' And the next thing you know, we won the game.

"With our togetherness on that team," Leach added, "we were all friends. Our wives were involved with everything we did off the ice. We had good times together. And now, more than forty years later, we're all still friends. We stay in touch. Our families are close. That's what kind of team we had."

The team also had a brilliant coach, who was an innovator, brought discipline to the club, introduced a system that took advantage of the players' different abilities, and who searched libraries for inspirational quotes. The players trusted Fred Shero, and he trusted them. Shero, who would eventually earn a place in the ice hockey Hall of Fame while posting a 308–151–95 record in seven seasons with the Flyers, was especially remembered for a sign he hung in the locker room prior to the 1974 Stanley Cup Finals. "Win today, and we walk together forever," it said.

"Shero always gave us a goal," Schultz said. "The key was, we always played as a team. We knew what we had to do, and he made sure we focused on that. We had great leadership from him. We had all the ingredients of a championship team. Nobody wins a championship without a great coach, great forwards, great goal-tending, great defense, and great ownership. We had it all. You name it, we had it."

Rather unexpectedly, Shero had been offered over the winter a $100,000 contract to coach the Minnesota Fighting Saints of the World Hockey League. He was only earning $25,000 at the time, but Snider kept him in Philadelphia by giving him a $50,000 raise. Snider, whose insight and vision were extraordinary, also became the sole owner of the Spectrum when he bought out his brother-in-law Earl Foreman.

As the 1974–75 season unfolded, the Flyers were generally considered to be the favorites to win another Stanley Cup. No one believed this any stronger than the players themselves.

"Initially, we never thought we could win the first time," said Clarke. "But we were favored to win the second time, and we all thought we would. We had talent, good coaching, everybody worked hard and made sacrifices for each other, and we approached every game thinking we would win."

"Frankly, it was quietly assumed that our first championship was not a fluke, even though there were a lot of things people didn't give us credit for," added Van Impe. "But we had an even better team the second year, and we figured we had a good chance to win again. Of course, the loss of Ashbee didn't help, so we had to look for some new people. Larry Goodenough was one who helped fill the void on defense. And we had a real good defense. Everyone did what he had to do to help us win."

The Flyers season started dramatically at the Spectrum when the Stanley Cup banner was raised, and then twelve-year-old Frankie Hudson dropped the first puck. Hudson had been kicked by a horse during the Stanley Cup parade after the previous season.

The game, however, put a damper on the evening as the Flyers dropped a 5–3 decision to the Los Angeles Kings. Three nights later, the Flyers entered the win column with a 3–2 victory over the first-year Kansas City Scouts.

From there, the Flyers went on to win twelve of their first seventeen games (with two ties). In the midst of that streak, the Flyers lost a 4–1 decision to the California Seals in a game marked by numerous brawls. In one, Saleski and Bob Kelly battered the Seals' Mike Christie in a bench-clearing brawl that resulted in the California player needing eleven stitches in his face. The game produced an NHL-record 237 penalty minutes between the two teams.

In another game, Clarke's goal in the final minute of the third quarter gave the Flyers their first victory over the New York Rangers at Madison Square Garden since 1968.

Leach got his first Flyers hat trick in a 6–2 defeat of the Detroit Red Wings on November 27, and from there through December 29, the Flyers won 12 of 15 games with two ties to build a 24–7–5 record. Included was a 10–0 thrashing of Kansas City.

In early January, the New York Islanders grabbed their first win at the Spectrum with a 3–1 victory. Then, after a 6–0 loss to the Montreal Canadiens, the Flyers won five straight games, including a 4–0 shutout of the new Washington Capitals.

In early February, the Flyers dropped a season-high three straight decisions, losing 3–1 to the Rangers, 5–0 to the Minnesota North Stars, and 3–1 to the St. Louis Blues. The Flyers ended February with their only losing month, posting a 5–7–2 record.

The gloom quickly ended, however, when the Flyers staged their best month of the season, dancing through March with a 13–1–1 record. Among their wins were a 9–2 rout of Minnesota and a 2–1 victory over Montreal that broke the Canadiens' 23-game road winning streak. Parent recorded four shutouts during the month.

The Flyers opened April with a 1–1 tie against the Rangers on a night in which Ashbee was honored as he headed into retirement. Tragically, the talented defenseman would pass away just two years later after being diagnosed with leukemia.

The Flyers went on to finish the season with two more wins, ending the campaign with 16 wins in their final 19 games and giving them a final record of 51–18–11, the best mark in the league and one win better than their team one year earlier. The Rangers finished second in the Patrick Division with a 37–29–14 record, followed by the Islanders with a 33–25–22 mark.

During the season, the Flyers did not lose a game to Washington (4–0), Kansas City (4–0–1), the Buffalo Sabres (3–0–1), or the Toronto Maple Leafs (3–0–1). They had a 1–2–1 mark against the Boston Bruins.

The Flyers scored 293 points and allowed 181. Clarke led the team with 116 points on 27 goals and 89 assists. MacLeish tallied 79 points (38–41), while Leach had 78 (45–33), and Barber 71 (34–37). MacLeish performed four hat tricks during the season and Leach recorded three. Parent registered 12 shutouts while playing in eighty games.

Clarke, still the team's all-time leader in scoring, won his second in what would become three Hart Trophy awards as the league's Most Valuable Player, and Parent captured the Vezina Trophy as the league's top goalie.

"We knew we could do it," said Terry Crisp about winning the division title. "1974 was a great year, but this season we said, 'hey, we're set for another run.' And we did it."

But the season wasn't over yet. The Flyers were still way off from becoming the first Philadelphia team to win back-to-back championships since the 1948–49 Eagles.

"There was no question in our minds what we were going to do," said Joe Watson. "We were very sure of ourselves. You could call us cocky. We knew we would win, and nobody was going to stop us. It was the same the year before, and it was the same the year after when we went to the finals again, but lost to Montreal. That was the season when we beat the Russians (the Flyers downed the Soviet Red Army team, 4–1, in an exhibition game at the Spectrum) in a game that was seen all over the world and by many people who had never seen a hockey game before."

One of the key players on the Flyers' defense was Joe Watson. The Flyers had the top defense in the NHL.
Courtesy of the Philadelphia Flyers

Playoff rules in the NHL had been changed for 1975, with the winners of each of the league's four divisions drawing byes in the first round. In addition, the league now allowed twelve teams to enter the playoffs. So the Philly guys had to wait until the quarterfinals to make an appearance in the playoffs. Their opponent was Toronto, which had advanced after whipping the Kings.

In the first game played at the Spectrum, MacLeish scored twice in the first period, but the Maple Leafs rallied to take a 3–2 lead into the third period. The Flyers stormed back with goals from Barber, Leach, and Jim Watson before MacLeish closed out the 6–3 victory with a hat trick.

Parent moved to the forefront in the next two games, as the Flyers blanked the Maples Leafs, 3–0, at the Spectrum, and 2–0 as the series moved to Toronto. Two goals by Crisp and one by Dupont assured the victory in Game Two, and Dornhoefer and MacLeish put the puck in the net in the third game when Parent registered 31 saves.

In the fourth game, the Flyers got goals from Leach and two by Barber before Toronto tied the score on Ron Ellis's shot with 6:37 left in the third period. The Flyers closed out the series with a 4–3 victory in overtime as Dupont scored the winning goal with an assist from Schultz with 1:45 on the clock.

The win set up a Flyers-Islanders meeting, which had the makings of a ferocious battle. The Islanders, in just their third year in the NHL, had knocked out the Rangers in the preliminary round, then rallied from a three-games-to-none deficit to win four straight and beat the Pittsburgh Penguins in the quarterfinals. The Islanders were not only the second team ever to overcome a 3–0 deficit in the playoffs, but were just the second expansion team to defeat one of the original NHL clubs in the postseason.

The Flyers had enjoyed a week off, but now they were ready. Yet disaster awaited them. While warming up before the first game, a shot by Dornhoefer slammed into the unprotected knee of Parent, causing the goalie to collapse in severe pain on the ice.

Although x-rays on Parent's knee would turn out to be negative, Stephenson, who had played just 12 games all season, was inserted into the lineup. He played magnificently, stopping 21 shots and posting a 4–0 shutout as Saleski, Barber, Clarke, and MacLeish scored goals for the Flyers.

Stephenson was in goal again for Game Two at the Spectrum, but this time, the results were somewhat different. The Flyers were ahead, 4–1, on goals by Dornhoefer, Leach, Tom Blandon, and Barber, but the New Yorkers rallied in the third period to tie the score. In overtime, Clarke knocked in a shot to give the Flyers a 5–4 decision.

Game Three moved to Long Island, and with Parent back in the lineup, the two teams battled to a 0–0 score until early in the third period when Leach slammed home a shot that gave the Flyers a 1–0 victory.

The Islanders were now down three games to none for the second straight series. But they weren't done yet. In the fourth game, they jumped out to an early 3–0 lead. The Flyers bounced back with second period goals by Lonsberry and MacLeish. Then a third period goal by MacLeish tied the score. A shot by Barber as time ran out was nullified, sending the game into overtime. At 1:53, Jude Drouin found the net and the Islanders skated away on top, 4–3.

Unbelievable as it may have been, the Islanders overcame another large deficit, as they had done in the last series, when they came back with three straight wins to tie the Flyers. They took the verdict in Game Five, 5–1, and then won Game Six, 2–1.

That set the stage for the seventh game played at the Spectrum. With Kate Smith called to town to sing "God Bless America," after which the Islanders graciously formed a line to shake her hand, and a nearly hysterical sellout crowd of 17,077 packing the stands, the Flyers jumped out to a 3–1 lead in the first period on goals by Dornhoefer and two by MacLeish. Another goal by MacLeish in the third period gave him the hat trick and the Flyers a 4–1 victory.

It was back to the Stanley Cup finals for the second straight year. This time, the opponent was Buffalo, and the series would be the first finals between two teams that weren't among the league's six originals and the only finals between 1965 and 1979 that didn't feature either the Bruins or the Canadiens.

The Sabres were one of the teams the Broad Street Bullies had handled with ease during the regular season, with two wins and one tie. What's more, the Sabres, playing in their fifth season and having reached the finals by beating Montreal in six games, had never won a game at the Spectrum.

The Flyers certainly didn't lack confidence. "We enjoyed winning the first one, but we wanted the second one real bad," said Van Impe. "And we knew the fans wanted it, too. We figured we could win it."

"We always had success against Buffalo," added Joe Watson. "They were good, but we were better. We had no thoughts of losing."

The first game supported that view. Neither team scored in the first two periods, but in the third session, Barber, Lonsberry, Clarke, and Barber again all scored and the Flyers rode home with a 4–1 victory.

The Flyers took a two-games-to-none lead in the series in Game Two with a 2–1 triumph. Leach scored to put them ahead in the first period, and Clarke whacked home the winning goal at 6:43 of the third period.

The teams traveled to upstate New York for Game Three. As it turned out, though, this would be more than a hockey game. And shortly after it was over, it became known as "The Fog Game."

Because it was now spring and a heat wave had made temperatures considerably warmer while Memorial Auditorium had no air conditioning, and fog began to rise from the ice. Ultimately, the whole rink was covered with fog. Play had to be stopped twelve times as players and employees carrying bedsheets skated around the ice trying to dissipate the fog. The fog was so thick that some spectators couldn't even see what was happening on the ice. At one point, a bat flew into the rink (perhaps unrelated, or possibly related to the warm temperature), and for much of the rest of the game circulated around the players, until one Sabre killed it with his hockey stick.

Despite the fog, the Flyers took a 3–2 lead in the first period on goals by Dornhoefer, Saleski, and MacLeish. Leach scored in the second session, but the Sabres scored twice, with Bill Hajt's third period goal sending the game into overtime. With

Terry Crisp gets hammered, but manages to get off a shot against the Buffalo Sabres during the Stanley Cup finals.
Courtesy of the Philadelphia Flyers

fatigue starting to take a heavy toll on the players, the overtime lasted for 18:29 before Buffalo won 5–4 on Hajt's goal.

The Sabres evened the series in Game Four with a 4–2 victory. The teams then returned to the Spectrum with the Flyers winning the fifth game, 5–1, on two goals from Schultz and one each from Dornhoefer, Kelly, and Leach.

Back in Buffalo for Game Six, the teams played without a goal for the first two periods. Then Kelly scored 11 seconds into the third period, and Bill Clement added another goal a few minutes later as the Flyers captured a 2–0 victory and their second straight Stanley Cup, the oldest championship trophy in professional sports, dating back to 1892. As the players celebrated deliriously on the ice, the often-reclusive Shero walked quietly to the locker room.

In the final game, Parent was again brilliant, racking up 32 saves, and becoming the first player to win two straight Conn Smythe Trophies as the playoff's Most Valuable Player. The rest of the Flyers defense also played masterfully, allowing just 12 goals.

"You dream about winning a Stanley Cup all your life," said Van Impe. "You want to be the best there is. Then you win it, and it's like being on top of a mountain. The emotion is overwhelming."

NHL commissioner Clarence Campbell presented the Stanley Cup to the Flyers, including (left to right) Bobby Clarke, Rick MacLeish, and Orest Kindrachuk.
Courtesy of the Philadelphia Flyers

The Flyers celebrated joyfully on the plane ride home. Then after arriving home at 2:30 a.m. they continued the merriment at the Spectrum. No one left for home before 4:30 a.m.

As happened the year before, later that morning, another gigantic parade celebrated the Flyers' victory. An estimated crowd of 2.3 million fans, some 300,000 more than the previous year, lined the route. This time the players rode on flatbed trucks starting at 18th and Locust Streets, then down Broad Street to a rally at JFK Stadium, where a crowd of 100,000 jammed the old venue. There, the trucks circled around the inside of the stadium twice before stopping at a platform in the middle of the field where they were greeted by Pennsylvania governor Milton Shapp.

"It was huge," recalled MacLeish. "We knew we could beat Buffalo and there would be a parade, but this was incredible. People were everywhere, hanging out of windows, on rooftops, blowing horns in their cars. It was amazing."

At the ceremony at what used to be known as Municipal Stadium, Shero told an audience swallowed in pandemonium, "This city is beautiful." The crowd responded with cheers that probably could be heard halfway to Buffalo.

They were cheers that undeniably celebrated what had been the second of the greatest ice hockey seasons in Philadelphia history. Since then, the Flyers have appeared in six more Stanley Cup finals (1976, 1980, 1985, 1987, 1997, and 2010) without a win. That makes the 1974 and 1975 seasons even more spectacular in the annals of the city's ice hockey history.

WORLD SERIES WINNERS AT LAST

15 There was pandemonium in the stands as 64,839 fans stood screaming at the tops of their lungs. Policemen—some with dogs, some on horseback—rimmed the field. Players stood breathlessly on the top steps of the dugouts. The tension at every level was virtually unbearable.

It was 11:29 p.m. on October 21, 1980. Phillies versus Kansas City Royals. Sixth game of the World Series at Veterans Stadium with the Phillies holding a 4–1 lead in the game and a 3–2 edge in the Series. Top of the ninth inning. Two outs. Bases loaded.

Out on the mound, Phillies reliever Tug McGraw took a deep breath and got set to deliver a 1–2 pitch to Willie Wilson. Just one batter earlier, Pete Rose had reached under the outstretched glove of Bob Boone to snatch a foul popup in front of the Phillies' dugout. Then, summoning one more pitch from his exhausted left arm, McGraw, admittedly "out of gas," struck out Wilson to climax what up to that point was the greatest moment in Phillies history.

What kind of pitch had he thrown? McGraw was asked afterward. "A fastball," he said. "The slowest fastball in baseball history." What made it the slowest? "Because," said Tug, "it took 97 years to get there."

Ninety-seven years. That's how long it took the Phillies to win their first World Series. The team, which was formed in 1883, had not only never won a World Series before, but in their only two previous appearances in the Fall Classic had won just one game. McGraw's torpid fastball forever changed the perception of Phillies history.

It was a history that had been mostly inglorious. But in 1976 they had launched a streak of three straight East Division titles. Although they lost each time—once to the Cincinnati Reds and twice to the Los Angeles Dodgers in the National League Championship Series—the Phillies had become a team that seemed on the verge of something big.

Team president Ruly Carpenter, who had taken over for his father, Bob, in 1973; general manager Paul Owens; and minor league director Dallas Green had developed a team that was a striking combination of exceptional products of the Phillies' farm system and superb talent acquired from other teams. And although the Phillies had staged an unexpected backslide in 1979 when they tumbled to fourth place, the elements of a championship team were firmly in place.

Among the top players on the roster, third baseman Mike Schmidt, left fielder Greg Luzinski, shortstop Larry Bowa, and catcher Boone, along with youngsters Lonnie Smith and Keith Moreland, and pitchers Dick Ruthven, Larry Christenson, Randy Lerch, Bob Walk, Marty Bystrom, Dickie Noles, and Kevin Saucier had all come up through the Phillies farm system. First baseman Rose had been signed as a free agent before the 1979 season. Center fielder Garry Maddox, right fielder Bake McBride, second baseman Manny Trillo, utility-men Del Unser and Greg Gross, and pitchers Steve Carlton, McGraw, and Ron Reed had all come in trades made (except for Carlton) by the ultra-astute Owens.

"We were mostly an experienced team," Schmidt recalled. "We had a lot of talent and an inner confidence. When you have a guy like Rose on the team, you're going to have confidence. We were not a young team, although during the season some of our young players really came through. We had a great defensive team, too, with a lot of Gold Glovers."

Initially, the pitching staff had Carlton, Ruthven, Christenson, and Lerch as the starters. McGraw, Reed, Noles, and Saucier were the primary relievers. After Christenson was hurt and Lerch was ineffective, Walk joined the starting rotation, as did Bystrom late in the season.

"Our pitching staff was really good," said Boone. "Everybody did his job. At the end of the season, our pitchers were pretty worn down. But our staff was still better than everybody else we faced in the postseason. Carlton was one of the greatest pitchers in history. That year, he was sensational."

The final piece of the team had been added when Green was called down from the front office to replace Danny Ozark as the team's manager at the end of August 1979.

"Paul's main thrust in having me manage," Green said, "was to find out those last thirty days in 1979 who had the real desire to be a winner. We had talent. But we had just never gotten to the big dance. We were getting a little long in the tooth, and we thought this might be our last go-around."

"Danny was a great manager, but he couldn't get us over the hump," said Bowa. "From 1975 on, we had a shot. Overall, I think our best team was in 1977. We had great defense, great speed, great hitting. Our pitching wasn't deep, but we had some really good pitchers. Then in 1980, Dallas planted the seed and we wound up with a great team. But I always thought that if the team hadn't won that year, they were going to blow it up and start all over."

With Green in place and a team that the city had come to love, the Phillies were ready to rumble when the 1980 season began.

"Coming off the '79 season, the Pittsburgh Pirates had won the World Series," Schmidt recalled. "They were in our division and we had to get through them first. And that was going to be tough to do. They were favored to win the NL East again. Plus Montreal had a star-studded young team. So, it was going to be a race between the Pirates, the Expos, and us."

When the season started, though, the race wasn't ready to begin. Behind the pitching of Carlton and Ruthven, the Phillies won their first two games of the season, but then they lost nine of their next thirteen games. One of the wins, however, was a 14–8 victory over the New York Mets with Schmidt hitting a two-run homer and a grand slam. Nearly two weeks later, the Phillies bowed to the Los Angeles Dodgers, 12–10, in a game that featured 28 hits by the two teams and eleven pitchers.

In the beginning of May, the club found itself in fourth place. Then, after bouncing back and forth between fourth and third through the first two weeks of the month, they jumped up to second (despite the fact that in one game against the Reds, Luzinski bashed two homers and Schmidt and McBride each hit one, en route to a 7–6 loss). By the end of the month, though, the Phils had spent two days in first place with the help of a 7–0 whitewash of the Chicago Cubs in a game in which Carlton allowed four hits and struck out 11 in seven innings.

By mid-June, the Phils were back in third place, four and one-half games out of first, when Carlton stretched his record to 11–2 with a 13-strikeout, 3–1 win over the San Diego Padres. That was part of a six-game winning streak, but soon afterward, the Phils lost eight of ten games. Walk stopped the skid with a 5–2 victory over the Mets. That launched a streak in which the Phillies won 12 of 18 games.

In early August, the Phils bowed to the St. Louis Cardinals, 14–0, in the second-most-lopsided shutout loss in Phillies history. That was one of five losses in six games as the club fell to six games behind. Then, starting with an 8–5 victory over the Cubs in 15 innings, the Phillies won eight of their next nine games.

Two days after the streak ended, the Phils nipped the Padres, 9–8 in 17 innings. Six days later, Carlton won his twentieth, a 4–3 win over the Los Angeles Dodgers. But the Phillies were still dividing most of their time between second and third places.

Over the years, some of the veteran Phillies had been accused of being too complacent. Plus, this was not exactly a team overloaded with camaraderie. Green did not tolerate these kinds of attitudes. More than once during the season, he threw clubhouse tantrums.

"It took a long time to get those guys to buy into what we wanted to do," Green recalled. "I did a lot of screaming and yelling. I kept preaching pride and work ethic. I said we have to play together as a team. We want to play the game right, and we want to win. I want to do that, and you guys want to do that. So, I'm going to pound you. I'm going to hound you. I will not let you forget what our goal is. "

Green had a memorable clubhouse tirade in late August when he tore apart the team from bottom to top. "The Pope [Owens's nickname] backed me up on that," he said, "and then he had one of his own screaming sessions. From then on, the guys realized that they better wake up and play hard and play right. And they played their hearts out. They played as well as any team I've ever seen."

The team moved into first place on September 1 for the first time since it was tied for the lead on July 11 as Boone's hit drove in the winning run in a 6–4 decision over the San Francisco Giants. But they stayed there for only four days. A few more brief climbs to first followed, but the Phils spent most of September in second place.

On September 17, they began a five-game winning streak, moving into first place for one day after a 3–2 decision over the Cardinals. Two losses to Montreal dropped them out of first before four straight wins over the Cubs that included Bystrom's fifth win and a two-hitter by Carlton put them one-half game out of first.

On October 3, the Phillies went back into first place as Schmidt's sacrifice fly and home run knocked the Expos out of the lead, 2–1. Then, on the next to last day of the season, the Phillies clinched the division title. After a three-hour, ten-minute rain delay, Schmidt's two-run homer in the 11th inning and McGraw's three innings of one-hit relief gave the Phils a 6–4 win over Montreal. They finished the season the next day with a final record of 91–71.

The Phils won the division crown, but it was also a big year for individual awards. Schmidt led the league in home

On a team packed with star players, Garry Maddox, Mike Schmidt, and Steve Carlton were all big winners in 1980. Maddox won a Gold Glove, Schmidt was the league Most Valuable Player and also won a Gold Glove, and Carlton was winner of the Cy Young Award.
Courtesy of the Philadelphia Phillies

runs (48), which was more than any third baseman in baseball history had ever hit, and RBIs (121) while hitting .286. In what some said was the greatest season of his career, he won his first of three Most Valuable Player awards. Along with Maddox, he also won a Gold Glove.

"A lot of individual honors came to me," Schmidt said. "But the most important thing that happened was we won the championship."

Carlton won his third of four Cy Young Awards, posting a 24–9 record (2.34 ERA) while leading the league in wins, strikeouts (286), and innings pitched (304). Smith was named Rookie of the Year after hitting .339 in 100 games.

While the Phillies had the second-highest team batting average with a .270, McBride hit .309, followed by Trillo (.292) and Rose (.282). Luzinski, despite missing a big chunk of the season with a cartilage injury, smacked 19 homers. Gross and Unser proved to be invaluable pinch-hitters with numerous clutch hits during the season.

Among the other pitchers, Ruthven (17–10) and Walk (11–7) posted the top records while McGraw recorded 20 saves and a 1.47 ERA. Bystrom won all five of his starts after being called up in September. Reed, a major contributor throughout the season as a set-up man, had a 7–5 record with nine saves.

"The last six weeks of the season, we played as well as any team could play," Rose said. "Everybody helped. But Dallas Green was the reason we won because we rallied around him. We believed in what he was trying to tell us. And he had the kind of discipline that we needed. He was a no-nonsense manager."

The National League Championship Series against the Astros has often been labeled the greatest pre-World Series playoff there ever was. It went five games, and every game was a thriller. The last four games were all decided by one run and all played into extra innings.

Houston had won the West Division regular-season title in a torrid race with the Dodgers. The two had ended the season tied for first place, and in a one-game playoff, the Astros won to move into the league championship series.

In the first game, played October 7 at Veterans Stadium, Luzinski, who had hit safely in all eleven of the Phillies' previous playoff games, walloped a sixth inning drive into the upper deck in left-center field for a two-run homer that led to a 3–1 victory. Carlton got the win and McGraw a save.

The Astros came back to take the next two games. Despite a fine job by Phils starter Ruthven, who allowed three hits and two runs in seven innings to outshine Houston starter Nolan Ryan, the Phils bullpen fell apart and the Astros won Game Two, 7–4, with a four-run rally in the tenth inning that featured a two-run triple by pinch-hitter Dave Bergman.

Then, moving to the Astrodome in Houston, Phil Niekro gave up just six hits in ten strong innings, and the Astros captured a 1–0 victory in the 11th on Joe Morgan's triple and a sacrifice fly by Dennis Walling off McGraw in his third inning of relief following Christenson and Noles.

The Phillies rallied in Game Four to take a 5–3 decision in ten innings. Down 2–0 with Carlton on the mound, the Phils went ahead with three runs in the eighth. Then after Houston had pulled to a 3–3 tie in the ninth, Rose singled and then bowled over Astros catcher Bruce Bochy to score on Luzinski's double in the bottom of the 10th. Trillo's double added an insurance run. There were five double plays in the game, four started by outfielders, as Warren Brusstar got the win and McGraw another save.

Game Five in Houston turned out to be one of the most memorable games in Phillies history. With Ryan on the mound, the Astros held a 5–2 lead after seven innings. Then it happened. The Phils kayoed Ryan with a five-run eighth that featured Unser's RBIs, pinch-hit single that tied the score and Trillo's two-run triple that gave the Phillies a 7–5 lead. Houston came back with two runs in the ninth off McGraw, but the Phils won in the tenth as Unser doubled and scored on a double by Maddox. Ruthven, pitching hitless ball in two innings of relief, got the win, Trillo was named the NLCS MVP, and the Phillies were off to their first World Series appearance in thirty-five years.

"We had a team that was special because it took twenty-five guys to get us to the World Series," recalled Luzinski, who battled the flu during the early part of the Series. "The hard part was getting there. Once we did get there, the pressure kind of lifted off and we were able to enjoy ourselves a little bit."

The World Series opponent was the Kansas City Royals, a team that with a 97–65 record had won the West Division regular-season title, finishing 14 games ahead of the second-place Oakland Athletics. In the playoffs, the Royals had swept the New York Yankees in three games.

American League batting champion George Brett, who had hit above .400 most of the season before settling for a .390 average while clubbing 24 homers and driving in 118, led the Royals. Willie Aikens recorded 20 homers and 98 RBIs, and Willie Wilson hit .326. Six KC pitchers won in double figures, with starters Dennis Leonard (20–11) and Larry Gura (18–10) and reliever Dan Quisenberry (12–7 with 33 saves) leading the pack.

"Getting to the World Series was highly emotional," Green said. "It had been such a dogfight, and the league playoffs had been such a nail-biter. I remember Rose came to me during the Houston series, and said, 'If we can get through this thing, the World Series will be a piece of cake.' It wasn't exactly a piece of cake. The tensions and frustrations had taken a heavy toll. But that all disappeared when we beat Houston. We felt very comfortable going into the World Series."

The first game was played on October 14 at Veterans Stadium. With a then-record crowd of 65,791 watching, the Royals took an early 4–0 lead against Walk, but the Phillies came back with a five-run third inning that featured McBride's three-run homer. Boone added two RBI doubles before the Phils got a sacrifice fly in the fifth by Maddox that proved to be the winning run. KC came back on Aikens's second home run of the game, a two-run blast in the eighth, but McGraw stopped the rally as the Phillies won, 7–6.

The Phillies had to come from behind again in Game Two. After taking a 2–0 lead on a sacrifice fly by Trillo and an RBIs single by Bowa, the Royals grabbed a 4–2 lead with the help of Amos Otis's two-run double in the seventh off Carlton. The Phillies, however, bounced back with four runs in the eighth on RBI doubles by Unser and Schmidt and run-scoring singles by McBride and Moreland to give them a 6–4 victory.

Two days later, the Series resumed in Kansas City. The city didn't agree with the Phillies, as they lost the first game in 10 innings, 4–3, and the next game, 5–3. In Game Three, Schmidt hit a solo home run and Ruthven hurled nine good innings, but that wasn't enough as U. L. Washington's bases-loaded single off McGraw in the tenth drove in the winning run in a game in which the Phils tied a Series record by leaving 15 men on base.

Game Four carved a lasting place in Phillies history when, after Christenson had allowed four runs in the first inning, a fourth-inning brushback pitch by Noles sent Brett flying onto his back. A heated argument followed in which Royals manager Jim Frey and Rose nearly came to blows. Ultimately, Noles struck out Brett, who would get just three more hits in the rest of the Series.

It was claimed that Noles knocked down Brett intentionally and that one pitch turned the whole Series around. Both players, however, denied that assertion in later years, Noles saying he "was really just trying to move him off the plate," and Brett stating that the pitcher "was just trying to intimidate me."

As for the game itself, Aikens again hit two home runs, the first time in Series history that a player hit multiple homers in two different games, while Quisenberry shut the Phils down in his fourth straight game.

The Phils regained the Series lead in the fifth game with a 4–3 decision. Schmidt's two-run homer in the fourth gave the Phils a 2–0 lead, but the Royals came back with the help of an Otis four-bagger, and took a 3–2 lead into the ninth. The lead vanished after Unser drove in the tying run with a pinch-hit double and then scored on Trillo's infield single. McGraw had to escape a three-walk, bases-loaded jam in the bottom of the ninth to preserve the lead.

Back in Philadelphia, Game Six became the most memorable game in the Phillies' ninety-seven-year history. Schmidt's two-run single gave the Phils a 2–0 lead in the third. Then in the fifth Lonnie Smith doubled, went to third on a sacrifice fly by Rose, and scored on McBride's infield grounder. One inning later, Bowa doubled and came home on Boone's single.

With a record crowd of 65,839 at the ten-year-old Veterans Stadium, Carlton, who had yielded just four hits in seven innings, was replaced during the eighth by McGraw, who had to escape a bases-loaded jam to get out of the inning.

Then, the Royals loaded the bases again in the ninth.

"When he was warming up," Boone remembered, "he threw everything high. He had me really worried. I watched him like a hawk, trying to figure out his mechanics. I knew I had to say something to him, but I didn't know what to say. Finally, I went out to the mound, and I said to him, 'Tuggles, everything is high.' Then I turned and went back to the plate. After that, he became the old Tug again."

With one out, a foul popup in front of the Phillies dugout by Frank White hit the glove of Boone, but bounced out. Rose caught it underneath Boone's glove for the second out.

"As a catcher," said Boone, "it was my territory. When I got over there, I thought, *Where's Pete? He's not there.* Then he came flying down, and I thought he'd knock us both into the dugout. At that moment, I wanted to kill him. Then after he caught the ball, I wanted to kiss him."

In a play that few will ever forget, Pete Rose catches a pop foul that had bounced off the glove of Bob Boone for the second out in the ninth inning of the final game of the World Series.

Courtesy of the Philadelphia Phillies

Then Tylenol Tug, his left arm racked with pain, struck out Wilson. The Phillies had a 4–1 win and their first Series victory.

The ballpark exploded with joy. McGraw leaped skyward with his hands in the air. Then the Phillies, led by Schmidt, jumped on McGraw in a wild demonstration of sheer ecstasy. The stands shook. And the whole city went berserk as people throughout the Delaware Valley poured out of their homes to launch a celebration that lasted throughout the night.

"It was obvious the town was hungry for a winner," said Luzinski. "The fans had supported us in the past, and they continued to support us that year. There was a lot of excitement. As a team, we all anticipated it was going to be a good

As two million watched, the Phillies held a victory parade down Broad Street. Paul Owens (left) and Dallas Green celebrated in the lead truck.
Courtesy of the Philadelphia Phillies

year, but we knew that a lot of guys were getting older and would be moving on soon. So it was a very crucial year for us."

One day later, a crowd estimated to number two million jammed into every available space along Broad Street to watch the Phillies parade in open trucks from City Hall to South Philly. At the end of the route, the Phillies and 100,000 fans swarmed into Municipal Stadium to continue the festivities. Jubilation reigned like it never had before as McGraw held up a newspaper with the headline, "We Win."

"I'll have that memory the rest of my life," said Bowa about the day's dramatic events. "People were crying as we

Ace reliever Tug McGraw, who got the final outs in the sixth game, gave a rousing victory speech during a raucous celebration at Municipal Stadium.
Courtesy of the Philadelphia Phillies

came down Broad Street. It was a big thing for the city and for us. We took the big elephant off of everybody's shoulders."

Indeed, they did. "It was the greatest thing that ever happened to me, and I think everybody on the team would say the same thing," said Green. Up to that point, it was also the greatest thing that had ever happened in the ninety-seven-year history of the Phillies.

76ERS DOMINATE THE NBA FOR THEIR SECOND TITLE

16 When the 76ers assembled for the start of the 1982–83 season, there was a strong feeling around town that this might be the year the championship drought would end. The team had gone to the NBA finals in two of the last three seasons, and although it had lost each time, the upcoming season figured to be different. The 76ers' first title in sixteen years seemed like a distinct possibility.

The biggest reason for such optimism was the changes that had been made to the starting lineup. While Julius Erving was the centerpiece of the club's roster, and had been since he was bought from the New York Nets for $3 million in 1976, the Sixers made a major addition to their lineup when they signed center Moses Malone.

In addition, Andrew Toney, a reserve the previous two years, was inserted into the starting lineup as a guard, and twenty-six-year-old rookie Marc Iavaroni, who had played the previous three seasons in Italy, took over as a starting forward. Maurice Cheeks, in his fifth season with the team, completed the starting lineup.

The bench consisted of Bobby Jones, Clint Richardson, Earl Cureton, Franklin Edwards, and rookies Mark

It was called "Dr. J's team," and with good reason. Julius Erving was a dominant force on a 76ers team that ran away with the NBA championship.
Courtesy of the Philadelphia 76ers

McNamara and Reggie Johnson. Clemon Johnson joined the team near midseason in a trade with the Indiana Pacers for Russ Schoene, who with Mitch Anderson had seen limited action earlier in the season.

Among the most noted players gone from the previous team were Darryl Dawkins, Caldwell Jones, Lionel Hollins, Steve Mix, and Mike Bantom. The first three were traded and the last two were not offered new contracts.

Since winning their first championship in 1966–67, the 76ers had reached the NBA finals in 1976–77, 1979–80, and 1981–82. But each time, they had lost the best-of-seven finals four games to two, first to the Portland Trailblazers and then twice to the Los Angeles Lakers. Even though they lost in three final rounds, the 76ers' most devastating defeat had occurred in 1980–81 when they owned a three games-to-one lead over the Boston Celtics in the Eastern Conference Finals, but, needing only one more win to reach the league finals, lost three straight games to get slammed out of the playoffs.

The losses had become so distressing to 76ers fans that the team had adopted a slogan. "We owe you one," it proclaimed. At least, that was better than the previous slogan, "Let George Do It," after the team had signed star forward George McGinnis in 1975, but swapped him for Jones after three seasons with no championships.

"We had an enormous history of falling short," recalled Pat Williams, the team's general manager from 1974 to 1986. "When Moses arrived, it gave us a sense of extreme confidence. We felt confident from the first day of training camp and had the feeling that this time, we were not going to be denied."

With Williams having put all the pieces together, the addition of Malone gave the Sixers a much-needed boost under the basket. An eight-year veteran, most recently with the Houston Rockets, he had long been at the top of the list among the league's rebounders, leading the NBA four times in that category while also ranking annually among the league's top scorers. In 1981–82, he had averaged 31.1 points and 14.7 rebounds per game.

"We knew that the cost of signing him would be prohibitive," said Williams. "But our owner, Harold Katz, took a deep breath and dangled $13.2 million in front of him. We signed him to a six-year contract and sent them Caldwell as part of the deal."

Katz, who had made a fortune in the weight-loss business, had purchased the team for $12 million in 1981 from F. Eugene Dixon. He was the second of a string of five different club owners over a twenty-two-year period. Katz realized that without a dominant big man, the 76ers were never going to rule the NBA. "We were two games away from the championship last year," he said. "You'd think Moses would be worth two games, wouldn't you?"

It was still Erving's team, however. A twelve-year veteran of professional basketball who had led the old American Basketball League in scoring four straight years and who was now in his seventh season with the 76ers, the former University of Massachusetts star now called "Dr. J" had revolutionized the game of basketball with his exquisite physical prowess that included dunks, swoops, and flights through the air. In the process, he had etched his name on the list of one of the all-time greatest athletes in Philadelphia sports history.

"I hadn't seen anything like him since Wilt Chamberlain," Tom Gola, a member of the last 76ers championship team, told a writer. "The difference was, Erving was flying around the rim while Wilt was hanging out next to it."

Even Phillies superstar Mike Schmidt got on the bandwagon. "Whenever I went into the locker room after a game to joke around with the guys, I'd find myself stealing glances over at Julius Erving," he said. "Jocks were jocks, but this was Dr. J. Being around him made me feel like a little kid."

Erving was not only the team's star point-getter, but one of the league's highest scorers. And he also played with class and dignity. "He came to represent the essence of citizenship and sportsmanship," *Philadelphia Inquirer* columnist Bill Lyon wrote, "the forceful, ever-present reminder that there is room up there on the marquee for compassion and humanitarianism."

Cheeks, a West Texas A & M graduate, was the playmaker who led the 76ers in assists in each of his eleven years with the team. Toney, a nearly flawless shooter out of Southwest Louisiana, added a scoring weapon to the arsenal. Iavaroni, from the University of Virginia, proved to be a strong rebounder, while Jones, the sixth man from North Carolina University, was a skilled defensive player and rebounder who usually got as much time on the court as some of the regulars.

"It was a revamped roster," recalled Richardson. "But we all had the same expectations. And everybody was very businesslike and very methodical. We respected each other, we enjoyed each other, and we all stuck together. There was no off-court drama, either. It was a very conservative team as far as behavior goes. No big egos and nobody was pompous."

Billy Cunningham was then in his sixth of eight years as the 76ers mentor. Cunningham, who had been the sixth man on the previous Sixers championship team, was noted for his intensity and his intimidating style. A hard-driving perfectionist with what was described as "zero tolerance," he was seldom reluctant to display his hot temper, and would sometimes scream at his players while they were on the court.

Williams, who in more than forty years in the NBA would have a highly successful career while also serving as an executive with the Chicago Bulls, Atlanta Hawks, and Orlando Magic, was ably supported by John Nash, the club's assistant general manager, who would become a longtime member of the local sports community.

Still on the scene was the iconic public address announcer Dave Zinkoff. A fixture in Philadelphia sports since he first went behind the mike with Eddie Gottlieb's SPHAS in the 1930s, Zink had been with the Warriors throughout their tenure in Philadelphia and then moved to the 76ers when they came to town. Known for his special calls, his deep bass voice was at its peak when he would announce goals such as "Malooone Alooone," or "Field Goal Errrrrrving."

Another popular member of the club's game-day lineup was noted musician Grover Washington Jr. A native Philadelphian who had become one of the nation's top saxophone players, Washington regularly played the national anthem before Sixers games, a performance that was enormously popular among the team's fans. One night after watching Erving slam a ball through the hoop, Washington went home and wrote a song for the 76ers star entitled "Let It Flow."

The 76ers held their training camp once again at Frank lin and Marshall College in Lancaster. They opened the season on October 29 with a 104–89 victory over the New York Knicks at Madison Square Garden in a game in which Malone immediately demonstrated his value by scoring 21 points and pulling down 17 rebounds.

Over the next two weeks, the team won six straight games, including a 110–99 win over the New Jersey Nets in a game in which Cheeks tied Wilt Chamberlain's team record with 21 assists. In another win, the Sixers captured a 119–115 double-overtime victory over the Boston Celtics at the Spectrum in a contest in which Malone played fifty-six of the game's fifty-eight minutes while recording 28 points and 19 rebounds. In their next game, they walloped the Bulls, 145–108, at home.

"When the season started, we kind of knew we could win," said Richardson. "Pat had put a lot of thought and research into it and had put all the pieces together to build a machine that could disassemble any team it played. At first, we didn't talk much about winning the title. Because we were so focused, we took it one game at a time."

Losses were a rarity with the Sixers, and by the end of November, they sported a 13–3 record. Soon afterward, they clobbered the Hawks, 132–85, and as the year ended they owned a 24–5 record. Malone and Erving. Erving and Malone. The two formed a virtually unbeatable combination with invaluable help from the other starters and a standout group of reserves.

Erving, whose career would end four seasons later, was particularly devastating as a game neared its conclusion. "Late in the game, he seemed to have a different face," said Jack McCaffery, who covered the team for the Trenton *Times*. "He went into another personality. He didn't have to say he wanted the ball. He gave a walk and a little sneer, which meant, 'Give me the ball. I'm going to find a way for us to win.'"

At that point, the Sixers were in the midst of a fourteen-game winning streak, a franchise record that still stands. The streak, which included consecutive overtime victories over the Dallas Mavericks, 126–116, and Lakers, 122–120, ended on January 23 with a 107–96 loss to the Milwaukee Bucks. The 76ers' record was 34–6, and it appeared that there was nobody in the league who could touch them.

"This was a very dominant team," said Clemon Johnson, who had proved to be an invaluable reserve at both the center and forward positions. "When we picked up Moses, we had all the parts. That made the difference; we beat teams by 10 to 15 points and more. With our confidence level, we thought we could beat anybody. We felt we were the best."

From the start of December though the end of February, the 76ers lost just four games. After their fourteen-game winning streak ended with a 107–96 loss to the Bucks, they won sixteen of seventeen games, eleven of which were by 10 points or more and included a 127–98 rout of the Rockets and a 133–101 smashing of the Mavericks.

"Never since the old Boston teams has a team been so dominant in all aspects of the game as Philadelphia has been," Milwaukee coach Don Nelson told reporters. "I hope people understand that a dynasty is brewing in Philadelphia."

That may have turned into a slight exaggeration. But certainly noteworthy was the fact that for the All-Star Game in Los Angeles that year, Erving, Malone, Cheeks, and Toney were all selected to the East squad, the first time four 76ers had ever been named to one All-Star team. Erving scored 25 points to lead the East team to a 132–123 victory over the West. Afterward, he was named the game's Most Valuable Player, an award he had also won in 1977.

On March 1, the 76ers beat the Knicks, 106–94, to run their record to 50–7, a league record for the mark at that point of the season. In their next two games, the 76ers fell victim to an experience they would encounter just one other time during the season. They lost two games in a row, bowing to the Celtics, 115–110, and the New Jersey Nets, 112–106. A seven-game winning streak followed, and on the last day of March, the Sixers won their sixtieth game of the season with a 120–113 victory over Atlanta. The win gave the team a spectacular 60–12 record.

"They were a group that went for the jugular," remembered the highly regarded NBA referee Ed Rush, who worked the courts for more than thirty years. "Some teams go on cruise control once they get a lead. But with the Sixers, once you got down you didn't have a chance. They wouldn't let you up.

"I don't think they had a weakness," Rush added. "They had great offense. Great defense. The role players were stars in their own right. This team had explosiveness. It had unbelievable fire-power. It could dominate the paint. Teams like that are easy to referee. They were very efficient. It's the teams with deficiencies that are tough to referee."

The Sixers clinched the division title on March 30, nearly three weeks before the end of the season, then finished the campaign with a 65–17 record, the second-best mark in team history and one that included a 35–6 log at home. They wound up nine games ahead of the Celtics (56–26) in the Eastern Conference's Atlantic Division. The Nets were third with a 49–33 mark. A then-franchise record 612,203 people, which was second in the twenty-three-team league, attended 76ers games at the Spectrum.

Malone, called by Bucks' broadcaster Eddie Doucette as "the Clydesdale that pulled the wagon," led the league in rebounds with 1,194 (15.3 average) and placed fifth in scoring with an average of 24.5 points per game (1,908 total points). Erving scored 1,542 points (21.4), while Toney tallied 1,598 (19.7). Cheeks scored 990 (12.5) with 543 assists.

"When Moses arrived that year, he was at the peak of his career," recalled Williams, "and there was a sense that we were not going to be denied. As it turned out, we had the energy, the intensity, the drive, and everything we did broke right."

As the playoffs approached, it was announced that Malone had been elected the league's Most Valuable Player for the second straight year. When he was asked how he expected his team to do in the playoffs, he reportedly responded by saying "fo, fo, fo." Suggesting that the team would sweep each playoff, Malone's prediction would be nearly right.

Moses Malone predicted that the 76ers with win every game in the playoffs. He was nearly right as the club swept its first two opponents and lost just one game in the finals.
Courtesy of the Philadelphia 76ers

The Sixers received a bye in the first round, and then were pitted against the Knicks in the Eastern Conference semifinals. But one issue loomed large. Malone had missed the last four games of the regular season with tendinitis in one knee. When his other knee became inflamed during practice, panic was on the verge of appearing.

But Malone wasn't about to be sidelined. And in the first game at the Spectrum, he tied a season's high with 38 points, grabbed 17 rebounds, and led the 76ers to a 112–102 victory. "I didn't concentrate on the pain. I just concentrated on playing the game," he told reporters afterward.

In Game Two, despite injuries to Toney and Jones that put them out of action, the Sixers overcame a 20-point third quarter deficit to win, 98–91. Then, moving to Madison Square Garden, the Knicks, after being down 10 points with four minutes left in the game, fought back to tie the score in the final minute. But with two seconds left, Edwards sank a ten-foot shot that gave the Sixers a 107–105 victory. The series ended the next day when Malone's 29-point, 14-rebound showing gave the 76ers a 105–102 at New York.

Malone finished the four-game series with an astonishing total of 125 points and 62 rebounds. And for that, Cureton introduced him to a friend as "Al Capone Malone." "That's because he steals games," Cureton said.

With the first part of Malone's "fo, fo, fo" prediction now certified, the 76ers moved into the Eastern Conference finals against Milwaukee. The Bucks, who had won the Central Division and then blanked Boston in the four-game Eastern semifinals, fielded a team that featured standout center Bob Lanier.

In Game One, with the Bucks leading, 109–108, with 1:36 left in overtime, Jones blocked an inbounds pass by Al Lister, fired the ball to Richardson, and the reserve guard slam-dunked a shot. Ultimately, the Sixers won, 111–109.

Game Two turned into a defensive battle as the Sixers walked off with an 87–81 decision. Moving to Milwaukee, the Philly club overcame a seven-point Bucks fourth quarter lead to win, 104–96, with Erving scoring 26 points. Then Malone's prediction developed a flaw in the fourth game as the Bucks captured a 100–94 win. The Sixers, though, moved back into the win column three days later with a 115–103 victory at the Spectrum and a trip to the finals.

The opponent would be the Lakers, winners of the Pacific Division with a 58–24 record and playoff victors over Portland in five games in the Western Conference semifinals and the San Antonio Spurs in six games in the Western finals. Not only were the Lakers the defending NBA champs, but also they had beaten the 76ers in six games in the NBA finals one year earlier and also in six games in the NBA finals in 1979–80.

The Lakers were a strong team coached by Pat Riley and led by superstars Kareem Abdul-Jabbar and Earvin (Magic) Johnson. Starters Jamaal Wilkes, James Worthy, and Norm Nixon weren't too bad, either, serving as standout parts of the starting lineup.

In the first game played at the Spectrum, the weary Lakers, who had just completed a grueling series thirty-nine hours earlier, awoke to overcome a 10-point Sixers lead at the end of the first quarter to take a 57–54 edge into halftime. But the Philly guys came back with a strong second half and captured a 113–107 victory. Malone scored 27 points and snatched 18 rebounds, while Toney scored 25 and Erving 20.

Game Two had a vastly different twist as Cureton came off the bench after Malone had picked up his fifth foul, and virtually stopped Abdul-Jabbar through much of the fourth quarter. After trailing 55–51 at halftime, the Sixers outscored the Lakers 52–38 in the second half and coasted to a 103–93 triumph. Malone (24), Cheeks (19), and Toney (19) led the way in scoring.

The teams moved to LA for the third game, and the Lakers stepped out to a 32–21 lead after the first quarter. But an 18–7 run by the Sixers narrowed the gap to 52–49 at halftime. Then, coming off of a 72–72 tie at the end of the third period, a 14–0 explosion by the 76ers led them to a 111–94 victory. Malone, with 28 points and 19 rebounds, and Erving and Toney, each with 21 points, set the pace.

"We're going to win it," Erving proclaimed. "If we don't win it Tuesday [Game Four], we'll win it the next day [Game Five]. We have to work, but we are going to win it."

Now on the verge of a sweep, the Sixers nearly made Erving's prediction come true. The Lakers stormed to a 65–51 lead

Point guard Maurice Cheeks was a valuable member of the team as its playmaker and an excellent shooter.
Courtesy of the Philadelphia Inquirer

at halftime, but with Erving scoring seven points in the final two minutes of the game, the 76ers outscored their opponents 64–43 in the second half to win going away, 115–108. Malone again played a major role in the victory, dominating the fourth quarter and scoring 24 points with 24 rebounds. Toney (23), Erving (21), and Cheeks (20) also made big contributions.

"Moses had such confidence," Williams said. "He was going to control the ball at both ends of the court. He'd get the ball out to one of the guards, and off and running they'd go. He did everything you wanted a guy in his position to do. And he took no nights off."

"There was no way the Lakers were going to beat us," Richardson said. "When we won, it was such a great feeling. We won for ourselves and for our fans, we won for our owners, and we won for the city and the state of Pennsylvania."

In the final totals, Malone scored 103 points and pulled down 72 rebounds and was named the MVP of the series. Toney wound up with 88 points, while Erving scored 76, Cheeks 61, and Jones 48. Abdul-Jabbar scored 94 points, but was dominated under the basket by Malone. Johnson tallied 76 and Wilkes scored 74 for the Lakers.

It was a marvelous victory for the Sixers. "I'm standing here feeling so strong, so purposeful, so good because I know—we all know—that we came the long way, the hard way," Erving told the group of reporters assembled in the clubhouse after his team clinched the title. "I have nothing but respect and admiration for the people in this [locker] room who stayed together and did what had to be done."

Phil Jasner of the *Philadelphia Daily News* quoted Malone as saying, "We came to be the best, and we are. I want this team to be remembered as a great team, one of the greatest ever. I want to be able to look in the record books and find us."

The Sixers flew home the next afternoon, and when they landed at Philadelphia International Airport, a cheering crowd of 5,000, including Mayor Bill Green, was there to greet them. Cureton waved a broom symbolizing the team's sweep. "It was like New Year's Eve," Zinkoff said.

The following day, June 2, the city threw a parade. As an estimated 1.7 million fans lined the streets, the 76ers and their families rode on flatbed trucks from 18th and Market Streets to City Hall and then down Broad Street, where at the end they were carried in convertibles into Veterans Stadium, where a jubilant celebration attended by some 65,000 took place.

"To get to where we are today, we had to live through a whole lot more than four, five, four," Erving told the crowd. "There was nothing pretty about what we did to the NBA this year. It was beautiful."

"It [the turnout] showed the appreciation of the city for our team," Clemon Johnson remembered. "We owed them one, and now we had paid them in full. I was just grateful to be part of that celebration."

It was a celebration that those who were there would never forget. A perfectly constructed team had won the franchise's first championship in sixteen years and what would turn out to be their last one since then. Several decades later, the 1982–83 76ers would be named one of the ten greatest teams in NBA history.

PHILLIES END A TWENTY-EIGHT-YEAR DROUGHT WITH SERIES WIN

17 Not long after the twenty-first century began, it was starting to become every-so-slightly apparent that the Phillies might again be building for another run at a pennant.

The team hadn't finished atop the National League since 1993, and in the seven years after that, it had produced losing records in every season. But the face of the club was starting to change. In 2001, the Phillies jumped all the way up to second place. Two third-place finishes and three straight second-place finishes followed. And the Phillies had launched what would become the greatest era in team history—the Golden Era—which included two pennants and five straight division titles.

In 2004, the club had ended a thirty-three-year stint in the unglamorous, multipurpose Veterans Stadium, moving to the luxurious, baseball-only Citizens Bank Park. A modern ballfield that quickly became known as one of the best in the country, CBP, constructed on the site of one of the Vet parking lots, was built at a cost of $345 million and had a seating capacity of 43,651. By 2008, it had become an enormously popular venue for sports fans, and it would go on to set a club record with 257 straight sellouts.

Within a few years of the stadium's opening, the Phils had built a team around a collection of three young stars—first baseman Ryan Howard, second baseman Chase Utley, and shortstop Jimmy Rollins. The trio had all come up through the Phillies farm system, and each would go on to become the top player at his position in Phillies history.

The Phillies double-play combination of Jimmy Rollins (left) and Chase Utley was the best in the National League, not only on the field but also at the plate.
Photo by Al Tielemans

Two other home-grown products, outfielder Pat Burrell and catcher Carlos Ruiz, added their special talents to the starting lineup, while outfielders Shane Victorino and Jason Werth, and third baseman Pedro Feliz, had all come from other teams and proved to be extremely valuable additions.

On the mound, starters Cole Hamels, Brett Myers, and Kyle Kenrick and reliever Ryan Madson were also graduates of the Phils' minor leagues. Starters Joe Blanton and Jamie Moyer and relievers Brad Lidge, J. C. Romero, Chad Durbin, Tom Gordon, Clay Condrey, and Scott Eyre were all new to the system.

"This was a real good bunch of guys," said Howard, who had led the National League in home runs in 2006 with a Phillies-record 58. "We believed in ourselves and in each other, and we believed we had all the pieces together. We had a feeling that it was just a matter of going out and doing what it took to win."

Much of the Phillies roster and a solid farm system had been built by Ed Wade, who had served as the team's general manager from 1998 through 2005. Pat Gillick then became the Phils' general manager before the 2006 season.

"The core of the team had really been put together by Ed before I got here," recalled Gillick, a future Hall of Famer and general manager dating back to 1978, including a stint with the Toronto Blue Jays when they beat the Phillies in the 1993 World Series. "The main thing I did was to add some of the pieces so we could be more competitive."

Ironically, Lidge had been traded to the Phillies from the Houston Astros, where Wade had become the general manager. Lidge became the anchor of a stellar bullpen that turned into one of the Phillies' greatest assets.

Philadelphia was also a team that was highly competitive. That was due in part to Charlie Manuel. An ex-skipper of the Cleveland Indians and a former minor and major league player who'd had his best years in Japan, Manuel was a baseball lifer who had taken over the club's manage-rial duties in 2005 after serving for several years as a special assistant to Wade.

Manager Charlie Manuel, who would later become the winningest skipper in Phillies history, addresses the fans during the victory celebration at Citizens Bank Park.
Photo by Al Tielemans

Manuel had an outgoing personality, and despite a coun-try-boy exterior resulting from his having grown up in West Virginia, he was a guy who knew how to manage. Plus, he had the admiration and respect of his players, had built their con-fidence, and ran a clubhouse free of tension and distractions. He had made the game fun for his players, and although he was sometimes criticized for his strategical decisions, he ran his team with skill and determination.

Nevertheless, he shunned attention on himself. "It's not me, it's the players," he said. "They're the reason I won all these games. The game is a lot more important than me; I always tell my players when I stand up in front of them that the first priority is to win the game. That's why I manage. My philosophy is to win the game.

"Everybody on our team had a role," Manuel recalled. "And everybody stayed focused on what he had to do. Everybody was on the same page. It was the closest team I was ever around. We had a high caliber of players and all responded well. As they say, 'everybody got game.'"

Manuel, who with 780 wins later became by far the winningest manager in Phillies history before he was dismissed in August 2013, had replaced the fiery, hard-driving former Phils shortstop Larry Bowa as manager. Bowa, with a team that featured slugger Jim Thome, the 2003 National League home run king, had started the Phils on the road to victory in 2001, posting one second-place finish, two thirds, and another second before his exit.

Manuel, who would go on to become enormously popular with baseball fans in Philadelphia and the city's second-winningest manager behind Connie Mack, continued the run with two second-place finishes. Then the Phils burst into the postseason playoffs in 2007 after finishing first in the East Division. In the National League Division Series, the Phillies faced the Colorado Rockies.

Although the Phillies were wiped out in three games by the Rockies, who went on to the World Series, it appeared that something bigger and better might be on the horizon.

It certainly was, and in 2008 the Phillies finally won their sixth National League pennant and second World Series in the club's 126 years of operation. It was the team's first World Series victory in twenty-eight years. The team that had become one of Philadelphia's all-time favorite sports teams had finally given the city its first major championship in twenty-five years.

"It didn't start off like a championship season," remembered Rollins, the National League's Most Valuable Player in 2007, who would later become the Phillies' all-time leader in hits. "But coming off the 2007 season, we knew how to maintain ourselves and what it took to get to the playoffs. This team had been in a long drought for many years before this, so we were determined to win. And this team was good enough to do that."

That view was not obvious as the season got under way. After losing their opener, 11–6, when the Washington Nationals scored five runs in the top of the ninth inning, the Phils were one-hit the next day by the Nats' Tim Redding in a 1–0 loss. Despite an 8–7 win over the Cincinnati Reds in a game that featured two Utley home runs, the Phils went on to lose six of their first 10 games. By April 19, they were in fourth place with an 8–10 record.

By the end of April, though, the Phillies had moved up to a tie for second place with the help of Utley's four-RBIs, two-homer game in a 5–4 win over the New York Mets, and

Hamels's 7–4 victory over Greg Maddux and the San Diego Padres.

Then in May, a five-game winning streak and 17 wins in 29 games landed the Phils in first place. In one game, Werth drilled three homers and tied a club record with eight RBIs as the Phils whipped the Blue Jays, 10–3. In another game, Utley drove in six runs and Moyer became only the sixth pitcher ever to beat all thirty major league teams with a 20–5 slamming of the Rockies.

"We had a good personality in the clubhouse, and we laid it out every night," recalled Utley, the league's best second baseman and eventually a six-time All-Star. "Our expectations were getting higher, and we were all pulling together all the time. We hit home runs, ran the bases well, scored a lot of runs, and we were keeping the other teams in line. Everything was working just right."

The Phillies roosted in first place throughout June during a month that included Utley homering in his fifth straight game in a 5–4 win over the Reds, a 5–0 victory over Cincinnati giving Hamels his second complete game shutout of the year, consecutive homers by Utley, Howard, and Burrell that gave the Phillies a 20–2 walloping of the St. Louis Cardinals, and Rollins's club-record 28th leadoff home run in an 8–2 decision over the Boston Red Sox.

Burrell joined Mike Schmidt as only the second Phils player to hit 20 homers in eight straight seasons as the Phils started July with an 8–3 win over the Atlanta Braves. But by then, the club was in the midst of a slump that would see them lose 19 of 31 games and slip to a tie for second, two games behind the Mets.

The Phils returned to first on July 30 when Moyer became only the fourth pitcher in major league history to win at least ten games in one season at age forty-five or older, beating Washington, 8–5. But two weeks later, the Phils were back to second, where they would stay for all but one day until September 16, at one point in early September falling as far back as three and one-half games behind.

"The Mets were hot, but it looked like we might be headed the same way as 2007 [when the New Yorkers collapsed in the final weeks of the season, losing 12 of their final 17 games after leading most of the way, while the Phillies won thirteen of their last seventeen, and rallied to take the title]," said Rollins.

He was exactly right. Howard's hitting and a standout relief outing by Madson led the Phillies to an 8–7 win over the Braves on September 16, and the Phillies were back in first place. Rookie J. A. Happ earned his first Phillies win the next night with a 6–1 victory over the Braves. The Phils fell briefly out of first after a 14–8 loss to the Florida Marlins, but coming down the final two weeks, they won 13 of their last 16 games, while the Mets lost 10 of their final 16. The Phils clinched the East Division title on September 27 with a 4–3 victory over the Nationals, in which Moyer got the win and Lidge notched his 41st save.

"We knew we could do it," Gillick remembered. "We had a great offensive team, but we were also a good defensive club. And our pitchers usually got us into the late innings, and then we were really tough to beat. We really played well throughout the season."

The Phillies finished with a 92–70 record, and a three-game lead over the Mets, who crashed at the end of the season. The Phils' winning total was the highest since the 1993 team won 97 games, and it was their sixth straight winning season since 2003. An all-time Phillies record crowd of 3,422,583 flocked to Citizens Park, including fifty sellouts.

Howard, the league's MVP in 2006 and Rookie of the Year in 2005, led the majors in home runs (48) and RBIs (146). Utley hit .292 with 33 homers and 104 RBIs, while Victorino went .293–14–58. Rollins was .277–11–59, Werth .273–24–67, Burrell .250–33–86, and third baseman Feliz .249–14–48. Pinch-hit star Greg Dobbs hit .301, and reserve catcher Chris Coste had a mark of .263–9–36.

"Throughout the season, our hitting was really big," said Manuel. "Our offense was definitely what got us to the post-season. But our defense was tremendous, too. Nobody talked much about that. And we had some really good pitching. Some of those saves Lidge had came in really big games."

On the mound, the forty-five-year-old Moyer led the staff with a 16–7 record (3.71 ERA), while Hamels was 14–10, Kendrick 11–9, and Myers 10–13. En route to being named Relief Pitcher of the Year, Lidge had a sensational season with 41 saves in 41 opportunities.

"All season, we had a combination of good health, good players, and good chemistry," Ruiz recalled. "We had a special kind of magic. That's not to say it hadn't happened with some of our other teams, but this team was very special. It wasn't quite the same kind of team as the others."

The National League Division Series began on October 1, and in the opener in Philadelphia, Hamels retired the first fourteen batters he faced and gave up two hits while pitching eight shutout innings to beat the Central Division wild-card winners, the Milwaukee Brewers, 3–1. Victorino's grand slam sparked a five-run second inning that gave Myers and the Phillies a 5–2 win before a ballpark record crowd of 46,208 in Game Two. Then, after the Brewers beat Moyer and the Phils, 4–1, at Milwaukee, the Phillies clinched the series with a 6–2 victory behind Blanton's pitching and two homers by Burrell and one each by Rollins and Werth.

Moving on to the National League Championship Series against the Los Angeles Dodgers, the West Division winners who had swept the Central Division's Chicago Cubs in three games in the NLDS, the Phillies came from behind in the opener to take a 3–2 decision behind Hamels and sixth inning home runs by Utley and Burrell.

In Game Two, Myers got the win with the help of his own bat as he became the first hurler in postseason history to slam three hits and collect three RBIs in one game as the Phils topped LA, 8–5. Lidge fanned the side in the ninth to record his fourth save of the postseason. Then, the Dodgers came back to win the fourth game with a 7–2 verdict over the

Phils and Moyer at Dodger Stadium in a game in which both benches emptied after Hiroki Kuroda brushed back Victorino with a high, inside pitch.

Pinch-hitter Matt Stairs became the hero of Game Four when his two-out, two-run homer in the top of the eighth, just two batters after a two-run four-bagger by Victorino, handed the Phillies a come-from-behind 7–5 victory, with Madson notching the win.

Two days later at Dodger Stadium, the Phillies clinched their sixth National League pennant with a 5–1 victory. Rollins hit a leadoff home run to give the Phils an early lead in the first, and Hamels gave up five hits in seven innings to get his second win of the series. For his work, the Phillies' lefthander was named the NLCS Most Valuable Player, an award he said was one that was really "for the whole team. I'm just happy to be a part of this," he said.

In the nine postseason games to date, Burrell (.300–3–7) and Victorino (.281–2–11) were the batting stars along with Dobbs, who went 6-for-11 as a pinch-hitter. Hamels had won three games, Myers two, and Lidge had relieved in seven.

"We knew this was going to be one of the greatest teams in Philadelphia sports history," Victorino remembered. "This was a team where we all had each other's backs. We were all part of one team, and we knew the only way to play was to give 100 percent. As for me, I understood how blessed and lucky I was to be part of that team. I always said that my teammates made me a better player."

In the World Series, the Phillies met the Tampa Bay Rays, managed by Hazleton, Pennsylvania, native Joe Maddon. The Rays, owners of the worst record in baseball the previous year, had won the American League's East Division during the regular season with a 96–65 record and a one and one-half game lead over Boston. Then, advancing to the playoffs for the first time in the club's eleven-year history, Tampa had beaten the Chicago White Sox in four games in the ALDS, then downed the Red Sox in a seven-game ALCS.

The Rays had a lineup led by third baseman Evan Longoria (.272–27–85), who was later to be named American League Rookie of the Year; B. J. Upton (.273–9–67), who had homered seven times in the postseason; and Carlos Crawford (.273–8–57). Edwin Jackson (14–11), James Shields (14–8), Andy Sonnanstine (13–9), and Scott Kazmir (12–8) headed a formidable pitching staff. As good as they were, though, the Rays turned out to be no match for the Phillies.

"We were the best team in baseball that year, and we just kept carrying it all the way through and into the World Series," Lidge recalled. "We were all very confident. I remember Charlie Manuel saying that if we played for another two months, we'd still be creaming everybody. Every one of us, to a man, thought we were going to win the Series."

Because the ALCS was late getting finished and the NLCS was done early, the Phillies had to sit around for six days before the World Series began. Nevertheless, in the first game at Tampa's Tropicana Field, Utley's two-run homer in the first off Kazmir and an impressive five-hit performance over seven innings by Hamels led the Phils to a 3–2 win.

Tampa came back the next day to even the Series with a 4–2 win. Myers yielded three runs in the first two innings as sloppy play dominated the Phils' performance. A pinch-hit homer in the eighth inning by Dobbs was the biggest hit for the Phillies, who left eleven men on base in Shields's win.

Two days later, the teams had moved to Philadelphia for the city's first Series game in fifteen years. A ninety-one-minute rain delay at the start set the game back, and it wasn't finished until 1:47 a.m. Meanwhile, Moyer became the second-oldest pitcher ever to start a game in the Fall Classic. Ruiz homered in the second and back-to-back four-baggers in the sixth by Utley and Howard, all off Mike Garza, gave the Phils a 4–1 lead. But Tampa rallied to tie the score before the Phils won in the bottom of the ninth on Ruiz's bases-loaded single. Romero got the win.

Game Four featured Howard's two homers and five RBIs as the Phils bombed the Rays, 10–2. Winning pitcher Blanton, who allowed four hits and two runs in six innings, hit the first home run of his career, while Werth added a two-run homer as the Phils laced 12 hits off Sonnanstine and three others. Crawford and pinch-hitter Eric Hinske both homered for Tampa.

The win was followed by one of the strangest games in World Series history. Victorino's two-run single in the first gave the Phillies an early lead. But a Longoria single in the fourth and a single by Carlos Pena in the sixth produced a

2–2 tie off Hamels. By then, however, a cold, hard rain was drenching not only the ballpark but the whole Philadelphia area, and as the bottom of the sixth was about to begin, the game was stopped at 11:10 p.m.

The storm continued unabated, leaving the field underwater and the fans soaked. Ultimately, Commissioner Bud Selig decided that the game would be suspended and resumed when conditions were playable. It was the first World Series game ever suspended.

It continued to rain hard the following day. As a result, play was not resumed until October 29, two days after the game had been stopped. Following a delay of forty-six hours, the Phillies went to bat, and quickly scored as pinch-hitter Geoff Jenkins doubled and scored on a single by Werth. Rocco Baldelli homered to tie the score in the seventh, but the Phils regained the lead in the bottom of the seventh as Burrell doubled, and pinch-runner Eric Bruntlett scored on a single by Feliz.

The Phillies had a 4–3 lead, and soon afterward, Romero, who got the win, and Lidge, who registered his second save of the Series and seventh in the postseason, blanked the Rays. After striking out Hinske for the final out at 8:58 p.m., Lidge fell to his knees in what now ranks as one of the most unforgettable scenes in Phillies history. After a nearly three-decade wait, the Phillies had finally won another World Series.

"It was a complete feeling of elation," Lidge said. "I remember looking up and saying, 'Oh My God.' Or at least that's what I think I said. You're in awe of what just happened.

You dream when you're a kid about winning a World Series, and then it happens. It's a feeling that will stay with you for a very long time."

Lidge said he struck out Hinske with a slider. "My slider was really on that night," he remembered. "I knew I could get him out. I just had to make sure that the slider stayed in the strike zone long enough to appear as a fastball."

Brad Lidge was ecstatic as he fell to his knees after striking out the final batter in the last game of the Phillies' World Series victory.
Photo by Al Tielemans

A Citizens Bank Park record crowd of 45,940, which had paid a total of $7,521,808 to get into the ballpark, went berserk. The stadium shook, horns, bells, and sirens went off, people poured into the streets in neighborhoods in and around the city, and Philadelphia had its first championship team in twenty-five years.

"We knew we could do it," said Howard six years later. "We played 27 outs every game, and we never thought we were going to be out of a game, even if we were down eight or nine runs. We played until the last out. We never said, 'hey, are we going to beat these guys,' but 'by how much are we going to do it?' This is the way we felt throughout the playoffs."

Hamels was named the Series Most Valuable Player. "Hamels was absolutely outstanding," Manuel understated. "You couldn't have had better pitching than what he gave us."

Six years later, Hamels looked back and said the MVP awards raised his confidence level as a pitcher. "It made me feel that I could definitely pitch at the major league level," he said. "I could get out the best batters, and I could extend myself beyond pitching just six or seven innings. Winning the awards was really special and it had a major impact on my career."

Werth, with a .444 batting average; Ruiz, who hit .375; Feliz (.333); and Howard, who batted .286, led the team in hitting.

"It was an epic run," Werth recalled. "We were a very special group. For me, it was the kind of accomplishment I'd dreamed about since I was a little kid when my grandfather [Dick (Ducky) Schofield] used to show me the ring he got with the Pittsburgh Pirates for winning the 1960 World Series. I remember looking at it and really wishing that someday I could have something like it."

Two days after the Series ended, Philadelphia staged a wild victory celebration. Some two million deliriously joyful fans lined the parade route on Market Street and then down Broad Street as the Phillies, showered by confetti, rode in flatbed trailers. Afterward, another 40,000 fans jammed into Citizens Bank Park to salute the team at a program led by Phillies announcer Harry Kalas and made especially memorable by Utley's unexpected remark when during his turn at the mike he excitedly shouted, "World Champions. . . . World f—ing Champions."

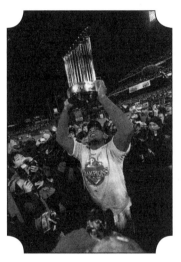

Surrounded by the media and others, slugger Ryan Howard, who led the major leagues in home runs and RBIs, raises the World Series trophy after the Phillies' final victory over the Tampa Bay Rays.
Photo by Al Tielemans

World Champions indeed. Although the team had won pennants in 1915, 1950, 1980, 1983, and 1993, this was only its second Series victory. The Phillies would appear in the Fall Classic again the following year against the New York Yankees, but the 2008 victory would prove to be impossible to duplicate.

OTHER PRO TEAMS THAT WON CHAMPIONSHIPS

18 Since the start of the twentieth century, nearly fifty professional teams have called Philadelphia their home. These teams have played at many different levels, and cover a variety of sports, including baseball, football, basketball, ice hockey, soccer, tennis, and lacrosse.

Many of Philadelphia's professional teams are not as well known as the ones from the major league sports. But a number of these less-familiar clubs did win championships, too. There may not have been parades down Broad Street for them. Yet, every title was important to the team that won it and to its fans, and it rates a special place in the city's sports history.

Foremost among this group are Philadelphia teams that played Negro League baseball. During some fifty years of black professional baseball in the city, there were three main teams. Each won championships.

The first was the Philadelphia Giants, a team that played in the city from 1902 to 1917. The Giants, whose principal owner was Walter (Slick) Schlichter, a Caucasian who was the sports editor of a daily newspaper called the *Philadelphia Item*, played as a pro team from 1902 to 1912.

Although there was no formal league, between 1902 and 1904, the Giants beat the Cuban X-Giants, a team from New York, each year in what was called "The World's Colored Championship." The Philadelphia team, managed by Sol White, one of the premier early black players, featured Andrew (Rube) Foster, a pitcher with tremendous talent, Grant (Home Run) Johnson, and Charlie Grant, a light-skinned second baseman whom John McGraw had once unsuccessfully tried to sign for the New York Giants, passing him off as a Native American.

The Philly club, which played most of its home games at the Athletics' Columbia Park, would go on to post what would be claimed as a 426–149 record between 1903 and 1906.

In 1906, it won the championship of the first formal black baseball league, the International League. Led by sparkling future Hall of Fame shortstop Henry (Pop) Lloyd, the Giants, who had beaten the Cuban team in ten out of fifteen games during the regular season, downed them again in a one-game series played before a crowd of 10,000 at the Phillies' Philadelphia Park to win the league's first title.

After that season, Foster, another future Hall of Famer for his many contributions to Negro League baseball, moved to the Chicago American Giants, where he eventually became the team's owner and then an enormously powerful president of the league. The Philadelphia Giants continued to play in what had become the Negro National League, but they would never win another championship.

Another champion, however, appeared in the area in 1925 when the Hilldale Daisies (or Giants, as they were also called) captured the Colored World Series while defeating the Kansas City Monarchs.

The Daisies, a team that had been formed in 1910 as an independent club for young men from Darby and Southwest Philadelphia, had gone pro in 1917, playing as an independent team at a ballpark in Yeadon. Hilldale joined the Negro National League in 1920, a year in which it played a series of games against a team of major league all-stars, including Babe Ruth.

In 1921, Hilldale played in a six-game league championship series against the American Giants, and won three games while losing two and tying one. Then, two years later, after feuding with the NNL, owner Ed Bolden, a post office employee, pulled his team out of that league and became one of the driving forces in the formation of the Eastern Colored League. The Daisies then won the league's first pennant, but there was no postseason series.

The Daisies featured future Baseball Hall of Famers Judy Johnson at third base and Biz Mackey and Louis Santop at catcher, plus the brilliant but aging shortstop Pop Lloyd, slugging outfielder Clint Thomas, and ace pitchers Phil Cockrell and Nip Winters. With that lineup, they won the pennant again in 1924, but lost to the NNL's Monarchs five games to four in the championship series.

The following year, however, Hilldale won the ECL title with a 52 15 record, and again faced the Monarchs, owners of

Judy Johnson, a native of Wilmington, Delaware, was considered one of the greatest Negro League players of all time, and was inducted into the Baseball Hall of Fame in 1975.

Art by Michael Mellett, courtesy of the Judy Johnson Memorial Foundation

a 62–23 log, in the Colored World Series. This time, the Daisies won, defeating their rivals in five of six games, including the last two at the Phillies' Baker Bowl. The winners were awarded $69 per man.

That would be Hilldale's last title. The ECL disbanded after the 1927 season, and the Daisies played an independent schedule until joining the newly formed American Negro League in 1929. After that league dissolved, Hilldale again played independent ball before folding after the 1931 season.

Two years later, another African-American team was formed. Called the Philadelphia Stars, the squad was again put together by Bolden with sports entrepreneur Eddie Got-tllieb financing the operation. Gottlieb was a long-time prominent figure in local sports and the future coach and owner of the Philadelphia Warriors. The Stars originally played as an independent team.

Over the years, outfielder Gene Benson, first baseman Jud Wilson, catcher Bill (Ready) Cash, and pitchers Stuart (Slim) Jones and Cockrell led the Stars. Future Hall of Famers Buck Leonard, Mackey, and Oscar Charleston, who also served as manager, played briefly for the team.

In 1934, having joined the Negro National League, the Stars, who played most of their early games at Passon Field

Biz Mackey, a Hall of Famer, was arguably the greatest catcher in Negro League history.
Courtesy of John Bossong

at 48th and Spruce Streets and occasionally at Shibe Park and Baker Bowl, finished second in the first half of a divided season. Then, after finishing the season with a 23–13 league record and winding up in first place in the second half, they met the first-half winners, the team now known as the Chicago American Giants.

In a hotly contested seven-game championship series, the Stars lost the first two games, then won three of the next four. In the seventh contest, the game was called off after a Giants player whacked an umpire with his bat following a called third strike. In the rescheduled game at Passon Park, the Stars captured a victory and the championship.

Like their predecessors, the Stars would win no more titles. Ultimately, they moved to Penmar Park at 44th Street and Parkside Avenue, but the winning seasons dwindled. Attendance declined, too, and finally, with African-American players moving into major league baseball and further reducing the crowds and the quality of Negro League baseball, the Stars played their last game in 1952.

It was not only the Stars' last season, but the final season of Negro League baseball in Philadelphia.

Perhaps somewhat ironically, Gottlieb by then had become one of the most powerful figures in another sport—pro basketball. Actually, basketball had provided his first connection with organized sports when he, Hughie Black, and Harry Passon had started an amateur team for young Jewish players.

In 1919, the team officially became known as the SPHAS, which stood for South Philadelphia Hebrew Association, and turned pro with players earning $5 per game. The scores of games back then were typically ones like 18–15 or 12–9.

With players mostly in their early twenties, the SPHAS joined a new pro circuit called the Philadelphia League in 1921. In their second season, the SPHAS won the league championship. By then called "Gotty's Goal Gatherers," they won it again in 1923–24 and 1924–25, after which the league disbanded.

Over a twenty-two-year period, while playing in three different leagues, the SPHAS appeared in eighteen championship series and won thirteen of them. Playing many of their games on Saturday nights at the downtown Broadwood Hotel, where crowds often number around 4,000 and dances were held after

Red Klotz was one of the greatest SPHAS players of all time. He played with the team and later was its coach. Klotz also played with the BAA champion Baltimore Bullets and played with and coached the Washington Generals.

Courtesy of Ronee Klotz-Groff

games, the SPHAS for much of the first half of the twentieth century were the crown jewel of Philadelphia basketball.

Not only did they win titles in the Philadelphia League, they also took home championships in the Eastern and American Leagues, each at the time being the top professional basketball league in the country. Teams the SPHAS beat along the way included the Original Celtics, the Harlem Renaissance (Rens), and the Cleveland Rosenblums, all premier clubs in the early years of pro basketball.

Over the years, the SPHAS had some of early basketball's all-time greats. In addition to Black and Harry and Chickie Passon, they included players such as Mockie Bunin, Davey Banks, Cy Kaselman, Harry Litwack, Jerry Fleisman, Inky Lautman, Shikey Gotthofer, Red Rosan, Petey Rosenberg, Ossie Schectman, Ralph Kaplowitz, and Red Klotz. Some of these stalwarts went on to play with the Warriors and others in the Basketball Association of American, which later merged with the National Basketball League to become the National Basketball Association.

One of the SPHAS's most noteworthy titles came in 1929–30 in the Eastern League. After posting a 30–7 record during the regular season, they met in a best-of-five series for the title against their bitter rivals, the Philadelphia Elks. The Elks were led by former Germantown High School standout William (Bucky) Walters. The SPHAS won the series three games to two, then went on to win titles the next two seasons. As for Walters, he went on to become a star big league pitcher with the Cincinnati Reds, a three-

One of the SPHAS top teams was the 1940 club. Joining Eddie
Gottlieb (left) were a group of star players, including (from left)
Harry Litwack, George Wolfe, Inky Lautman, Lou Forman, Gil Fitch,
Shikey Gotthoffer, and Cy Kaselman.
*Courtesy of the Special Collections Research Center, Temple
University Libraries*

time twenty-game winner, and the National League's 1939
Most Valuable Player.

Gottlieb, by then heavily entrenched with the Warriors,
pulled the SPHAS out of the American League in 1949. Afterward, with baseball funnyman Max Patkin playing and putting on comedy routines, the team played exhibition games,
often prior to Warriors games. Eventually, with Klotz serving as player-coach, the SPHAS became one of the opposition teams that traveled around the world with the Harlem
Globetrotters. The SPHAS played their final season in 1954,
ironically the same season that the Athletics performed their
last game in Philadelphia.

While the SPHAS were Philadelphia's winningest pro team in terms of championships, the city had another squad that captured titles with regularity. Betweeen 1986 and 2014 the Philadelphia Wings won six championships as an indoor box lacrosse league team.

The Wings, with rosters consisting mostly of American players, unlike some of the other teams, were one of four original franchises in the Eagle Pro Box Lacrosse League formed in 1987. Later, the league was renamed the Major Indoor Lacrosse League and then the National Lacrosse League. The Wings, playing in Philadelphia for twenty-eight years, first at the Spectrum and later at the Wells Fargo Center, won championships in 1989, 1990, 1994, 1995, 1998, and 2001 while also capturing division titles in 1993 and 1994.

Among their most noteworthy wins were 26–15 and 19–16 victories over the Buffalo Bandits in the finals of the 1994 and 1995 playoffs. Over a five-year period, the Wings and Bandits would face each other in four of the five championship games.

In 1998, the Wings downed the Baltimore Thunder in the league's only best-of-three series with 16–12 and 17–12 victories. Their next and last crown came in 2001 when they downed the Toronto Rock with a 9–8 upset victory.

While drawing crowds of 12,000 in their early years, the Wings were led by three-time Most Valuable Player Gary Gait. He, Paul Gait, Russ Cline, Christ Fritz, Mike French, Tom Marecheck, Dallas Eliuk, and coach Tony Resch are all members of the NLL Hall of Fame. In 2008, Athan Iannucci set a league scoring record with 71 goals during his MVP season.

After the 2014 season, the Wings were sold to the Native American Mohegan tribe and moved to Uncasville, Connecticut.

Although it is not widely known, Philadelphia has been the home of eleven professional ice hockey teams. The first was the Philadelphia Arrows, a team that was formed in 1927 and initially played in the Canadian-American League. Along the way, other teams that played in the city included the Comets, Falcons, and two teams known as the Ramblers. Even after the Flyers arrived, pro teams such as the Blazers, Firebirds, and Phantoms called Philadelphia their home.

The city had its first National Hockey League team in 1930–31 when former light-heavyweight boxing champion Benny Leonard moved a team from Pittsburgh to Philadelphia and named it the Quakers. The team lasted just one season.

The city's first ice hockey championship arrived in 1935–36 when the first Ramblers team won the Canadian-American League title. A farm team of the New York Rangers, the Ramblers posted a 27–18–3 record during the regular season, and then downed Providence, 3–1, in the title game. The Ramblers, whose lineup included Bryan Hextall, the grandfather of future Flyers goaltender and present general manager Ron Hextall, became the Philadelphia Rockets in 1941–42 in their final season as an ice hockey team.

Another team to carry home a trophy was the Firebirds.. With Hall of Fame and former Phillies pitcher Robin Roberts as a part-owner, the Firebirds, who played at Convention Hall in Philadelphia from 1974 through 1980, were winners of the Lockhart Cup in 1975–76 in the North American Hockey League. At the time an affiliate of the Flyers, the Firebirds were led by future NHL star goalie Rejean Lemelin and high-scorers Bobby Collyard and Gordie Brooks. The Firebirds posted a 45–29–0 record before advancing to the playoff finals, where they defeated the Beauce Jaros, 4–2.

One other Philadelphia ice hockey team wore championship crowns. That was the Philadelphia Phantoms, another Flyers farm team that played in the American Hockey League from 1996 through 2009 and won two Calder Cups

After drawing a record 425,900 fans for the season, the Phantoms, headed by leading scorer Peter White, defenseman Jamie Heward, and goalie Neil Little, went 47–21–10 during the season. They then posted an 11–3 record in the playoffs before going to the finals and winning the 1997–98 Cup with a four-games-to-two triumph over the Saint John Flames. Mike Manekuk scored 34 points in the playoffs and was named Calder Cup MVP.

The Phantoms won the Cup again in 2004–05. Top scorer R. J. Umberger, Freddy Meyer, and defensive players John Slaney, Dennis Seidenberg, and goalie Antero Niittymaki led the team to a regular season record of 48–25–0. Then, after going 12–5 in the first three rounds of the playoffs, the Phantoms swept the Chicago Wolves in four games, winning the last game, 5–2, before a record crowd of 20,103 at the Wachovia Center.

The Philadelphia Kixx, a member of the Major Indoor Soccer League, also won two championships during a local stint that went from 1995 through 2010. The Kixx played originally at the Spectrum then in their final season at the Liacouras Center at Temple University.

Originally a member of the National Professional Soccer Association, the Kixx, after finishing second during the regular season with a 30–14 record, won the first championship in the new Major Indoor Soccer League in 2001–02, beating the Milwaukee Waves two games to one in a best-of-three game series with all-star goalie Pete Pappas leading the way. After winding up in third place during the regular season with a 17–13 mark, the Kixx won the MISL title again in 2006–07 with a 13–8 win over the Detroit Ignition in a one-game championship final.

Another soccer team to win a title was the Philadelphia Atoms of the North American Soccer League. While playing

Bob Rigby (with ball) was a standout goalie with the Philadelphia Atoms when they won a soccer championship in 1973.
Courtesy of Rich Pagano

from 1973 through 1976, they won the NASL crown at Veterans Stadium in their first year of operation, defeating the Dallas Tornado in a one-game final, 2–0, before a crowd of 11,501. Atoms goalie Bob Rigby not only shut out the opposition, but became the first soccer player ever shown on the cover of *Sports Illustrated*. Chris Dunleavy, Jim Fryatt, and Andy Provan were among the other team stars.

Three other Philadelphia football teams have won professional titles. In 1926, the Philadelphia Quakers, led by All-American and future West Chester State legendary coach Glenn Killinger and former NFL players Century Milstead, Bull Behman, Butch Spagna, and Charlie Way, defeated the New York Yankees, 13–7, for the American Football League title at the later-named Municipal Stadium. It was the first and last season not only for the Quakers, but also for the AFL, which finished the year with just four teams.

In 1984, the Philadelphia Stars defeated the Arizona Wranglers, 23–3, before a crowd of 52,622 at Tampa Stadium to win the United States Football League championship. The Stars, featuring quarterback Chuck Fasina, running back Kelvin Bryant, and linemen Irv Eatman and Bart Oates, had won the regular season title with a 16–2 record. Following their title, they moved to Baltimore and the league would fold the following year.

The Philadelphia Soul, members of the Arena Football League, originally owned by singer Bon Jovi, defeated the San Jose SaberCats, 59–56, in New Orleans, Louisiana, to win the AFL championship in 2008 in what was the twenty-second and final title game in the indoor league's history. Led by quarterback Matt D'Orazio, wide receiver Chris Jackson, and defensive lineman Gabe Nyenhuis, the Soul had posted a 13–3 record during a season in which they scored a one-game high of 77 points. The Soul, founded in 2004, played its home games at the Wells Fargo Center.

Another championship for a local squad came in 2001 when the Philadelphia Freedoms won their first of two titles in the World Team Tennis league. Owned by former tennis star Billie Jean King and with national star Jimmy Connors as one of the players, the Freedoms were a coed team that beat the Springfield Lasers, 20–18, to win their first crown. Led by Rannae Stubbs and Chanda Rubin, they won their second title in 2006 when they downed the Newport Beach Breakers, 21–14.

The Philadelphia Barrage won three Steinfeld Cup championships in an outdoor league that was called Major League Lacrosse. After moving from Bridgeport, Connecticut, the Barrage played in Philadelphia from 2004 through 2008. They beat the Boston Cannons, 13–11, for their first title in 2004. In 2006, the Barrage won again with a 23–12 triumph over the Denver Outlaws. A third crown came in 2007 when they downed the Los Angeles Riptide, 16–13. With heavy financial problems, they team became a traveling team in 2008, but folded after the season.

In the long history of Philadelphia sports, there have been many other professional teams, including the present soccer team called the Philadelphia Union, a member of Major

League Soccer. Others played successfully in leagues below the major league level. The Bulldogs, Liberty Belles, Tapers, Rage, Fusion, Thunder, Sting, Fury, Fever, and Spartans were among the many that performed in various sports. They did not win championships, but together, they have all contributed to making Philadelphia one of the top sports cities in the country.

Other Books by Rich Westcott

The Phillies Encyclopedia (with Frank Bilovsky), first, second, and third editions

Diamond Greats: Profiles and Interviews with 65 of Baseball's History Makers

Phillies '93: An Incredible Season

Masters of the Diamond: Interviews with Players Who Began Their Careers More Than 50 Years Ago

Mike Schmidt

Philadelphia's Old Ballparks

No-Hitters: The 225 Games, 1893–1999 (with Allen Lewis)

Splendor on the Diamond: Interviews with 35 Stars of Baseball's Past

A Century of Philadelphia Phillies Baseball: 1900–1999

Great Home Runs of the 20th Century

A Century of Philadelphia Sports

Winningest Pitchers: Baseball's 300-Game Winners

Tales from the Phillies Dugout (first, second, and third editions)

Native Sons: Philadelphia-area Baseball Players Who Made the Major Leagues

Mickey Vernon: The Gentleman First Baseman

Veterans Stadium: Field of Memories

Phillies Essential

The Mogul: Eddie Gottlieb, a Philadelphia Sports Legend and Pro Basketball Pioneer

The Fightin' Phils: Oddities, Insights, and Untold Stories

Philadelphia Phillies: Past and Present

Back Again: The Story of the 2009 Phillies

Shibe Park-Connie Mack Stadium

Philadelphia's Top 50 Baseball Players

Great Stuff: Baseball's Most Amazing Pitching Feats

SOURCES

Baseball Hall of Fame. *Cooperstown: Where the Legends Live Forever*, Gramercy Books, 1999.

Campbell, Donald. *Sunday's Warriors: The Philadelphia Eagles History*, Quantim Leap Publisher, 1995.

Charlton, James. *The Baseball Chronology*, Macmillan Publishing, 1991.

Didinger, Ray, and Robert Lyons. *The Eagles Encyclopedia*, Temple University Press, 2005.

Greenberg, Jay. *Full Spectrum: The Complete History of the Philadelphia Flyers*, Triumph Books, 1997.

Mack, Connie. *My 66 Years in the Big Leagues*, 2nd edition, Dover Publications, 2009.

Romanowski, Father Jerome. *The Mackmen*, Graphic Press, 1979.

Rosin, Jim. *Philly Hoops: The SPHAS and Warriors*, Autumn Road Publishers, 2003.

Sabin, Lou. *Great Teams of Pro Basketball*, Random House, 1971.

Sherman, David. *The Philadelphia Flyers Encyclopedia*, Sports Publishing, 2003.

Westcott, Rich. *A Century of Philadelphia Sports*, Temple University Press, 2001.

Westcott, Rich. *The Fightin' Phils: Oddities, Insights, and Untold Stories*, Camino Books, 2008.

Westcott, Rich. *The Mogul: Eddie Gottlieb, Philadelphia Sports Legend and Pro Basketball Pioneer*, Temple University Press, 2008.

Westcott, Rich and Frank Bilovsky. *The Phillies Encyclopedia*, 3rd edition, Temple University Press, 2004.

Williams, Pat, and Gordon Jones. *Tales from the Philadelphia 76ers*, Sports Publishing, 2009.

Others sources

A Documentary Scrap Book of Football in Frankford, The Historical Society of Frankford

Baseball-Almanac.com

Basketball-Almanac.com

Baseball-Reference.com

Basketball-Reference.com

"History of Philadelphia Soccer" by Steve Holroyd

Along the Elephant Trail (The Philadelphia Athletics Historical Society)

Media Guides: Philadelphia Eagles, Flyers, Phillies, 76ers, Oakland Athletics

New York Times

Pennsylvania Center for the Book (Frankford Yellow Jackets)

Philadelphia Daily News

Philadelphia Evening Bulletin

Philadelphia Inquirer

Pro Football-Reference.com

Sports Illustrated

The Baseball Encyclopedia, Macmillan Books

The Pro Football Encyclopedia, Macmillan Books

The Official NBA Basketball Encyclopedia, Villard Books

"The Team That Time Forgot" by William Nack, *Sports Illustrated*

Wikipedia.org